T0330024

Innovation, Competition and Collaboration

Edited by

Dana Beldiman

Professor, Bucerius Law School, Hamburg, Germany and Professor-in-Residence, UC Hastings College of the Law, San Francisco, USA

Edward Elgar
PUBLISHING

Cheltenham, UK • Northampton, MA, USA

Published by
Edward Elgar Publishing Limited
The Lypiatts
15 Lansdown Road
Cheltenham
Glos GL50 2JA
UK

Edward Elgar Publishing, Inc.
William Pratt House
9 Dewey Court
Northampton
Massachusetts 01060
USA

A catalogue record for this book
is available from the British Library

Library of Congress Control Number: 2014959501

This book is available electronically in the **Elgar**online
Law subject collection
DOI 10.4337/9781784715779

ISBN   978 1 78471 576 2 (cased)
ISBN   978 1 78471 577 9 (eBook)

Typeset by Columns Design XML Ltd, Reading
Printed and bound in Great Britain by T.J. International Ltd, Padstow

Contents

Contributors

Dana Beldiman, Professor, Bucerius Law School, Hamburg, Germany; Professor-in-Residence, UC Hastings College of the Law, San Francisco, USA.

Michael W. Carroll, Professor of Law and Director, Program on Information Justice and Intellectual Property, American University, Washington College of Law.

Séverine Dusollier, Professor, Sciences Po, Paris, France.

Gustavo Ghidini, Professor, University of Milan and LUISS Guido Carli University, Rome, Italy.

Annette Kur, Senior Research Fellow, Max Planck Institute for Innovation and Competition Law, Munich, Germany.

Timo Minssen, Associate Professor, LLD, LLM, Centre for Information and Innovation Law, University of Copenhagen, Denmark.

Ansgar Ohly, Professor, Dr, LLM (Cantab.), Chair in Civil Law, Intellectual Property and Competition Law, Ludwig-Maximilians-Universität of Munich; Visiting Professor, University of Oxford.

Andrea Stazi, Aggregate Professor of Comparative Law, European University of Rome, Italy.

Thomas Vinje, Attorney, Clifford Chance, Brussels, Belgium.

Jacques de Werra, Professor of Intellectual Property Law and of Contract Law, University of Geneva; Faculty Associate, Berkman Center for Internet and Society, Harvard University (2013–2014).

Jakob B. Wested, University of Copenhagen, Denmark.

Preface

This book is the second publication of the Center for Transnational IP, Media and Technology Law and Policy at Bucerius Law School, Hamburg, Germany. I would like to thank the contributing authors Michael Carroll, Séverine Dusollier, Gustavo Ghidini, Anette Kur, Timo Minssen, Ansgar Ohly, Andrea Stazi, Thomas Vinje, Jacques de Werra and Jakob Wested for having provided the insightful and intellectually stimulating contents of this book. I am further grateful to Constantin Blanke-Roeser for his outstanding editorial assistance and to Edward Elgar Publishing for the highly professional and friendly assistance provided. I wish to thank Bucerius Law School's management and the members of the Bucerius IP Center and the Center's Academic Advisory Committee for their advice and support. On a personal note, my deepest appreciation goes to my husband, Justs Karlsons, for his ongoing patience and encouragement.

Dana Beldiman

Abbreviations

BBF	BioBricks Foundation
CFREU	Charter of Fundamental Rights of the European Union
CJEU	Court of Justice of the European Union
EMA	European Medicines Agency
ETSI	European Telecommunications Standards Institute
FDA	US Food and Drug Administration
FRAND	fair, reasonable, and non-discriminatory
FTC	US Federal Trade Commission
ICT	information and communication technology
IOS	International Organization for Standardization
IP	intellectual property
IPR	intellectual property right
ITU	International Telecommunications Union
NAC	non-assertion covenant
OHIM	Office for Harmonization in the Internal Market
pma	*post mortem auctoris*
PSTC	Predictive Safety Testing Consortium
R&D	research and development
SB	synthetic biology
SEP	standard essential patent
SSO	standard setting organization
TFEU	Treaty on the Functioning of the European Union
TRIPS	Agreement on Trade-Related Aspects of Intellectual Property Rights
WIPO	World Intellectual Property Organization

Introduction: exclusion and inclusion – the role of IP laws in a shared knowledge environment

Dana Beldiman

FROM INNOVATION TO COLLABORATION

The past few decades have brought profound changes to all aspects of the innovation process. In the past, scientific and technological research and development (R&D) was mainly performed within manufacturing industries, usually as part of vertically integrated R&D and product innovation processes. Knowledge was generally produced in-house and maintained in a closed, internally proprietary, and localized environment, within large enterprises, universities, or think tanks.[1]

This paradigm began to change as the pace of technological development accelerated and technologies became more complex and fragmented. Difficulties in covering all stages of the innovation and production process internally led firms to seek complementary expertise and disciplines from outside their immediate chain of production and supply.[2] Research tools became more specialized and their cost decreased. This allowed new and, in many cases, small- and medium-sized enterprises to enter the R&D field and caused the number of players and overall participation in the innovation process to increase.

---

[1] *WIPO Intellectual Property Report 2011*, ch. 1, section 1.2, p. 23, available at www.wipo.int/export/sites/www/freepublications/en/intproperty/944/wipo_pub_944_2011.pdf.

[2] See Gustavo Ghidini and Andrea Stazi, Chapter 1.

One of the cornerstones of the open innovation[3] environment is the ability to make free and massive use of Internet-based communication platforms. This ability, which is largely taken for granted, is the result of key policy decisions made in the early days of the Internet to shield providers of information society services from infringement liability.[4] This model, which was adopted by legislators on both sides of the Atlantic[5] and spread to other geographic areas as well, has allowed society to take full advantage of the opportunities created by networked technologies and the communication facilities they provide.[6] Upon this foundation, numerous successful innovative services have been built, which provide the technological basis for the functioning of the open innovation paradigm.[7] The unrestricted emergence of new communication platforms thus enabled the interaction with new players, which previously had been beyond a firm's traditional supply and production environment and its localized geographic boundaries. Fuelled by these developments, open innovation emerged as an environment in which knowledge-based industries tend to abandon the vertical integration model in favor of a horizontal one and to rely on knowledge and skills from outside sources to complement their own internal resources.[8]

---

[3]   The term 'open innovation' generally refers to models of collaborative knowledge generation, largely enabled by new technology platforms which allow access to information from and collaboration with a wide circle of participants, including competitors, universities, customers, consumers, and so on. This should not be confused with the concept of 'open source', a movement prevalent primarily in the field of software development, which promotes an ethos of free sharing.

[4]   See Michael W. Carroll, Chapter 8, for a description of the evolution of this policy.

[5]   DMCA, 17 USC s. 512(a); Directive 2000/31/EC of the European Parliament and of the Council of 8 June 2000 on certain legal aspects of Information Society services, in particular electronic commerce, in the Internal Market ('Directive on Electronic Commerce') [2000] OJ L178/14.

[6]   See generally, D. Beldiman, 'Introduction' in D. Beldiman (ed.), *Access to Information and Knowledge: 21st Century Challenges in Intellectual Property and Knowledge Governance* (Cheltenham (UK)/Northampton, MA, Edward Elgar, 2013).

[7]   See Michael W. Carroll, Chapter 8.

[8]   Open innovation has been defined as 'the use of purposive inflows and outflows of knowledge to accelerate internal innovation and to expand the

This new paradigm requires a new type of interaction among the participants in the innovation process. Traditional rigid organizational structures are abandoned and dividing lines between firms' functions become more fluid. Close collaboration in innovation and production generates a variety of new relationships among firms, ranging from simple contract R&D, licensing in and out, to acquisition or dissemination of new technologies, cooperative R&D, cross licenses and collective R&D by industry associations or government supported institutions.[9] Openness accelerates innovation[10] and spawns new fields of research and new industries and endeavors, of increased complexity, often cross-disciplinary in such diverse fields as synthetic biology,[11] information technology,[12] creative industries,[13] and others.

In short, open innovation enables new paths for creation and dissemination of knowledge, more players in the market and new forms of relationships. It gives rise to a paradigm in which competitive advantage no longer necessarily rests on exclusive knowledge, instead primarily on the ability to access the right kind of knowledge at the right time.

These developments require a rethinking of the role that intellectual property (IP) laws should play in order to meet the needs of open innovation effectively. The individual chapters of this book will highlight developments in various areas of IP law, prompted by the realities of an open and shared knowledge environment.

---

markets for external innovation, respectively': *WIPO Intellectual Property Report 2011*, p. 47, quoting Henry Chesbrough, 'Open Innovation: A New Paradigm for Understanding Industrial Innovation' in Henry Chesbrough, Wim Vanhaverbeke and Joel West (eds), *Open Innovation: Researching a New Paradigm* (Oxford University Press, 2006); Gustavo Ghidini and Andrea Stazi, Chapter 1.

[9]   Other forms of collaboration include R&D consortia, ventures co-production, comarketing, coauthorship with universities, research organizations, and so on: *WIPO Intellectual Property Report 2011*, ch. 1.

[10]   *Ibid*. p. 47.

[11]   See Timo Minssen and Jakob B. Wested, Chapter 3.

[12]   Michael W. Carroll, Chapter 8.

[13]   See Dana Beldiman, Chapter 6.

EXCLUSION AND INCLUSION: THE ROLE OF IP IN A SHARED KNOWLEDGE ENVIRONMENT

IP laws grant exclusive rights to inventors so that they can position their inventions in the market advantageously. Yet in an open innovation environment, competitive advantage tends to reside less and less in the exclusive right to knowledge. How is this apparent conflict to be reconciled?

Neoclassical economic theory teaches that the exclusionary nature of IP laws is dictated by the need to avoid a market failure that would cause undersupply of knowledge products.[14] IP laws provide inventors with a temporary competition-free environment to allow them to derive economic gain from their invention.[15]

Open innovation does not detract from the ability for economic gain. Instead, open innovation relates to the proper allocation of IP resources among players in the economy and creates an environment which facilitates reallocation. A system based on private arrangements for allocation of IP rights leads to greater efficiency in the use of knowledge and thus furthers innovation.

For policy-makers it is notoriously difficult to determine the proper quantum of exclusivity that should granted by any particular IP right. The law therefore approximates the quantum of exclusivity based on a variety of economic assumptions. Individual IP owners, on the other hand, have the advantage of knowing the specific circumstances in which an IP asset is used. They are in a position to assess, with greater accuracy, the point at which ownership and exploitation of a particular IP asset is no longer of value, or is of greater value when traded for other benefits. Once that point is reached, a rational IP owner can relinquish exclusivity in exchange for a benefit, and at the same time, free the asset up for use by third parties.[16]

---

[14]   See generally, W. Landes and R. Posner, *The Economic Structure of Intellectual Property Law* (Cambridge, MA, Harvard University Press, 2003).

[15]   See *ibid.*

[16]   From a public policy perspective, it should be noted that a certain amount of sharing/access is considered to be in the interests of public welfare, by making valuable intellectual achievements available to the common benefit.

The option to relinquish IP rights is based on the fact that the law provides for, but does not mandate, the right to *exclude*. In other words, the right to *include* remains in the owner's discretion. Once considered from the perspective of inclusion and relinquishment of exclusivity, it becomes clear that, given their non-rivalrous nature, IP assets are particularly suitable for shared use, as they enable an asset's simultaneous use by multiple parties, without the risk of depletion. The interplay between the right to exclude and the right to include forms the theoretical basis for creating a privately ordered knowledge environment.

Many different paths lead to the shared use of knowledge. One of the more prevalent mechanisms is the use of contractual relations as a vehicle for transferring knowledge, operating against the background of IP laws.[17] Contract law and IP law serve as its primary legal instruments.

Contract law doctrines enable the structuring of malleable relationships between parties in knowledge transfer agreements. They establish the parties' rights and obligations vis-à-vis each other, including the terms of use, exploitation and transfer of IP assets. While contract law allows a great deal of flexibility in the allocation of IP rights, this flexibility brings with it certain risks due to the non-rivalrous nature of information. Open innovation involves a multitude of relationships among different players, seeking to share in the most recent inventions and know-how. Use of IP assets among multiple players gives rise to the risk of IP interdependence, in other words, the possibility of inconsistent contractual rights over IP assets, arising in the course of relationships such as outsourcing of R&D, joint ventures, licensing, sublicensing, and so on.[18]

Turning to IP laws, it becomes apparent that they play a dual role. First, by virtue of their *erga omnes*[19] effect, IP doctrines transform knowledge from a public into a privately appropriable,

---

[17] Gustavo Ghidini and Andrea Stazi, Chapter 1.
[18] The concerns arising out of this situation are discussed by Jacques de Werra, Chapter 5.
[19] Entitlement enforceable against all third parties, in contrast with the right to enforce only against contracting parties, conferred by contractual relationships.

merchandisable asset,[20] defining and delimiting the scope of rights and making them defensible vis-à-vis third parties. Second, by virtue of the ability to exercise exclusivity selectively, IP laws enable parties to structure arrangements that meet their respective economic goals, in terms of use, exploitation, geographic scope, subject matter scope, assignability, and so on. In particular, in the context of open innovation, their role is to enable collaboration between different players, by channeling knowledge among them in accordance with the structure and rules of the respective collaborative venture.[21]

These doctrines form the core theoretical legal framework that underlies the business relations and knowledge transfer agreements in an open innovation environment. The following discussion illustrates some of the issues raised by the interplay of contractual and IP norms in the context of shared use of IP assets.

INTERSECTION OF STANDARDS, FRAND AND COMPETITION LAW

Standardization of technologies poses one of the most significant challenges to IP laws, in particular to patent law. Standards require shared use of technologies in order to ensure interoperability and to allow establishment of common platforms in the context of complex technologies. Technology standards are mostly used by competitors, each seeking to secure a share of the product market for the respective technology. Thus, in addition to complex IP and contract issues, standardization may raise antitrust/competition problems as well, although, absent a dominant market position by the patent holder, in most instances no such issues are present.[22]

---

[20] See H. Ullrich and A. Heinemann in U. Immenga and E.J. Mestmäcker (eds.), *Wettbewerbsrecht*, vol. 1, EU Part 2, 5th edn (Munich, C.H. Beck, 2012), p. 1986 *et seq.* (GRUR B. annot. 22) with references.

[21] This includes rules on contribution of capital and/or capacities, on the division and/or centralization of work and on the distribution of results, including the 'rights' of exploitation, see *ibid.*

[22] Standards may be created by regulation, institutions or standard setting organizations which operate on a national, regional or international basis and may be found in all types of industries and businesses from railroads to business conduct, Timo Minssen and Jakob B. Wested, Chapter 3.

However, patents that are essential to a particular technology (standard essential patents or SEPs)[23] may raise serious antitrust/ competition concerns, as such patents confer on their owner the ability to restrict competing innovation in the licensing market, as well as downstream markets. In recognition of this fact, competition laws and standard setting organizations (SSOs) impose on licensors of SEPs the obligation to deal with license seekers on terms that are 'fair, reasonable, and non-discriminatory' (FRAND).[24] SSOs generally include FRAND commitments in their license agreements, thereby subjecting owners of declared SEPs to such commitments.

Issues surrounding SEPs and FRAND terms have presented challenges to courts for a number of years and are far from being resolved. One of the thornier issues facing courts and competition authorities is whether a SEP holder who is subject to a FRAND commitment has the right to enjoin an implementer (license seeker) from use of the SEP.[25]

In general, under most countries' patent laws, the grant of injunctions does not give rise to antitrust implications. In the case of SEPs, however, competition authorities are concerned that injunctions may have adverse competitive effects, leading to the distortion of licensing negotiations and to competition-restrictive licensing terms, and ultimately have a negative impact on consumer choice and prices.[26] Particularly in industries where time is of the essence, such as tablet computers and mobile phones, the delay caused by an injunction could be tantamount to precluding the

---

[23] A 'standard essential patent' (SEP) is a patent that is essential to the implementation of a particular standard and which cannot be designed around. European Commission, *Google/MMI*, COMP/M.6381.

[24] See EC proceeding against Qualcomm for excessive pricing, concluded without resolution, available at http://europa.eu/rapid/press-release_MEMO-09-516_en.htm?locale=en.

[25] Under European law, SEP owners are generally held to occupy a dominant position in the licensing and downstream market of the respective technology, and therefore to be subject to competition law.

[26] European Commission, Motorola Mobility and Samsung Electronics: Frequently Asked Questions, 29 April 2014, available at europa.eu/rapid/press-release_MEMO-14-322_en.pdf; see also European Commission antitrust proceeding in the *Apple Samsung* case, available at http://europa.eu/rapid/press-release_IP-13-971_en.htm. The European Commission takes the position that when seeking injunctions in the context of SEPs, the hold-up exists regardless of whether the effects are likely or actual.

license seeker from entering the market. In such cases, the mere seeking of injunctions may 'hold up' implementers of the particular technology and be sufficiently threatening to implementers to cause them to pay royalties in excess of FRAND rates, to relinquish certain rights, such as the right to challenge the validity of the SEP, or to agree to terms that they otherwise might not have agreed to. EU law views this an abuse of a SEP holder's dominant position.[27] Chapter 2 provides an in-depth discussion of the risks of the hold-up effect.[28]

Some initial guidance on the issue of injunctions in a SEP setting was provided by a German court. The *Orange Book* case held that the implementer of a SEP can successfully defend against an injunction sought by a SEP holder if (a) the implementer makes an unconditional offer to conclude a license agreement, (b) refusal of which by the SEP holder would be unfair or discriminatory, and (c) the implementer fulfills its contractual obligations by, for instance, paying or depositing appropriate royalties.[29] This standard was, however, viewed with skepticism by the European Commission. The concern voiced was that requiring the implementer to make an 'unconditional offer' would unreasonably strengthen a SEP holder's negotiation position and would risk forcing implementers into restrictive license agreements. In other words, the hold-up risk would remain present.[30] Thus the *Orange Book* rule might easily lead to the worst overall outcome, namely that an implementer would be precluded from use of a technology, despite its willingness to take a license.

---

[27]   TFEU Art. 102 prohibits the abusive exploitation of the dominant market position by an undertaking. The holder of a SEP occupies a dominant market position under antitrust law in both the license market and the downstream market, see European Commission, IP/13/406 06/05/2013, available at http://europa.eu/rapid/press-release_IP-13-406_en.htm.

[28]   See Thomas Vinje, Chapter 2.

[29]   German Federal Court of Justice, Orange Book Standard Decision, KZR 39/06 (2009).

[30]   '[T]he worst-case scenario [namely that] a company *willing to take a license* for standard-essential patents on FRAND terms is hit by an injunction' (emphasis added): J. Almunia, Vice President of the European Commission responsible for Competition Policy, EC Press Release, 20 September 2012, available at http://europa.eu/rapid/press-release_SPEECH-12-629_en.htm.

Under a more balanced standard, the implementer should merely have to demonstrate willingness to enter an agreement. This requirement would pose less danger to competition than an 'unconditional offer', in that it would eliminate the hold-up risk. Implementers who demonstrate a willingness to submit to the licensing framework provided for by the FRAND commitments could thus benefit from a safe harbor protecting them against injunctions sought by SEP owners.[31] This solution would balance 'the interests of SEP holders to be appropriately remunerated for their IP and the interests of implementers of standards to get access to standardised technology on FRAND terms'.[32]

This solution is not entirely devoid of risk. 'Willingness to negotiate' is a vague and unreliable standard. One can envision the reverse risk – that of a hold-out – where an implementer engages in lengthy non-committal negotiations without being subject to firm obligations. Meanwhile, the SEP holder would have to tolerate the unlawful use of its patent for an unforeseeable time, its remedy being limited to damages in a remote future.[33]

The issue of SEP injunctions in a FRAND context provides a good illustration of how proper interpretation of a specific IP law can facilitate shared use of an IP asset and can channel its use to the parties who are in a position to make beneficial use out of it. In the policy space between the extremes of (a) prohibiting use by the implementer and (b) allowing the implementer's use without adequate compensation to the SEP owner, one of the standards discussed above[34] or a modified version thereof, is likely to reach a balance point that places the parties into reasonably equal negotiating positions so that a deal can be reached. It is up to courts and SSOs to work out where that point lies, taking yet another step

---

[31] European Commission, Motorola Mobility and Samsung Electronics: Frequently Asked Questions, n. 26 above.

[32] *Ibid.*

[33] *Huawei* v. *ZTE*, Case no. 4b O 104/12, District Court Dusseldorf, Germany, 21 March 2013, referral to the Court of Justice of the European Union (CJEU) for clarification of the proper standard for evaluating injunctions involving SEPs subject to a FRAND commitment.

[34] Orange Book 'unconditional offer' and the 'willingness to negotiate' standard in defending against injunctions relating to a FRAND encumbered SEP.

toward facilitating the smooth flow of information required for an open innovation environment.[35]

An effective and comprehensive resolution of licensing in the FRAND context and the right to injunctions is also crucial for newly emerging fields of expertise, such as synthetic biology, discussed in detail in Chapter 3, whose overall IP treatment is still under debate. Synthetic biology is the field that deals with design and construction of new biological parts, devices and systems, and the re-design of existing natural biological systems.[36] It illustrates the questions arising in a new and promising, but legally largely uncharted field, in which the approach to innovation is yet to be defined. Some stakeholders view open innovation as a necessity to tackle innovation gaps, while others view it as an opportunity of 'free sharing' that would allow them to challenge traditional IP rights-based innovation models. Standardization is, of course, key to developing an IP model that allows synthetic biology as a field of research to move forward on solid bases. While efforts have been made in this regard, they are in an incipient phase. Much work is required to help synthetic biology reach its expressed goal of effective translational exploitation, in an open, standardized, and safe innovation system. Given the immense security risks of this new technology, effective legal strategies and regulations are critical for both the industry and society.

TRADEMARK LAW AND THE CONCEPT OF 'OPENNESS'

Trademark law issues may arise out of shared use as well, albeit of a slightly different nature. Unlike patents and copyright, trademarks are not assets in the nature of public goods[37] and therefore are not characterized by non-rivalry and non-excludability. The incentive and exclusivity rationale present in patent and copyright doctrine therefore does not apply. Yet, trademark law requires a different, and perhaps more stringent sort of exclusivity. Trademarks are unique indicators of commercial source, in that a trademark is

---

35   Thomas Vinje, Chapter 2.
36   Timo Minssen and Jakob B. Wested, Chapter 3.
37   Landes and Posner, n. 14 above.

capable of designating only one single source without giving rise to likelihood of confusion. Third party use would inevitably undermine the mark's uniqueness and prevent it from fulfilling its purpose.[38] Possibly, because of the apparent obviousness of this conclusion, the question of shared use of trademarks has received little attention.

Still, as pointed out in Chapter 4, in the trademark area private ordering resulting in shared use of trademarks tends to occur with increasing frequency. Such use takes the form of delimitation agreements, which demarcate the parties' mutual areas of exclusivity, by limiting the use of respective signs to particular product sectors, geographic areas, target groups, get-ups, and so on. Given their flexibility in the face of changing business relations, such private coexistence agreements fulfill an important business need.

To what extent such agreements are objectionable from the perspective of trademark policy remains to be determined. In principle, the main function of trademarks, avoidance of confusion, is likely ensured by the fact that in an arm's length transaction, each contracting party would affirmatively seek not to have the goodwill of its mark diverted to the other party.[39] As long as the agreement does not seek to apportion markets it would also be unobjectionable from a competition standpoint. Still, the concern remains that such agreements, which are usually not captured by the trademark offices or other public records, might undermine the public notice function of trademark law, which requires economic operators to inform the public with 'clarity and precision' of the nature of the protected subject matter.[40]

Nonetheless, it appears that the general axiom that shared use of a trademark is unacceptable is undergoing modification, and the notion that coexistence of marks in the market does not necessarily cause harm is gaining traction. Scholars and courts would have to focus on defining the circumstances in which coexistence can be tolerated and those in which it cannot, and articulating measures apt to provide appropriate and sufficient means to rule out serious risk to the public.[41]

---

[38]   See Annette Kur, Chapter 4.
[39]   See *ibid.*
[40]   See *ibid.*
[41]   See *ibid.*

CREATION AND SHARED KNOWLEDGE

Other models of knowledge sharing exist which, even though not collaborative, lead to accelerated innovation. This is well illustrated by the case of the fashion industry. Deviating from the classical exclusionary IP model, the fashion industry operates on a broadly shared knowledge basis, mostly without contractual restrictions. A possible explanation for the success of this model is sought in the effect of the expressive dimensions of design, self-expression and social expression, which, in the presence of massive knowledge spillover within the industry, accelerate consumption and increase demand for products.[42] This leads to the hypothesis that product demand, fuelled by the combined effect of disclosure of the product's IP content and the expressive dimensions of design, is capable of providing sufficient incentive to create, independent of the incentive provided by IP laws.

CONCLUSION

These and other models of knowledge sharing will be dealt with in detail in the various chapters of this book. However, within the general trend towards increasingly open innovation environments, a wide variety of other models exist. Furthermore, as new technologies develop, as new pathways for dissemination knowledge emerge and new players appear on the innovation scene, the ways in which knowledge can be shared will evolve as well. We are merely starting out on the path of shared knowledge.[43]

---

[42]   See Dana Beldiman, Chapter 6.
[43]   See generally *ibid.*

PART I

The intersection of standards, FRAND and competition law

1. Coopetition: the role of IPRs

Gustavo Ghidini and Andrea Stazi

1.1 THE GENERAL PHENOMENON: ITS DRIVING FACTORS, ITS BASIC CONTRACTUAL EXPRESSION

More and more typically, collaboration between competitors (hence: coopetition) is the way of creating innovation, and doing business at large, in a contemporary economic scenario which increasingly requires that both R&D and production of goods and services be based on multiple technological contributions.

Coopetition is an expression of contractual freedom, a functional profile of the 'freedom to conduct business' as per Article 16 of the Charter of Fundamental Rights of the European Union (CFREU), which translates into the right to choose if, when, how, and with whom to cooperate for entrepreneurial purposes and projects.

In particular, such collaboration is pursued in order to create 'value networks'[1] that:

- achieve lower costs and higher research and development (R&D);
- develop and expand markets;
- address major technological challenges;
- comply with new regulations; and
- develop new industry standards.[2]

---

[1]   See E.G. Carayannis and J. Alexander, 'The Wealth of Knowledge: Converting Intellectual Property to Intellectual Capital in Co-opetitive Research and Technology Management Settings' (1999) 18 *Int. J Technology Management* 326.
[2]   K. Blind, B. Ebersberger and A. Lorenz, *Coopetition, Cooperation and Competition as Determinants of Companies' Appropriation Strategies*

The philosophy of sharing as a prerequisite for the achievement of more advanced efficient industrial models stretches well beyond the field of information technologies and those *lato sensu* related to communications, which we usually think of in terms of network industries. That philosophy indeed permeates also more traditional sectors, in which industries have established – 'silently', in order not to tarnish the image of 'uniqueness' of products – production models largely based on projects developed in common, where the distinctive/competitive function is primarily entrusted to differentiation in design, trademarks, marketing policies, and so on.

Coopetition is built on a delicate, often fragile, balance of two opposite logics of interaction: the competitive paradigm driven by conflicting interests, which 'under the surface' nurture opportunistic, when not 'hostile' behavioral temptations, and the collaborative paradigm driven by common interests in a certain area.[3]

1.2   COOPETITION-FOR-INNOVATION: THE ROLE OF IPRs

Coopetition is particularly relevant and critical (even from a juridical perspective), when aimed at technological innovation. The challenges posed by such factors as shrinking product life cycles, the need for heavy investments in research and development, convergence of multiple technologies and paramount importance of technological standards, as well as similar features of the contemporary 'speed-based' multifaceted technological scenario, typically forbid that a single firm can create all the innovations needed to successfully compete. Conversely, firms that are capable of, and available for, peer collaboration have better chances to outperform competitors than those which rely only on internal resources and expertise.[4] Thus, in sum, mutual access and sharing amongst agreed

---

(February 2013), p. 3 *et seq.*, available at http://ssrn.com/abstract=2145165 or http://dx.doi.org/10.2139/ssrn.2145165.

   [3]   See *ibid.* p. 5.
   [4]   See D. Lim, 'Beyond Microsoft: Intellectual Property, Peer Production and the Law's Concern with Market Dominance' (2008) 18 *Intell. Prop., Media and Entertainment LJ* 291, especially 327.

partners emerges as an optimal, possibly 'the' optimal, paradigm for producing innovation.

Self-evidently, in technological coopetition, intellectual property rights (IPRs), patents in particular, play a crucial role. (The role is 'crucial', not 'indispensable', as it is quite possible, and not infrequent, that the collaboration concerns unpatented, even unpatentable, technology.)

Indeed, as the most important knowledge is normally covered by IPRs, patents and copyrights enhance the competitive value of the coopetitor's contribution to the collaborative venture,[5] thus making cooperation with patent and/or copyright holders reciprocally more attractive. This is due to:

(a) the *erga omnes* defensive power, which makes IPRs protected technology more valuable as enforceable against any free-riders, including third parties possibly benefiting in some manner from a violation of a contractual duty concerning the use of the patented technology – thus, the entitlement of patents provides a much stronger ('absolute') protection than the 'relative' one ensured by contractual remedies;

(b) the intrinsic 'certification' of innovative value that patents express: a value maximized when patents are standard essential patents (SEPs):[6] in other words, when they have no actual substitutes for achieving, or achieving efficiently, a specific purpose, as will be discussed below.

In sum, entitlement of IPRs interacts with the exercise of freedom of contract, acting both as *economic* incentive to seek-and-choose partners and to be sought-and-chosen by partners, and as legal

---

[5] See K.M. Saunders, 'The Role of Intellectual Property Rights in Negotiating and Planning a Research Joint Venture' (2003) 7 *Marquette Intell. Prop. L Rev.* 75; D.R. Gnyawali and B.J.R. Park, 'Co-opetition Between Giants: Collaboration with Competitors for Technological Innovation' (2011) 40 *Research Policy* 650.

[6] SEPs are 'patents that are essential to the standard (in that they must be practiced to accomplish the standard)' (Judge J. Robart, Order No. C101823JLR, in *Microsoft* v. *Motorola*, 24 September 2013, p. 3).

instrument for reciprocally granting, and being granted, partners of the collaborative venture, an *erga omnes* protection against free-riders.

We wish to emphasize the reference to 'inclusion' as the other face of Janus. We disagree with the current *vulgata* that identifies and symbolizes in the exclusive/excludent profile, almost exhausting in it, the content, and the very function, of IPRs. Indeed, while the exclusive/excluding 'face' of the patent acts as a Damocles' sword against *possible*, *occasional* contractual and non-contractual violations of the patent or the patent-related covenants, 'inclusive/ including' profile is instrumental to the *ordinary*, *permanent*, day by day entrepreneurial activity aimed at the cooperative development and exploitation of innovation.[7]

1.3 DUAL LEVEL OF REGULATION OF PATENT (ALSO SEPs) BASED COOPETITION: THE CONTRACTUAL RELATIONS AMONGST COOPETITORS

The subject matter evokes a systemic framework built at two basic legal levels:

(1)   at an internal level – in other words, a contractual one – related to the covenants and duties reciprocally binding the parties of the coopetitive venture;
(2)   at an external level, related to the impact of the same venture on the market, in particular on dynamic competition.

Let us synthetically check the main tenets of each of such levels of discipline.

(1)   The first level focuses on duties grounded on objective 'good faith' in the pre-contractual phase, the framing and interpretation of the contract, the execution thereof. Duties, thus, stemming

---

7   See G. Ghidini and A. Stazi, 'Freedom to Conduct a Business, Competition and Intellectual Property' in C. Geiger (ed.), *Research Handbook on Human Rights and Intellectual Property* (Cheltenham (UK)/Northampton, MA, Edward Elgar, 2015), pp. 410–20.

from the overarching principle of 'fairness and loyalty' (as translation of the German concept of *Treu und Glauben*), requesting that each party, in pursuing its own interest, 'preserve' – instead of boycotting – the contractual interest of the counterpart(s); and in this sense 'protect' the other party's trust in the establishment of a fairly balanced equilibrium of interests. Indeed, said duties, including reasonableness in fixing conditions, transparency/disclosure, and so on, are poignantly called by German doctrine 'protection duties' (*Schutzpflichten*), normatively stemming from section 241.2 BGB.[8]

This is equally true of other continental European national legislation, such as articles 1337, 1366, 1375 of the Italian Civil Code, and it is equally true, in substance, of common law contractual regimes. Such 'protection duties' were acknowledged by Judge Robart in his Order no. C10-1823JLR, in *Microsoft* v. *Motorola*, 24 September 2013, as duties based on the *Restatement (Second) of Contracts*, Section 205 'Duty of good faith and fair dealing' (on the concept of 'good faith' of the Uniform Commercial Code, Section 1-201).

1.4 PROCOMPETITIVE BOUNDARIES TO COOPETITIVE AGREEMENTS

(2)   The various forms of coopetition do not generally exclude the involved firms maintaining a reciprocal effective degree of competition, particularly, but not solely, as concerns 'downstream' market level. This is true not only because coopetitive relations are unstable, as nurturing opportunistic and hostile 'temptations' of reciprocally competing partners, nor 'just' because of antitrust constraints. Indeed, coopetitive initiatives may well *per se* have a positive impact on the prospects of dynamic competition. When competing firms cooperate, not only do they facilitate their own technological and product/service development and leverage the knowledge across related businesses within the firms' activity, but they also have a strong incentive to benchmark each other and

---

[8]   Buergerliches Gesetzbuch (BGB), in the text defined by the *Gesetz zur Modernisierung des Schuldrechts*, 26 November 2001, in force 1 January 2002.

prepare for future competition, which is enhanced because they become more 'informed', and richer in innovative capacity. Thus, present peace may well prepare for future 'dynamically competitive' (healthy) wars.

Moreover, as a consequence of the institution of a coopetitive venture, excluded followers may imitate and respond to industry leaders' actions, giving rise to a sort of 'group-to-group' competition.[9]

Thus, at the end of the day, these kind of 'alternative' cooperative initiatives may create new dynamics in the value chain, hence result in less concentrated 'one-sided' market dominance, with consequently less need for intervention by antitrust authorities.[10]

However, as hinted, antitrust authorities, carrying their big stick while not always speaking softly, keep a watch that the collaborative venture does not exceed its virtuous aims and does not transform itself into an agreement in restraint of trade, from the perspective of Article 101 of the EU Treaty. In European Union law, such control is normatively ensured by the discipline of specialization agreements and exchanges of technology, a discipline that tends to favor cooperation agreements while preventing the risk of degenerating into an appreciable restriction of competition.

This 'separation of the wheat from the chaff' is entrusted to the well-known exemption Regulations on R&D (Regulation (EU) 1217/2010) and technology transfer agreements (Regulation (EC) 772/2004 and related Guidelines, both under review by the European Commission). According to the new draft version of the Guidelines, in particular, the creation and operation of a technology pool falls outside Article 101(1) of the Treaty on the Functioning of the European Union, irrespective of the market position of the parties, if, among other conditions:

- sufficient safeguards are adopted to ensure that only essential technologies (which therefore by necessity are also complements) are pooled;
- sufficient safeguards are adopted to ensure that exchange of sensitive information is restricted to what is necessary for the creation and operation of the pool;

---

9   See Gnyawali and Park, n. 5 above, p. 652.
10   Lim, n. 4 above, p. 301 *et seq.*

- the pooled technologies are licensed out to all potential licensees on fair and non-discriminatory (FRAND) terms.[11]

1.5 THE CASE OF SEPs

Whenever the cooperative venture profits from either patents that embody or contribute to build a standard, and in particular in the hypothesis of standard essential patents (SEPs),[12] the antitrust perspective stretches to that of Article 102 TFEU. There must be an analysis of dominance, since SEPs *presumably*[13] confer dominance /market power (see the recent US-EU cases *Apple* v. *Samsung* and *Microsoft-Apple* v. *Motorola*). In recent years the number of SEPs-related litigation has been increasing.[14] Now, in such cases, and upon finding of market power, the antitrust authorities require that FRAND access to the resulting standards and related IPRs be granted even to third party competitors.[15]

1.6 A FINAL QUESTION

Finally, we leave open to doubt the possibility that access to SEPs might be systemically equated to the access that the patentee of a high-tech derivative invention may claim to the previous, 'original'

---

[11] See Draft Communication from the Commission: Guidelines on the application of Article 101 of the Treaty on the Functioning of the European Union to technology transfer agreements, C(2013)924 draft, paras 234–9 and 243 *et seq.*

[12] See n. 6 above.

[13] We disagree with the Commission's assumption that SEPs confer dominance *per se*. True, SEPs 'are a market' on their own. But the test for market power should be the absence of valid substitutes, based on different standards, for achieving the same functional result. Aspirin enjoyed market power until other drugs based on different pharmaceutical standards (for example, Tylenol = paracetamol) proved to be valid remedies for the same kind of illnesses.

[14] See K. Blind and T. Pohlmann, 'Trends in the Interplay of IPR and Standards, FRAND Commitments and SEP Litigation' (2013) *Les Nouvelles* 177.

[15] The subject obliged to grant such access will be, if the SEP remains owned by a single firm, the same firm; if the SEP is conferred in a patent pool, the access duty will fall on the pool.

patent she has worked on, in order to obtain green light to industrially realize and market her invention. Such hypothesis, as is well known, is foreseen by Article 31.1 of the Agreement on Trade-related Aspects of Intellectual Property Rights (TRIPs), which (as many national legislations, even *ante*-TRIPs, do) allows the derivative inventor to obtain a FRAND license (possibly crossed with that obtainable by the original inventor on the improvement). The effect of this mechanism is that both patentees will be able to compete offering an overall more advanced technology (A+B = B+A). This enhances innovation and consequently dynamic competition, and benefits consumers who will 'immediately' have access to the technological advancement – also at duopoly, rather than monopoly, prices. All this without any need of ad hoc investigations as to whether the original patentee has market power.

Hence, our question whether, whenever access to a SEP is requested for the purpose of developing and marketing a downstream (and thus 'derivative') innovation, the TRIPs norm might be applied by analogy *without*, as hinted, the need for an assessment of dominance/market power (and related costly proceedings).

Might such analogy be denied due to the difference of objectives (the TRIPs patent law rule 'just' aims at enhancing innovation, whereas antitrust aims at enhancing competition)? We doubt it. On one side, as shown, the TRIPs rule enhances dynamic competition. On the other side, however, isn't also the objective of enhancement of innovation an overarching goal of constitutional rank, just as much as defense of competition, thus allowing the interpreter to apply the rule that pursues it to substantially common scenarios of conflicting interests related to the sharing of essential technology?

That is our question, which we leave open. Should the answer be negative, we however express the wish that a future reform of the patent regime might expressly extend the Article 31.1 TRIPs mechanism to requests for access to SEPs for industrially realizing and marketing downstream innovation.

2. FRAND, hold-up and hold-out

Thomas Vinje

2.1 INTRODUCTION

This chapter will start out with an overview of the changes in the mobile telephony industry, how these changes have affected the patent litigation landscape, and in particular how they have given rise to the 'smartphone patent wars'. It will then describe how antitrust enforcement authorities, in particular the European Commission, have recently relied on the 'hold-up' theory[1] to limit the ability of a holder of a standard essential patent (SEP),[2] which is subject to a FRAND commitment,[3] to seek injunctive relief against potential licensees. In this context, the concept of 'willingness' will be addressed, including how it should be defined and whether it can serve as an appropriate criterion for determining the permissibility of injunctions.

2.2 LANDSCAPE OF STANDARD ESSENTIAL PATENTS IN THE MOBILE PHONE INDUSTRY

The relation between standard essential patents (SEPs) in the mobile telecommunications industry and antitrust law has not been

---

[1]   The hold-up theory as used by the European Commission is based on the concern that the threat of an injunction by the holder of a 'standard essential patent' (SEP) may have the effect of forcing a licensee out of the market.

[2]   A 'standard essential patent' (SEP) is a patent that is essential to the implementation of a particular standard and which cannot be designed around, see Google/MMI, COMP/M.6381.

[3]   A patent holder's commitment to fair, reasonable and non-discriminatory licensing terms.

an easy one. Competition authorities have already had to deal with issues of patent ambush, in other words, the failure to disclose one's patents reading on the candidate standard.[4] These issues have generally been resolved, with both antitrust law and the rules of standard setting organizations generally being understood as imposing an obligation to disclose in good faith patents that (are likely to) read on a candidate standard.[5] Similarly, the question of what constitutes FRAND licensing terms has been scrutinized, albeit without a conclusion having been reached. Hopes of greater clarity arose when the European Commission brought an action against Qualcomm for demanding excessive royalties in a FRAND context. However, the Commission ultimately chose not to pursue the difficult question of what constitutes FRAND terms, and no further clarification has been provided.

More recently, antitrust law has been facing the new challenge of the 'smartphone patent wars'. The background is that mobile telephony relies in large part on technology standards developed within the European Telecommunications Standards Institute (ETSI).[6] As most ETSI standard participants were both patentees (contributors) and implementers of the relevant standards, licensing negotiations could largely be based on bilateral, mutually-beneficial cross-license arrangements. In 2008, this equilibrium was distorted when Apple, which had not taken part in the ETSI standards development process, introduced its iPhone, which relied on ETSI standards and thus required a license from ETSI standard contributors.

The ETSI smartphone technology used in the iPhone had mostly been invented by Nokia and other ETSI contributors. Indeed, in its Communicator phone, Nokia had put together an early smartphone, using the Symbian operating system. However, Nokia had been unable to fully implement and market its phone. From having held

---

[4]   For instance, the US Federal Trade Commission investigated Dell for not having disclosed certain patent technologies in the context of standard setting, which ended with a consent agreement in 1996, see FTC Docket C-3658 (1996).

[5]   See n. 4 above.

[6]   European Telecommunications Standards Institute, see www.etsi.org.

well over 50 percent of the mobile phone market, Nokia's share dropped dramatically following the entry of Apple's iPhone.[7] At present, the smartphone market is largely divided between Apple and Samsung, with Apple taking the lion's share of profits and Samsung much of the remainder. Only a few other handset manufacturers of significance, mainly relying on Google's Android operating system, are present in the market.[8] Many of the players in the handset market are involved in an effort to jockey for position in that market, and thus engaged in the 'smartphones wars', in the form of numerous patent lawsuits and countersuits. Apple is at the center of a large number of these suits. Two main factors explain the proliferation of this litigation. One is that Apple's former CEO, Steve Jobs, took a hostile view of the Android operating system used by most handset manufacturers competing with Apple, publicly declaring a 'thermo-nuclear war' on Android. His main weapons in that thermo-nuclear war were patents, specifically design patents. The main reason for this was, as mentioned, that Apple had not participated in the standardization process of ETSI and others, as Apple was a late entrant in the telephony business. Apple therefore does not own standard essential patents covering the communication technologies involved in smartphones, relying instead on design patents in its infringement actions. Apple's litigation strategy against Samsung in particular proved very successful in the United States. However, Apple has been less successful elsewhere in the world, where many of its design patents were held invalid, thus resulting in far fewer judgments in its favor.

While Apple filed suits against other players, which it argued infringed its designs, many of Apple's targets felt compelled to defend themselves by countersuing Apple. With many of Apple's targets being established ETSI participants, some of whom had failed to convince Apple to take a license to their SEPs used in Apple's iPhone, these companies relied on their ETSI SEPs to defend themselves. Indeed, Apple's targets believed that Apple was maintaining its high margins in the smartphone market in part by free-riding on the technology produced via the standardization

---

[7]   Nokia's handset division was subsequently acquired by Microsoft in the spring of 2014.

[8]   Whereas Apple smartphones are based on Apple's proprietary mobile operating system, iOS.

efforts of earlier players who, unlike Apple, had actively contributed to the ETSI standardization process. They felt that Apple had been 'unwilling' to engage in good faith negotiations with respect to taking licenses to the requisite SEPs and to pay for the technology upon which its products rely.

This constitutes, in part, the background of the smartphone wars and explains the relevance of SEPs and of licensing them. Next we will address some of the difficulties inherent in these licenses, specifically relating to a SEP holder's ability to obtain injunctions against licensee/implementers of SEPs.

2.3   INJUNCTIONS AS TO SEPs AND THE RISKS OF HOLD-UPS AND HOLD-OUTS

The basic concern, which antitrust authorities and in particular the Federal Trade Commission (FTC) in the United States and the European Commission in Brussels have raised in relation to SEP litigation, relates to the hold-up theory. According to the hold-up theory, the SEP owner, by seeking an injunction with respect to an SEP, can 'hold up' implementers of the patent; specifically, implementers can be forced to pay excessive royalties or can be excluded from the market.[9] Because each SEP is (at least in theory) essential to implementing the relevant standard, the standard can, by definition, not be implemented without access to the SEP. A successful injunction request in relation to even a single SEP could thus prevent the defendant from implementing the entire standard. This is said in order to render the injunction request sufficiently great a threat to the implementer to cause it to be willing to pay excessive royalties, or royalties inconsistent with the patentee's FRAND commitment. According to the hold-up theory, it is irrelevant whether the injunction request is ultimately granted by the court, as the defendant or potential licensee may feel forced to accept the patentee's royalty demands knowing that there is a risk that the injunction may issue. Hold-up can therefore be caused by the mere *threat* created by an injunction request.

---

[9]   An implementer of such patents could, for instance, be in the position of Apple.

The hold-up theory is said to apply not only irrespective of whether an injunction is ultimately granted, it is also said to apply irrespective of whether the underlying royalty request is actually 'non-FRAND'. So far, antitrust authorities, specifically the European Commission, have been unwilling to delve deeper into the thorny issue of deciding what constitutes FRAND, as demonstrated in the Qualcomm[10] case, as well as in more recent cases involving Samsung and Motorola.[11] Thus, the Commission has not taken a position on whether the actual demands made by the SEP holders with respect to any of these cases are excessive in the context of FRAND commitments. Rather, irrespective of what does and does not constitute FRAND, any royalty demand made using the leverage of an injunction request is seen to amount to hold-up.

This is not the first time that the issue of whether injunction requests covering SEPs should be permitted arises. It was mentioned in the context of the Commission's Horizontal Guidelines,[12] but the Commission chose not to take a position on it. Standards-setting organizations have also addressed this question. For instance, an early ETSI proposal would have expressly permitted members to seek injunctions with respect to SEPs.[13] However, a lively debate on this topic is still ongoing in the standards setting organizations, including in particular ETSI and the ITU.[14]

---

[10] EC proceeding against Qualcomm for excessive pricing, concluded without resolution, available at http://europa.eu/rapid/press-release_MEMO-09-516_en.htm?locale=en.

[11] In 2011, Samsung sought injunctive relief in various European jurisdictions against competing mobile device makers based on alleged infringements of certain SEPs involving mobile telephony. In January 2012 the Commission opened an investigation to assess whether Samsung has abused its FRAND commitment to distort competition in mobile device markets, in violation of EU antitrust rules. In April 2014, the Commission issued 'Motorola Mobility and Samsung Electronics: Frequently Asked Questions', 29 April 2014, available at europa.eu/rapid/press-release_MEMO-14-322_en.pdf; see also European Commission antitrust proceeding in the Apple Samsung case, available at http://europa.eu/rapid/press-release_IP-13-971_en.htm.

[12] Guidelines on the applicability of Article 101 of the Treaty on the Functioning of the European Union to horizontal co-operation agreements [2011] OJ C11/1.

[13] See ETSI IPR Policy, available at www.etsi.org/images/files/etsi-ipr-policy.pdf.

[14] International Telecommunications Union (ITU).

It is worth mentioning that the hold-up theory as pursued by the Commission is distinct from related, more established, theories of harm, notably (a) refusals to license essential intellectual property rights, and (b) vexatious litigation. With respect to the former, the Commission appears to take the view that the case law on refusals to license applies to *commercially* essential intellectual property rights and not to intellectual property rights that have been declared *technically* essential to a widely used standard adopted by a standard setting organization (SSO). The Commission also appears to take the position that the Court of Justice of the European Union (CJEU)'s General Court case law on vexatious litigation[15] has no bearing on requests before a court seeking injunctive relief in relation to SEPs.

2.3.1 'Foreclosure' and Injunctions in the Context of SEP

Having addressed the basic hold-up concern, the question arises to what extent this concern can be addressed under EU competition law. To that end, it seems appropriate first to clarify a key concept under EU competition law (and in particular Article 102 TFEU), namely that of foreclosure. In recent years, the Commission has proclaimed an 'effects'-based approach to competition law enforcement, in particular to dominance cases under Article 102 of the TFEU.[16] The Commission has taken the position that an abuse should be found under Article 102 only in case of a likelihood of anti-competitive foreclosure, in other words, foreclosure leading to consumer harm. Specifically, the focus of enforcement was said to be shifted from the *form* of an undertaking's conduct to its actual or likely anti-competitive *effects*.

Against this background, it is important to consider the question of the standard against which such foreclosure effects must be proved, and what this means in the context of SEP injunctions. If one looks at the broader picture relating to such injunctions, one

---

15   T-111/96 ITT *Promedia*; T-119/09 *Protégé International*. According to this case law, exercising one's fundamental right of access to court can only amount to an abuse of a dominant position if two cumulative conditions have been met: (i) the claims cannot reasonably be expected to succeed, and (ii) the use of court proceedings is part of a plan to eliminate all competition.

16   Article 102 TFEU.

will find that European courts have not granted SEP injunction requests lightly.[17] The interrelation between the notion of foreclosure and the handling of injunctions relating to SEPs thus gives rise to a spectrum of potential approaches. On the one hand, the Commission's view is that seeking injunctions constitutes an abuse if the seeking of the injunction is (merely) *capable* of creating hold-up, in other words, of causing the implementer to pay excessive royalties, regardless of whether there are any likely (let alone actual) effects. An alternative approach, which the Commission has not adopted, but which some commentators believe would be appropriate, is that the seeking of SEP injunctions is abusive where doing so gives rise to a *likelihood* of foreclosure.[18] And finally, at the other end of the spectrum, one might find abuse only in case of *actual* foreclosure. Clearly, the threshold for a finding of anti-competitive foreclosure will affect the question of whether the seeking of SEP injunctive relief could constitute an abuse. But this question will ultimately have to be addressed by the Commission and by the courts, as more cases on these issues arise.

2.3.2 'Willingness' Standard

Returning to the issue of seeking injunctions in a SEP context, even if it is established that seeking SEP injunctive relief can lead to foreclosure under the relevant standard discussed above, the question remains whether all such foreclosure is necessarily anti-competitive, or whether, instead, some SEP injunction requests

---

[17] Samsung, for instance, was denied all of its injunction requests.

[18] Article 102 TFEU prohibits the abusive exploitation of the dominant market position by an undertaking. In 2009 the Commission published Guidance on the Commission's enforcement priorities in applying Article 82 of the EC Treaty to abusive exclusionary conduct by dominant undertakings (2009/C 45/02), available at http://eur-lex.europa.eu/legal-content/EN/TXT/HTML/?uri=CELEX:52009XC0224(01)&from=EN. The holder of a SEP occupies a dominant market position under antitrust law in both the license market and the downstream market, see European Commission, IP/13/406 06/05/2013, available at http://europa.eu/rapid/press-release_IP-13-406_en.htm. Support for the 'likelihood' standard of foreclosure could be found in para. 20 of these guidelines, which states, 'The Commission will normally intervene under Article 82 where, on the basis of cogent and convincing evidence, the allegedly abusive conduct is likely to lead to anti-competitive foreclosure'.

might be said to be pro-competitive. Again, a spectrum emerges. One end of the spectrum would be that injunctive relief should always be permitted. This position would be based on the normal application of patent law on the availability of injunctive relief, without creating special rules applicable to SEPs – in other words, seeking SEP injunctive relief would be immune from the application of competition laws. The other end of the spectrum would prohibit injunctive relief altogether, because of the risk of hold-up.[19]

The Commission is exploring the middle road of the spectrum, specifically whether these concerns can be balanced by using a 'willingness' approach. If the goal is to avoid a hold-up and a willingness standard is applied, then an implementer (licensee) who can demonstrate a willingness to license, can be assured that it will not be excluded from the market.[20] Therefore, if a willingness test can be applied to prevent a hold-up, no injunctions should be permitted, as long as the implementer demonstrates willingness to license on FRAND terms.

In this context it is important to mention the concept of a hold-out,[21] or reverse patent hold-up, which is the opposite of a hold-up. A hold-out occurs in a situation where an implementer is essentially immune from the SEP holder's efforts to seek injunctive relief and simply refuses to pay royalties. This would place the SEP holder in the position to have to seek damages with respect to every single patent, in every jurisdiction in which it is infringed. Considering the considerable numbers of patents and jurisdictions involved in the smartphone industry, the burden on the patent holder of obtaining an appropriate return on its investment by way of FRAND royalties would become excessive, potentially leading to a disincentive to contribute technology to new standards.

This fact prompts the conclusion that a solution to the risk of *hold-up* must be crafted in such a manner as to avoid raising the risk of a *hold-out*. The risks of both hold-up and hold-out can be avoided by focusing on the concept of 'willingness', an approach

---

[19]   This position was taken, for example, by Microsoft, among others.
[20]   For a more detailed discussion of the concept of 'willingness' see 3.2 below.
[21]   In a hold-out situation an implementer engages in lengthy non-committal negotiations without agreeing to firm obligations.

that is also favored by the Commission. The theory would be that an SEP injunction request could be abusive when made vis-à-vis a willing licensee (thus avoiding hold-up), but potentially permissible when sought against an unwilling licensee (thus helping to avoid hold-out).

Yet, the precise meaning of 'willingness' remains unresolved. For example, one question is *whose* willingness matters. Most, including the European Commission, view the concept of 'willingness' as referring to the *licensee's* willingness to take a license and pay FRAND royalties. However, that is not the only possible approach. The US International Trade Commission (USITC), for instance, looks at the willingness of the licensor to *grant* a license on FRAND terms, rather than whether the licensee is prepared to take one.[22] The USITC thus found that Samsung, in its capacity as licensor vis-à-vis Apple, had been willing to grant Apple a license to its SEPs. Having established Samsung's willingness to do so, the USITC saw no reason not to grant an exclusion order. Willingness can be approached in different ways: one way is to follow the Orange Book rule,[23] another is the FTC-Google approach.[24] In short, there is no agreement on the definition of the term 'willingness'; a clear definition and consistent application of the term would eliminate the current legal uncertainty on this issue.

Regarding the institutional point as to where best to address the question of willingness, there are two basic approaches. One is a case-by-case approach, by way of individual declarations.[25] National courts, where SEP injunctions were first sought, have addressed issues of willingness; competition authorities have begun

---

[22]   USITC, *In the Matter of Certain Electronic Devices, etc.*, Inv. No 337-TA-794 (2013).

[23]   *Orange Book Standard Decision*, German Federal Court of Justice, KZR 39/06 (2009).

[24]   See Federal Trade Commission (FTC) proceeding against Motorola Mobility and Google, Docket No. C-4410, concluded by settlement, Decision and Order, 23 July 2013, available at www.ftc.gov/sites/default/files/documents/cases/2013/07/130724googlemotorolado.pdf.

[25]   For instance, Microsoft has declared that it will not enforce SEPs via injunctions; Apple has given a declaration, caveated in certain key ways; Cisco has basically gone along with Apple; and Google has issued its own declaration, which differs in some respects from those of the other companies.

to consider them, and have done so not only under (EU) competition law, but also under principles of (national) civil law. Thus, in the Apple and Samsung litigation, the courts rejected all of Samsung's requests for injunctions. However, the weakness of the case-by-case approach lies in its lack of consistency. Alternatively, the issue can be dealt with under antitrust law, by way of individual cases brought by the antitrust authorities, such as the Samsung or the Google/Motorola cases.[26]

In this regard, some headway has been made by the position stated by the Commission in a press release relating to these cases. The Commission suggests a safe harbor to the benefit of SEP implementers who demonstrate a willingness to submit to the licensing framework provided for by the FRAND commitments, protecting them against injunctions sought by SEP owners.[27] This approach has balanced the positions somewhat by alleviating the implementer's burden.[28] It also addresses the hold-up concern by eliminating the threat of injunction. Thus, a willing licensee would no longer run the risk of being excluded from the market and possibly being forced into terms that it otherwise would not agree to.[29] On the other hand, the risk of hold-out remains.

2.4 CONCLUSION

The foregoing discussion illustrates that, whatever the ultimate approach to the issue of injunctions involving SEPs may be, it would seem desirable for a common and consistent position to be

---

[26]   European Commission, 'Antitrust: Commission sends Statement of Objections to Motorola Mobility on potential misuse of mobile phone standard-essential patents: Questions and Answers', MEMO/13/403, 06/05/2013, available at http://europa.eu/rapid/press-release_MEMO-13-403_en.htm.

[27]   European Commission, 'Motorola Mobility and Samsung Electronics: Frequently Asked Questions', n. 11 above.

[28]   For instance, compared to the Orange Book standard, under which an 'unconditional offer' was required from the implementer, rather than mere 'willingness', see *Orange Book Standard Decision*, n. 23 above.

[29]   The interests of SEP holders to be appropriately remunerated for their IPRs and the interests of implementers of standards to get access to standardized technology on FRAND terms: European Commission, 'Motorola Mobility and Samsung Electronics: Frequently Asked Questions', n. 11 above.

found. Where would it come from? One source would, of course, be the courts. In this regard, the outcome of the pending *Huawei* preliminary reference to the CJEU is critical,[30] as it has the potential of resulting in a EU-wide solution to this issue. Whether sufficiently clear and detailed guidance will result from that decision, however, remains to be seen. Another source could be the standard setting organizations, which could provide industry-wide solutions. Finally, legislation would provide an across-the-board solution, although it may be too optimistic to expect that in the near future. Still, instruments of 'soft law', such as antitrust guidelines issued by the European Commission, could contribute to more clarity. However, regardless of the means of reaching a solution, a consistent approach remains key to resolving these disputes.

---

[30] *Huawei* v. *ZTE*, Case no. 4b O 104/12, District Court Düsseldorf, Germany, 21 March 2013, referral to the CJEU for clarification of proper standard for evaluating injunctions involving SEPs subject to a FRAND commitment.

3. Standardization, IPRs and open innovation in synthetic biology

Timo Minssen and Jakob B. Wested *

INTRODUCTION

Innovation finds itself embedded in an expanding milieu of openness these days, which is closely connected to the increase in knowledge flows across traditional boundaries of scientific disciplines, geography, languages, businesses, institutions, markets, professions and subjects. The general concept of openness assumes many forms and variations depending on the context. The idea of openness has also found its way to the emerging technological area of synthetic biology (SB).

SB applies the principles of engineering – abstraction, decoupling and standardization – to the study of biology. This includes the design and construction of new biological parts, devices and systems, and the re-design of existing natural biological systems.[1] Due to recent advances in nanotechnology, automated strain engineering, protein modification, DNA synthesis, and

* This chapter is based on 'Standardization and Open Innovation in Synthetic Biology', paper presented at the Bucerius IP Conference 2013, 'Innovation, Competition and Collaboration', Hamburg, 11 October 2013. We thank Prof. Dr Dana Beldiman and her team for this wonderfully organized conference. The authors are currently preparing a lengthier follow-up paper on this topic. Our studies were supported by the Danish Research Council as part of project 'User Generated Law: Re-constructing Law in the Knowledge Society', as well as by the 'BioSYNergy' project, available at http://synbio. ku.dk/biosynergy/, under the umbrella of the University of Copenhagen's Excellence Program for Interdisciplinary Research.

[1] See Stanford School of Medicine, 'About Synthetic Biology', available at http://igem.stanford.edu/aboutus.html.

related technical standards, these activities rapidly boost both the sophistication and scope of genetically encoded functions. This enhances the development of complex integrated biological systems that can be customized to optimize various industrial, medical, or agricultural applications. Spurred by the great promises of SB, public and private investments in SB have increased dramatically.

Meanwhile, the inherent dangers of this technology, as well as the numerous scientific, socio-economic, ethical, regulatory, and legal challenges posed by SB, remain a multifaceted conundrum. One of the many different legal issues concerns the questions of how to best enhance the scientific advances of SB and how to best stimulate and govern its translational exploitation towards useful applications.

Traditionally, scientific advances within emerging technological fields, such as biotechnology, have been protected, licensed, and transferred through intellectual property rights (IPRs) and IPR-related rights. However, the complexity, interdisciplinarity, interoperability, and risks of this technology pose a variety of challenges for IPR prosecution and litigation in the biotechnological field.

In patent law, for example, some commentators warn of potentially stifling effects for innovation in SB resulting from a thicket of property rights evolving around patent law's problem children, in other words, biotechnology and software.[2] Other commentators acknowledge that SB presents challenges to the patent system and patent quality with regard to proper prior art searches, costs, effective processes, speed, and transparency, but note that the technology would not pose any dramatically new problems and that SB would not require any fundamental changes to substantive patent law. Some authors also point out that many problems and solutions would probably have to be addressed in the post-grant phase, in other words, once the patent has been granted.[3] Moreover,

[2]   S. Kumar and A. Rai, 'Synthetic Biology: The Intellectual Property Puzzle' (2007) 85 *Texas L Rev.* 1745 (arguing for a parallel patent-free space operating as public domain or commons).

[3]   B. Rutz, 'Synthetic Biology and Patents: A European Perspective' (2009) 10 *EMBO Reports* 514.

the nature and applications of SB have fuelled debates on copyright protection, trademarks, and trade secrets.[4] In addition to these 'internal' IPR debates, many uses and users of SB are also challenging, or even ignoring the well-established paradigms of the IPR and technology transfer system as such. Some SB research communities and bio-hackers have embraced an ethos of 'open biology' in the sense of 'free sharing' and welcome it as an opportunity to challenge traditional IPR-based innovation models. Open innovation models in a business context are, however, often associated with the development of creative, user-generated approaches to managing and licensing *traditional* IPRs instead of protecting and defending them within the boundaries of one company. Some stakeholders, such as (bio-)pharmaceutical companies, have begun to cautiously approach the concept of openness as an unavoidable necessity to tackle innovation gaps, while others are mostly concerned by threats that openness might pose to well established innovation and business models.

Irrespective of these different perceptions of openness and IPRs, an effective and just sharing of resources for innovation needs a supportive infrastructure. One such infrastructure of both historic and contemporary significance is the development of standards. Considering recent developments within the software and information and communication technology (ICT) industries, it seems fair to assume that the process of standardization may also have significant impact on the development and adoption of SB.[5] Within SB different standardization efforts have been made, but none has assumed a dominance or authority in the area. Standardization efforts within SB may differ within various *technical areas*, and also the *basic processes* of standard creation can be divided into various categories. The different technical areas and processes for standardization differ in their *speed, handling of interests*, and *ability to dodge possible IPR concerns*.

Out of this notion arises, *inter alia*, the following questions: How comparable is engineering in SB to more traditional fields of engineering? What types of standards have emerged and what

---

    [4]   A.W. Torrance, 'Synthesizing Law for Synthetic Biology' (2010) 11(2) *Minn. JL Sci. and Tech.* 629.
    [5]   A. Rai, 'Unstandard Standardization: The Case of Biology' (2010) 53(1) *Comm. Acm.* 37.

bearing have IPRs on these? and How applicable are the approaches adopted by the standard setting organizations in information and communication technology (ICT) to biological standards? These and further legal issues related to IPRs, regulation, standardization, competition law, and open innovation require a careful consideration of new user-generated models and solutions.

Against this background this chapter seeks to describe the IPR and standardization aspects of SB in order to discuss them in the context of the 'open innovation' discourse. We concentrate on describing the technology and identifying areas of particular relevance. Ultimately we also sketch out open questions and potential solutions requiring further research. However, due to the limitations of this chapter we do not aim to create thorough theories or to propose solutions in more detail.

To achieve this modest goal, 3.1 commences with a brief introduction to the fascinating science of SB and a description of recent technological advances and applications. This will lead us to 3.2, in which we will address standard setting efforts in SB, as well as the relevance and governance of various IPRs for specific SB standards. This provides the basis for 3.3, in which we debate problematic issues and summarize our conclusions.

3.1 FROM DISCOVERY TO CONSTRUCTION: A NEW GENERATION OF BIOTECHNOLOGY

Section 3.1.1 of this scientific preface will commence by briefly summarizing the history and typical characteristics of synthetic biology, as well as the various actors engaged in it. This is followed by a description of the main research areas and applications of SB in 3.1.2.

3.1.1 What is Synthetic Biology and Who is Involved?

At the turn of the twenty-first century, a new cluster of technologies has emerged as a new frontline in biotechnology. Synthetic biology, system biology, nanotechnology, as well as improved sequencing, more sophisticated recombinant DNA technologies, and bioinformatics are all part of this cluster constituting the next generation of biotechnology.[6] Standing on the shoulders of new scientific discoveries, vast amounts of data and improved technologies, the skillful combination of these overlapping disciplines provides a fertile platform for innovation. The step into the new generation of biotechnology is characterized by the move from copies and recombinations of what is found in nature, to the design and construction of biological entities from scratch.[7] Furthermore, the application of engineering principles and the goal of creating artificial life are also considered as constituting factors of the area of synthetic biology that distinguishes it as a new generation of biotechnology.[8] However, many of the building blocks or 'parts' used for synthetic biology are identical to those used in other areas of biotechnology. In summary, the differences between synthetic biology and traditional biotechnology thus seem to reside more in the scale of modification of naturally occurring organisms and in the underlying concepts than in the actual technologies used.[9]

The idea of creating novel biological entities by applying engineering principles to biology was already presented by the Nobel Prize laureate Edward Tatum[10] in 1958. In the 1970s the term surfaced again in the writings of Polish geneticist Waclaw Szybalski,[11] and in 1980 Barbara Hobom used the term synthetic biology

---

6   McKinsey Global Institute, *Disruptive Technologies: Advances that will Transform Life, Business, and the Global Economy* (2013), p. 87, available at www.mckinsey.com/insights/business_technology/disruptive_technologies.

7   For detailed description of the progression from the first to the second and third generations of biotechnology, see T. Minssen, *Assessing the Inventiveness of Bio-Pharmaceuticals under European and US Patent Law* (Ineko AB/Lund University, 2012), pp. 69–105.

8   Rutz, n. 3 above.

9   *Ibid.* p. 515.

10   E. Tatum's Nobel Prize lecture, 11 December 1958, available at www.nobelprize.org/nobel_prizes/medicine/laureates/1958/tatum-lecture.html (the presentation of this idea is found in para. 28 towards the end of the lecture).

11   W. Szybalski, 'In Vivo and in Vitro Initiation of Transcription' in A. Kohn and A. Shatkey (eds.), *Control of Gene Expression* (New York, Plenum Press, 1974), p. 405 (published in relation to conference held on 27–30 March 1973).

to describe her work with genetically engineered bacteria and recombinant DNA technology.[12]

The emergence of contemporary synthetic biology has been catalyzed by a variety of sources. These include the increased focus on interdisciplinary approaches, the development of improved enabling technologies, institutionalization of the field in dedicated conferences, as well as research groups and community building through initiatives like the iGEM competition.[13] However, a specific commonly accepted definition of the discipline has not yet been established.

As mentioned above, a common feature in the existing definitions of synthetic biology is the application of engineering principles to biology and the goal of designing and creating useful biological parts and devices.[14] The engineering methodology is depicted as (1) the construction and description of *standard* biological parts; (2) *decoupling*, in other words, the separation of complicated problems into smaller and less complicated problems; and (3) *abstraction hierarchies* that also help to reduce complexity.[15] Especially the standardization of biological parts has been at the center of the efforts and hopes of the synthetic biology community. Initiatives such as the BioBricks Foundation[16] are trying to create an open access repository of standard biological parts; a venture that is creating a comprehensive infrastructure for research, development, and innovation. Efforts of making standardized biological parts freely available and the rapid decrease in the price of many of the enabling technologies has spurred and enabled

---

[12]   B. Hobom, 'Gene Surgery: On the Threshold of Synthetic Biology' (1980) 75(24) *Medizinische Klinik* 834.

[13]   M. Meyer, 'Assembling, Governing, and Debating an Emerging Science: The Rise of Synthetic Biology in France' (2013) 63(5) *Bioscience* 374.

[14]   For examples of definitions see for example, www.erasynbio.eu/index.php?index=32 or www.syntheticbiology.org.

[15]   D. Endy, 'Foundations for Engineering Biology' (2005) 438(24) *Nature* 449.

[16]   The BioBricks Foundation (BBF) is a public-benefit organization founded in 2006 by MIT and Harvard scientists and engineers who recognized that synthetic biology had the potential to produce big impacts on people and the planet and who wanted to ensure that this emerging field would serve the public interest; for further information see http://biobricks.org/about-foundation/.

a 'bottom-up' movement in research including in the field of synthetic biology, where people tinker with science in their spare time. These groups may be found under headlines such as Bio-Hackers, Bio-Punks, garage biology, Do-It-Yourself (DIY) biology, and citizen science.[17] But SB has, of course, also attracted the interests of many large companies and research institutions that are heavily engaged in exploiting the possibilities of SB and invest large sums to develop useful applications. This has resulted in SB having developed into a significantly diversified discipline regarding agents, interests, research, and applications.

The scope of applications and their potential encompasses a vast number of industries. The synthetic biology market in itself is estimated to reach a size of US$10.8 billion in 2016,[18] and the overall market for this next generation of biotechnology is estimated to reach a size of up to US$1.6 trillion in 2025.[19]

3.1.2   Main Research Areas and Applications of Synthetic Biology

Simply speaking, the research areas of synthetic biology can be divided into three general areas: (1) biological parts; (2) genomes; and (3) cells,[20] moving from the simplest to the more complex entities.

Biological parts encompass the construction of DNA circuits, synthetic metabolic pathways, unnatural components, and microbial consortia.[21] One of the key ambitions of this field of research is to create modular biological parts that may be combined into more

---

[17]   The terms are not clearly separated and are often used interchangeably. The general goal of these movements is to make accessible the tools and resources for scientists and non-scientists alike, to undertake biological engineering and experiments, see for example, http://diybio.org/.

[18]   BCC Research Report, *Synthetic Biology: Merging Global Markets* (2011), available at www.bccresearch.com/market-research/biotechnology/global-synthetic-biology-markets-bio066b.html.

[19]   McKinsey Global Institute, n. 6 above.

[20]   See C.M.C. Lam, M. Godinho, and V.A.P. Martins dos Santos, 'An Introduction to Synthetic Biology' in M. Schmidt, A. Kelle, A. Ganguli-Mitra, and H. de Vriend (eds.), *Synthetic Biology: The Technoscience and Its Societal Consequences* (Berlin/Heidelberg, Springer, 2009), ch. 3, p. 25.

[21]   See Lam, Godinho, and Martins dos Santos, n. 20 above, pp. 26–37.

complex biological systems. *DNA circuits* may be thought of as logic gates or on–off switches that may regulate the release of medicine, expression of a phenotype, or start a metabolic process. *Metabolism* is a process in the cell, where material is either broken down (catabolism) or constructed (anabolism) for the purpose of regeneration or as a response to stimuli from the cells environment. This biological function has been utilized in its natural form in for example, the making of cheese, beer, and soy sauce. Synthetic metabolic pathways may likewise be designed to break down or construct material in order for example, to produce a chemical or degrade chemicals or agricultural bi-products. To optimize synthetic metabolic pathways to a level of efficiency sufficient to make this technology interesting on an industrial level,[22] construction of *unnatural components* such as amino acids are necessary. Introduction of unnatural components also renders the synthetic systems easier to regulate and increases stability and fitness. Finally, the research into *microbial consortia* focuses on the interplay between the synthetic parts and devices. Design of microbial consortia is necessary to construct more sophisticated metabolic processes and at the same time obtain robust systems. This field of research overlaps with the field of systems biology that focuses on the function of whole biological systems. The general difference between the two is their research focus. While systems biology is aimed at understanding biological systems, synthetic biology is aimed at constructing biological systems.[23]

Engineering on a *genomic level* is a field that has increased rapidly in the last years due to new and improved enabling technologies that reduce the cost and increase the pace and accuracy of genome sequencing.[24] Techniques for editing in a genome existed since the 1970s, in other words, in recombinant DNA technology, where genetic information from multiple sources are put together and inserted into a host cell. In a strict synthetic

[22] See Y. Li, 'Beyond Protein Engineering: Its Application in Synthetic Biology' (2012) 192 *Enzyme Engineering* 1.

[23] K. Kastenhofer, 'Two Sides of the Same Coin? The (Techno)epistemic Cultures of System and Synthetic Biology' (2013) 44 *Studies in History and Philosophy of Biological and Biomedical Science* 131.

[24] See L. Liu *et al.*, 'Comparison of Next Generation Sequencing Systems' (2012) *J Biomedicine and Biotechnology* Article ID 251364.

biology approach the ambition is to construct an entire genome from synthetic genes. The challenge with creating whole synthetic genomes is the design. At the moment testing the design must be done empirically, which makes large-scale *de novo* synthesis of genomes a resource- and effort-consuming endeavor.[25]

Obviously the same challenge of design applies considering attempts to create a minimum *living cell*. The reason for creating a cell that only contains what is absolutely necessary to be alive relates to the idea of creating a host for synthetic biology devices that entails the smallest possible level of complexity. It is then hoped that this will improve predictability, robustness, and efficiency. Two research approaches known as top-down and bottom-up are pursued in this area. The top-down approach is based on the removal of content from a living cell to find out what is essential and what is contingent to perform the functions constituting life, in other words, reproduction and evolution. The bottom-up approach seeks to build a minimum living cell from scratch, a task that has been described as similar to trying to assemble an operational jumbo jet from its parts list without a manual.[26] This is also called a *protocell*. This line of research is indeed related to the study of how life came about millions of years ago, a puzzle that has not yet been solved and a functional protocell has not yet been constructed.

Such research endeavors undertaken in synthetic biology are often multifaceted, intertwined, and overlapping with each other and a variety of disciplines, as is illustrated in Figure 3.1.[27]

The broad scope of disciplines, interdisciplinarity, and cross-fertilization found in synthetic biology provides the foundation for a vast range of present and potential future applications of the technology. Chemicals, pharmaceuticals, medical treatment, food, energy, and materials are just some of the areas where SB is applied

---

[25]   K.M. Esvelt and H.H. Wand, 'Genome-scale Engineering for Systems and Synthetic Biology' (2013) 9(1) *Molecular Systems Biology* 7.

[26]   Comment by J. Collins in 'Opinion in Nature, Life after the Synthetic Cell' (2010) 465 *Nature* 424.

[27]   Figure 3.1 is a modified version of an illustration that can be found in Lam, Godinho, and Martins dos Santos, n. 20 above, p. 26.

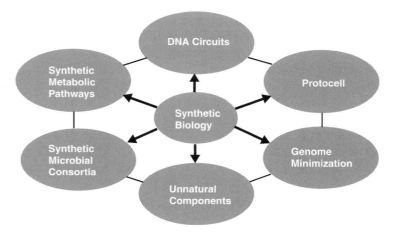

Figure 3.1 Research areas in synthetic biology

or products are in the pipeline.[28] So far, the most progressed field is relying on biological parts. Especially the construction of metabolic pathways has been utilized to transform biomass into a range of chemical products, such as surfactants[29] and acrylic,[30] subsidizing the petro-chemical production of these. Other applications have successfully produced medical compounds such as Artemisinin,[31] and a large industry transforming biomass into bio-fuels such as ethanol is already quite advanced.[32]

---

[28] See Synthetic Biology Project, 'Inventory of Synthetic Biology Products: Existing and Possible', available at www.cbd.int/doc/emerging-issues/ emergingissues-2013-07-WilsonCenter-SynbioApplicationsInventory-en.pdf.

[29] See K. Jarrell, 'Modular Genetics Demonstrates Production of Bio-Derived Glycinate, an Ultra-Mild Surfactant', available at www.businesswire. com/news/home/20130715006213/en#.UuAzG2SKZ-U.

[30] See OPX Biotechnologies Inc., 'Product Overview', available at www. opxbio.com/our-business/products/.

[31] D.-K. Ro *et al.*, 'Production of the Antimalarial Drug Precursor Artemisinic Acid in Engineered Yeast' (2006) 440 *Nature* 940.

[32] Biotechnology Industry Organization, *Current Uses of Synthetic Biology for Renewable Chemicals, Pharmaceuticals, and Biofuels* (2013), available at www.bio.org/sites/default/files/Synthetic-Biology-and-Everyday-Products-2012.pdf.

The harnessing of community-based innovation, open access, and the efforts invested in creating a foundation of standards to build on has made a deep imprint on the research and development agenda in synthetic biology. Commercialization of the inventive efforts will entail considerations of intellectual property rights (IPRs). Especially the emphasis on openness and standardization found in a broad range of contemporary synthetic biology activities raises several questions and concerns in relation to IPRs, questions that are becoming ever more pressing to answer for every step synthetic biology takes towards technological maturity.

3.2   STANDARDIZATION AND IPRs IN SB

In this section we first briefly explain what standards are and describe the different underlying rationales and incentives for standardization efforts. We also attempt to identify and categorize different situations and conditions, in which standards may emerge (3.2.1). This is followed by a summary of generally problematic issues in standardization (3.2.2). We will conclude this section with a brief description of particular standardization efforts in the pharma-, nanotech-, and SB sectors in order to discuss the relevance of IPRs for these areas and how they are addressed (3.2.3).

3.2.1   What are Standards, Where Do They Come From and Why Do We Need Them?

A standard may be based on a norm or requirement, specifying guidelines, specific characteristics of products or conducts, or – in the simplest definition – an agreed way of doing something.[33] Standards can be found in many technological endeavours, in other words, from railroad tracks and light bulbs to guidelines on business conduct and space shuttles.

---

[33]   British Standards Institution (BSI), 'What is a Standard?', available at www.bsigroup.com/en-GB/standards/Information-about-standards/what-is-a-standard/.

The establishment of standards is generally seen as an important step towards fostering innovation in any industry.[34] This general raison d'être of standards can be elaborated by applying the perspectives of economy, norms, strategy, and structure on standardization.

From an *economic* perspective standards bring down transaction costs, increase interoperability, and may create value through network effects. From a *normative* perspective standards may promote norms of environmental protection and safety through regulation or they may enable sharing and collaboration in communities based on such norms. Many synthetic biology communities embrace an ethos of openness, a norm that is indeed enabled and put into action by the development and adoption of standards. As a *strategic* tool standards may provide both variation and stabilization in a market. A common technological platform creates stability, but may also create technological variation by enabling competing down-stream innovation. Finally, a *structural* perspective on standardization may envision standards as a structure enabling dispersed innovation and collaboration in much the same way as the Internet enables communication and globalization.

Many standards are made by institutions or so-called standard setting organizations (SSOs). There are national, regional, as well as international SSOs. But standards also come into being through other channels such as regulation or general adoption,[35] also named *de jure* and *de facto* standards respectively. *De jure* standards may be found in for example, environmental regulation or regulation of safety measures. Examples of *de facto* standardization could be the use of Windows on computers or, before DVD and streaming came about, VHS.[36] The institution, regulation, or general adoption

---

[34] CEN Standard Compass, *The World of European Standards* (2010), p. 9, available at ftp://ftp.cen.eu/CEN/AboutUs/Publications/Compass.pdf. See K.M. Müller and K.M. Arndt, 'Standardization in Synthetic Biology' in W. and M. Fussenegger (eds.), *Synthetic Gene Networks: Methods and Protocols*, Methods in Molecular Biology (Berlin/Heidelberg, Springer, 2012), vol. 813, ch. 2.

[35] T.S. Simcoe, 'Open Standards and Intellectual Property Rights' in H. Chesbrough, W. Vanhaverbeke, and J. West (eds.), *Open Innovation: Researching a New Paradigm* (Oxford, Oxford University Press, 2006), p. 161.

[36] One example would be the battle of the 1980s between Betamax and the VHS format.

represents a *deliberative, authoritative,* or *pervasive* process of standardization.

Another line of distinction can be found between *formal* and *informal* standards. Definitions of standards that emphasize a standard as a document providing requirements, specifications, guidelines, or characteristics[37] are applying a more formal approach to standardization. But a more informal understanding of a standard may be conceived by the much broader approach that a standard is an agreed way of doing something[38] or that it may be constituted by a market's general adoption of a technology.[39] In Figure 3.2, on the basis of these distinctions (in white), we decided to divide the standardization process into six general categories (in grey).

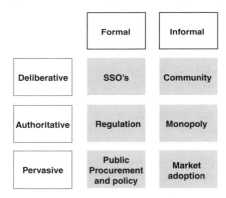

Figure 3.2   The general categories driving standardization

3.2.2   Problematic Issues in Standardization

In synthetic biology two inter-related standardization discussions are evolving. The first regards technological problems associated with standards, the second, the development of legal standards, and how to deal with the potential tension between proprietary rights such as IPRs and standardization.

---

[37]   This definition is found on the International Organization for Standardization (ISO) webpage, www.iso.org/iso/home/standards.htm.
[38]   See British Standards Institution, n. 33 above.
[39]   Simcoe, n. 35 above, p. 161.

First, the question of technological standards in synthetic biology is also a foundational discussion about whether synthetic biology is mostly biology or engineering. As a natural science, the standards used in biology are primarily processes such as guidelines for good scientific and laboratory practices. The purpose of these standards is to generate comparable and scientifically valid results, in other words, scientific knowledge. Being an applied science engineering standards are (generally speaking) more product oriented, with the purpose of creating modularity and interoperability, in other words, to promote usability rather than knowledge. Hence, the discussion of technological standards in synthetic biology is often discussed in two very differing perspectives, making the discussion somewhat ambiguous. What is clear is that technological standardization in synthetic biology is in the making[40] and will keep on evolving. The question is which side of the engineering–biology standardization dichotomy will get the upper hand.

Secondly, the inspiration the synthetic biology community draws from open source software and a general open innovation approach has challenged the development of legal instruments applicable to different standardization scenarios. Attempts have been made to adopt the legal standards developed within open source software, such as contributors and user agreements for standard biological parts. This approach is not unproblematic.

One problem relates to the fact that software is in general related to copyright protection, while biological parts are (at least so far) related to the realm of patents.[41] This entails great differences in the requirements and procedures for protection, as well as the content of the protection granted. Moreover, it must be realized that synthetic biology, as well as software, did not emerge out of the blue. They have both evolved from a technological background that influences the basic structures and dynamics of their respective fields. In the field of biotechnology, where synthetic biology has its roots, there is an existing and vast landscape of IPRs unique to this

---

[40] Most prominently, the BioBricks Foundation seeks to create open technological standards to empower open innovation within biotechnology and synthetic biology, see http://biobricks.org/programs/technical-program/.

[41] Copyright protection for biological parts has been suggested though, see for example, A.W. Torrance, 'Synthesizing Law for Synthetic Biology' (2010) 11(2) *Minnesota J Law, Science and Technology* 642.

area that synthetic biology has to manoeuvre in. The conditions for creating legal standards for open source software and open source biology may in this sense differ considerably.

A source of inspiration that is often mentioned in the debate over potential legal problems in SB standardization is the *user-generated* legal strategies developed in the ICT sector.[42] In this sector standardization has played a key role in the development of the technology, and legal problems arising in relation to standardization has been on the agenda for quite some time. Within this area, standard contractual tools, such as FRAND terms,[43] NACs,[44] clearing houses, and patent pools have been deployed.[45]

However, neither of these solutions has been shown to be unproblematic. Competition law issues and interpretation of the agreements are some of the obstacles that have caused trouble. A contractual remedy only has legal effect between the parties of the agreement, and hence does not rule out that a patent holder who is not part of the agreement may appear after a standard has been adopted and implemented. The owner of such a 'submarine patent' will get a strong market position and may claim excessive royalties or stifle competition.[46] A variant of this scenario is when a patent holder neglects to inform the parties to a standardization process about a patent right, and *after* the adoption of the standard claims that the patent is relevant to the adopted standard without having committed to licensing the patent on FRAND terms. This is also

---

[42]   See for example, A. Rai, 'Unstandard Standardization' (2010) 53(1) *Comm. Acm.* 37 (discussing the applicability of standardization strategies from the ICT sector to synthetic biology).

[43]   FRAND is the abbreviation of 'fair, reasonable and non-discriminatory'.

[44]   NAC is the abbreviation of 'non-assertion covenant'.

[45]   See R. Bekkers, E. Iversen, and K. Blind, *Emerging Ways to Address the Re-emerging Conflict Between Patenting and Technological Standardization, Industrial and Corporate Change* (Oxford, Oxford University Press, 2011), for an analysis of pros and cons of NACs, FRAND, and patent pools.

[46]   See the Federal Trade Commission (FTC) press release of 3 January 2013 concerning their agreement with Google to make certain standard technology available on FRAND terms to avoid stifling competition in the markets for smartphones, games, and tablets, available at www.ftc.gov/news-events/press-releases/2013/01/google-agrees-change-its-business-practices-resolve-ftc.

known as a 'patent ambush'.[47] Within the framework of contractual remedies, obstacles have been the interpretation of what is a 'fair and reasonable' royalty[48] and whether negotiations or an expressed willingness to negotiate a royalty cut off a patent holder's access to injunctive relief[49] or invoke infringement proceedings.[50]

Moreover, the feasibility of the solutions from ICT are likely to depend on whether synthetic biology is interpreted as an applied or natural science and hence which line of technical standardization is chosen. As will be discussed further below, the persisting lack of predictability of biological systems remains, despite recent technological advances, a major obstacle for widespread standardization and for simply transferring solutions from the ICT sector to SB. Also, the business environment and actors in SB are rather different as are the levels of maturity of the technologies.

3.2.3   Standardization in SB and the Relevance of IPRs

Before focusing on the more SB-specific standards, it makes sense to have a short look at how biological standards are organized and operated within the biotech, biopharmaceutical, and nanotech sectors. These types of standards may also be relevant in the field of synthetic biology.

---

[47]   See for example, the European Commission's Press Release of 23 August 2007, on their statement of objection sent to RAMBUS due to the level of royalties charged on their patents on the standardized DRAM technology, available at http://europa.eu/rapid/press-release_MEMO-07-330_en.htm?locale =en.

[48]   See Judge Posner's Opinion and Order of 22 June 2012 in *Apple* v. *Motorola*, No. 1:11-cv-08540, pp. 15–18, where Judge Posner discussed some of the difficulties of determining what a reasonable royalty on a SEP might be.

[49]   See Judge Posner's Opinion and Order of 22 June 2012 in *Apple* v. *Motorola*, n. 48 above, p. 18 *et seq.* with reference to FTC policy statement on the access to injunctive relief for SEP holders committed to licensing on FRAND terms.

[50]   See for example, the European Commission's press release, n. 47 above; C-170/13 *Huawei Technologies Co. Ltd* v. *ZTE Corp., ZTE Deutschland GmbH*, pending before the Court of Justice of the European Union (CJEU). The referred question concerns how a FRAND commitment may influence the evaluation of whether infringement proceedings relating to a SEP are misuse of a dominant position.

3.2.3.1 Standardization in the biotech-, pharma- and nanotech sectors

So far the most elaborated standardization attempts in the biological field could be found in the pharmaceutical sector. One of the typical fields where IPRs, and in particular patent rights, have been addressed concerns *biomarkers*. These are key molecular or cellular events that link a specific environmental exposure to a health outcome. Thus, biomarkers play an important role in understanding the relationships between exposure to environmental chemicals, the development of chronic human diseases, and the identification of subgroups that are at increased risk for disease.[51] There is wide consensus that biomarkers are and will be useful as evaluative tools in improving clinical R&D.[52] Since biomarkers can predict drug efficacy more quickly than conventional clinical endpoints, they hold the potential to substantially accelerate product development in certain disease areas.[53] Biomarkers also offer the potential to inform treatment decisions and to bring personalized medicine into clinical practice.[54]

Well aware of this enormous significance of biomarkers, pharmaceutical companies have established numerous associations and consortia that pool information and carry out collaborative research in order to detect and agree on biomarker standards. One of the most well-known consortia is the so-called Predictive Safety Testing Consortium (PSTC). This is a unique public–private partnership formed by the Critical Path Institute (C-Path) in collaboration with

---

[51] See the definition of biomarkers by the National Institutes of Health (NIH), available at www.niehs.nih.gov/health/topics/science/biomarkers/.

[52] See for example, FDA Critical Path Opportunities List (2006), available at www.fda.gov/oc/initiatives/criticalpath/reports/opp_list.pdf.

[53] See FDA, *Critical Path Opportunities Report* (2006), p. 18, available at www.fda.gov/ScienceResearch/SpecialTopics/CriticalPathInitiative/CriticalPath OpportunitiesReports/default.htm.

[54] See P. Sandell and T. Reuters, *Biomarkers: An Indispensible Addition to the Drug Development Toolkit*, White Paper (2010), available at http://thomsonreuters.com/products/ip-science/04_041/biomarkers-an-indispensable-addition-to-the-drug-development-toolkit.pdf (adding with further references: 'And because they help identify earlier those candidates that are likely to fail, they reduce drug development costs, giving life to the concept of "fail early, fail cheap". The FDA estimates that just a 10 percent improvement in the ability to predict drug failures before clinical trials could save US$100 million in development costs per drug.').

the United States Food and Drug Administration (FDA) to identify new and improved drug safety testing methods and submit them for formal regulatory qualification by the FDA, the European Medicines Agency (EMA), and the Japanese Pharmaceuticals and Medical Devices Agency (PMDA).[55] The FDA, EMA, and PMDA participate as advisors, along with more than 250 participating scientists across industry and academia.[56] Around 20 major pharmaceutical companies have already joined the PSTC, and in 2008, the PSTC obtained the first regulatory qualification of seven urinary renal preclinical safety biomarkers for use in rodent studies and on a case-by-case basis for inclusion into clinical development programs. These qualified biomarkers are now successfully informing drug discovery and development decisions.[57] The collaborative effort of multiple stakeholders promoted by the PSTC has resulted in significant cost savings and more rapid scientific consensus, leading to greater acceptance of these biomarkers by health authorities and pharmaceutical companies.[58]

Nanotechnology is a second more mature field with numerous private sector players that are engaged in standardization efforts. The standards that have been developed within this area are mostly governed by large established SSOs, such as the American Society

---

[55] E.H. Dennis *et al.*, 'Opportunities and Challenges of Safety Biomarker Qualification: Perspectives from the Predictive Safety Testing Consortium' (2013) 74 *Drug Dev. Res.* 112, available at http://onlinelibrary.wiley.com/doi/10.1002/ddr.21070/abstract.

[56] Further information is available on the homepage of the Critical Path Institute and the Predictive Safety Testing Consortium at http://c-path.org/programs/pstc/.

[57] Dennis *et al.*, n. 55 above (stressing that 'Regulatory qualification of a biomarker for a defined context of use provides scientifically robust assurances to sponsors and regulators that should accelerate appropriate adoption of biomarkers into drug development and, ultimately, clinical practice').

[58] *Ibid.* (adding that 'PSTC has expanded their qualification efforts into dogs, nonhuman primates, and humans and focuses on six areas of organ toxicity'). See also F.M. Goodsaidl, F.W. Fruehl, and W. Mattes, 'The Predictive Safety Testing Consortium: A Synthesis of the Goals, Challenges and Accomplishments of the Critical Path' (2007) 4(2) *Drug Discovery Today: Technologies* 47.

for Testing and Materials (ASTM), and the International Organization for Standardization (ISO), which also often have patent policies in place.[59] A third area with a well-developed standardization tradition relates to bioinformatics and the *development, presentation,* and *exchange* of biological data. With growing amounts of biological data and even more with the emergence of large-scale data generation experiments, it became apparent that the diversity and incompleteness of classical method publishing presented a roadblock for data comparison and data processing.[60] Thus, several life science sub-disciplines realized the need for traceable experiments and standardized sharing of information and consequently established rules on how to report experiments.[61] One of the earliest successful examples can be found in the Microarray Gene Expression Data Society (MGED). MGED's 'Minimum Information About a Microarray Experiment' (MIAME) standard has inspired similar efforts in many other biological fields, including proteomics, metabolomics, and RNA interference.[62] A more recent and also very successful example of such biological data standardization efforts with a direct

---

[59]   K. Maskus and S.A. Merrill (eds.), *Patent Challenges for Standard-Setting in the Global Economy: Lessons from Information and Communication Technology,* Study prepared for the Committee on Intellectual Property Management in Standard-Setting Processes of the National Research Council (2013), p. 19.

[60]   See Müller and Arndt, n. 34 above, p. 26 (adding that 'Electronic databases curated by teams also functioned as nucleation factor for standards in reporting methods and experimental results. A discipline, which early adopted rules of data reporting and submission to a database, was structural biology, namely, crystallography. A formal guideline from 1989 was widely adopted also by publishers. DNA sequence data were also among the first deposited in databases. In this case, only the final sequence was stored and recently new reporting standards in genomics were demanded').

[61]   See Müller and Arndt, n. 34 above, p. 26.

[62]   Rai, n. 42 above, p. 38 (adding that 'The Minimum Information for Biological and Biomedical Investigations (MIBBI) project takes standardization one step further by attempting to rationalize the varying data standards that have developed in different biological fields. MIBBI's goal is interoperability across data sets from different biological communities') (internal citations omitted).

effect on SB has been initiated by the Human Proteome Organization (HUPO).[63] In particular, the HUPO Proteomics Standards Initiative[64] defines community standards for data representation in proteomics to facilitate data comparison, exchange, and verification. Under the auspices of this initiative, various working groups have developed downloadable[65] guidelines, formats, and controlled vocabularies on important aspects of, for example, molecular interactions, mass spectrometry, proteomics informatics, and protein separations.

3.2.3.2 Specific standardization activities in synthetic biology

Since synthetic biology builds on several life science disciplines and adds its own dimension, it also requires a broad set of standards to enable productive collaboration.[66] Thus, all of the abovementioned areas, as well as additional areas of standardization from clinical and technical disciplines, can have a significant impact on SB. Considering further SB's general ambition to transform biotechnology into a science relying on standardized, well-characterized DNA 'parts' that could then be assembled into composite devices and systems with similarly well-defined behavior, it could be claimed that the emerging discipline of synthetic biology aims for 'the most comprehensive form of standardization'.[67] When transplanted into the standardized chassis of a suitable model organism, it is hoped that the composite systems would pave the way for many improved applications ranging from drug therapies to environmentally friendly fuels.[68] Ideally, not only

---

[63] Further information on the Human Proteome Organization is available at www.hupo.org/.

[64] See the homepage of the Proteomics Standards Initiative, available at www.psidev.info/.

[65] *Ibid.*

[66] Müller and Arndt, n. 34 above, p. 32 (adding 'Depending on the set goal, requirements for standardization can vary significantly. For example, the current challenge for biopharmaceuticals often falls within protein engineering while providing future solutions for regenerative medicine requires manipulation of cells and organs. As a consequence of this diversity, Synthetic Biology heavily relies on standards developed in various disciplines.').

[67] Rai, n. 42 above, p. 38.

[68] *Ibid.* p. 38.

parts and chassis would be standardized, but also the interfaces used to assemble parts and the interactions between parts and host cells.[69]

The most prominent standardization and organization effort of SB today can be found in the formation of the BioBricks Foundation (BBF),[70] the Registry of Standard Biological Parts,[71] and the International Genetically Engineered Machine (iGEM) competition.[72] The term 'BioBricks' was introduced by Tom Knight at MIT in 2003. Drew Endy, now at Stanford, and Christopher Voigt, at MIT, are also heavily involved in the project. BioBricks™ is a trademark protected standard for interchangable parts, developed for the construction of biological systems in living cells. These standard biological parts are often DNA sequences of defined structure and function. They share a common interface and are designed to be composed and incorporated into living cells. Bio-Brick *parts* can be assembled to form useful *devices*, through a process often referred to as 'Standard Assembly'. BioBrick parts are composable and may thus be combined and plugged together ('plug and play') in endless numbers to form complex *systems*.[73]

The BBF is a public-benefit organization founded in 2006 by scientists and engineers at MIT in Cambridge, MA, who recognized the potential of synthetic biology and wanted to ensure that this emerging field would serve the public interest on a global level. A main goal of the foundation is to enhance the worldwide cooperation of scientists and engineers in reducing the complexity and costs of SB by using freely available standardized biological parts that are safe, ethical, cost-effective and publicly accessible to create solutions to pressing problems.[74] The BBF is also the legal owner of the 'BioBrick' and 'BioBricks' trademark.

---

[69]   *Ibid.*
[70]   See the homepage of BioBricks Foundation, available at http://bio bricks.org/.
[71]   See the homepage of iGEM's Registry of Standard Biological Parts, available at http://parts.igem.org/Main_Page.
[72]   See the homepage of iGEM, available at http://igem.org/Main_Page#.
[73]   See http://parts.igem.org/Help:An_Introduction_to_BioBricks.
[74]   See http://biobricks.org/about-foundation/.

The Registry of Standard Biological Parts[75] (a.k.a. iGEM Registry) is a growing collection of genetic parts which, following a so-called 'BioBricks protocol' for cloning and physical linking with specific associated inputs and outputs, can be mixed and matched to build synthetic biology devices and systems. It received significant US federal funding and contains thousands of parts. As part of the synthetic biology community's efforts to make biology easier to engineer, it provides a source of genetic parts to iGEM teams and academic labs.[76]

The iGEM competition is the foremost and first undergraduate synthetic biology competition. Student teams are provided with a kit of biological parts at the beginning of the summer from the Registry of Standard Biological Parts. Working at their own schools over the summer, they use these parts and new parts of their own design to build biological systems and operate them in living cells.[77] Thus, iGEM educates future researchers in working with BioBricks, while it is at the same time the main provider of BioBricks.

Currently, the BioBricks Foundation is charting a technical standards framework that is envisaged to serve as the driver and promoter of a high-quality technical standards process for synthetic biology based on BioBrick™ parts.[78] It is envisaged that the framework will include the following components:

- teaching people, facilitation, and management of community;
- creating a mechanism for deprecation, promotion, and screening of standard biological parts;
- providing improved and expanded soft coupling to rewards for quality standards;
- developing a protocol for dealing with property rights around technical standards;
- recognizing and celebrating participants.[79]

---

[75] Registry of Standard Biological Parts for standard biological parts, available at http://parts.igem.org/Main_Page.

[76] *Ibid.*

[77] See homepage of the Biobricks Foundation, available at http://igem.org/About.

[78] See The BioBricks Foundation, 'RFC', available at www.openwetware.org/wiki/The_BioBricks_Foundation:RFC.

[79] See *ibid.*

The synthetic biology community is still discussing exactly how much information about a biological standard is necessary before a true standard can be said to have been established. However, some progress has been achieved.[80] Very much simplified, the standardization efforts in this area can so far be divided into the following basic categories.

The first category concerns attempts to standardize *designs*, in other words, the way(s) in which systems are designed from BioBrick parts. One example of such efforts can be found in the attempt to develop the most feasible 'standard abstraction frameworks' for engineered biological systems,[81] which often involves discussions on how to best cope with the design of increasingly complex biological systems.

A second and third category relates to efforts to develop *functional composition standards* and *reference standards* for making measurements of BioBricks, in other words, the way(s) in which the behavior and characteristics of BioBricks are described and measured.[82] This may range from mere preliminary notes on the characterization of parts to more detailed notes on generating absolute molecule number measurements.[83]

A fourth standardization activity is directed to the *fabrication or physical assembly* of and with BioBricks, in other words, the methods in which BioBricks are physically constructed, composed, and assembled together.[84] This may comprise general information on construction of new biological parts,[85] BioBricks construction tutorials,[86]

---

[80]   Rai, n. 42 above, p. 38.
[81]   See notes on 'standard abstraction frameworks', available at http://syntheticbiology.org/Abstraction_hierarchy.html.
[82]   See discussion on standard methods for part characterization, available at http://openwetware.org/wiki/Parts_characterization.
[83]   See Standardized GFP quantification, available at http://openwetware.org/wiki/Standardized_GFP_quantification.
[84]   See the homepage of SyntheticBiology.Org., available at http://syntheticbiology.org/BioBricks/Standardization.html.
[85]   See 'How-to Guide for Constructing Novel BioBrick Parts', available at http://syntheticbiology.org/BioBricks/Part_fabrication.html.
[86]   See 'BioBricks Construction Tutorial' available at http://openwetware.org/wiki/BioBricks_construction_tutorial.

more general 3A assembly approaches,[87] or specific Silver lab assembly strategies[88] for assembling existing biological parts. Moreover, this may relate to standardized information on the vectors in which BioBricks reside.[89]

Attempts to develop a common, *standardized language and documentation* of the manner and units of measurements in which BioBricks are documented represent a fifth category. This is a crucial category that is related to a sixth category of *data processing standards* and data exchanges formats that should enable large-scale data integration. It may range from barcodes[90] for information on signing BioBricks parts, to device datasheet examples[91] for a working example of documenting a BioBrick or a semantic web ontology[92] for biological parts.

Finally, the seventh category concerns efforts to reach a consensus on standards for the *operation of biosystems*, in other words, the conditions under which systems from BioBricks are operated. These activities involve standard vectors[93] for information on the vectors in which BioBricks reside; standard cellular chassis[94] for notes on constructing a novel strain in which all BioBricks would operate; and standard culture media[95] for information on a culture media in which all constructs would operate.

---

[87] See '3A Assembly Tutorial', available at http://syntheticbiology.org/BioBricks/3A_assembly.html.

[88] See 'Silver BB Strategy', available at http://openwetware.org/wiki/Silver:_BB_Strategy.

[89] See 'Notes on Vectors', available at http://syntheticbiology.org/Vectors.html.

[90] See 'Tutorial on Barcodes', available at http://openwetware.org/wiki/Barcodes.

[91] See 'Data Sheet Examples', available at http://openwetware.org/wiki/Endy:F2620.

[92] See for example, Open Biological and Biomedical Ontologies, 'Foundry', available at www-obofoundry.org/ (an umbrella organization to coordinate ontologies development).

[93] See 'Notes on Vectors', available at http://syntheticbiology.org/Vectors.html.

[94] See 'Standard E. coli Strain for BioBricks', available at http://openwetware.org/wiki/Standard_E._coli_Strain_for_BioBricks.

[95] See 'Discussion on Culture Media', available at http://syntheticbiology.org/Media.html.

The core mission for synthetic biology will now be to determine the abstraction hierarchies and rules of how to bring together these aspects or to reformat previously developed standards to better fit the general idea of building biological systems.[96] In doing so, special attention will have to be given to the classical standardization requirements for science: (1) results need to be comparable between samples; (2) results need to be comparable between labs; (3) experiments need to be repeatable in several labs; (4) researchers need to use the same language/naming; (5) data need to be amenable to electronic data processing.[97]

As will be discussed further below, SB is facing several challenges in this regard: in addition to the challenges posed by the persisting unpredictability of biological organisms/systems, the other key challenge to standardization is the sheer heterogeneity of biological device types.[98]

An additional question is, of course, to what extent such standardization efforts will have to consider IPRs, and if these are relevant, how they should be addressed.

3.2.3.3 Relevance and governance of IPRs in these standard efforts

Due to the principal availability of patents for inventive methods and products related to biomarkers and nanotechnology, various standard organizations in these areas have adopted quite well-elaborated policies on patent rights. The guidelines, procedures, and rules adopted by these associations may (at least to a certain degree) sometimes resemble those of SSOs in the ICT industries. The PSTC, mentioned above, has for example adopted rules that deal very carefully with potential future patents directed to biomarker standards that may emerge.[99] Under this system, PSTC members assign any future patent rights relevant to an emerging standard originating from the PSTC efforts to the non-profit trusted intermediary Critical Path. Critical Path must then license these rights on 'fair, neutral, and commercially reasonable' terms to

---

[96]   See also Müller and Arndt, n. 34 above, p. 32.
[97]   See *ibid.* p. 32.
[98]   See A. Arkin, 'Setting the Standard in Synthetic Biology' (2008) 26 *Nature Biotechnology* 771.
[99]   Rai, n. 42 above, p. 38.

members of the Consortium as well as third parties. It could thus be argued that the PSTC addresses potential *future* patents in terms somewhat similar to those used by ICT SSOs for background patents.[100] However, in contrast to many SSOs in the ICT sector, biomarker standard organizations, including the PSTC, often do not sufficiently address the licensing of 'background' patents. Consequently, firms with standard-relevant patents could participate in collaborative research, without having to comply with detailed prior rules on such (perhaps not fully disclosed) patents, which increases the risk of patent ambushes and further unwanted scenarios.

Data standardization efforts have so far mostly not been so much engaged in the adoption of formal policies on patents. One reason for this is that in the case of data standards, the administrative costs associated with establishing an SSO-type apparatus may exceed any challenges that patents pose.[101] Another reason can be seen in the simple fact that the field of bioinformatics has evolved largely within academic and governmental research centers. Most of the standards here have been developed for data structures and exchange, primarily in small, academically focused groups. Patent issues have therefore not received much, if any, attention and it does not appear that patenting has yet occurred with any frequency in this field, although the potential for filings in some subfields, such as genetic data structures, as well as copyright issues and (at least in Europe) problems related to database protection, could increase in the future.[102]

But the patent situation with BioBricks, and the SB products and SB methods contained in the Registry of Standard Biological Parts is more problematic. These developing standards could infringe thousands of US and European Patents on DNA and protein-related inventions. Both in Europe and in the United States, tens of thousands of patents have been granted on isolated DNA sequences. It could, of course, be claimed that many of the first generation patents on isolated DNA will soon expire and the US Supreme Court has (in contrast to the European Biotech Directive) recently

---

[100]   *Ibid.* p. 38.
[101]   *Ibid.* p. 38.
[102]   See Maskus and Merrill, n. 59 above, p. 18 *et seq.*

declared isolated genomic DNA to be ineligible for patent protection.[103] But, this prohibition would normally not apply to cDNA and synthetically modified biological processes or compounds due to sufficient human interventions, which in turn might also provide the basis for meeting the inventive step/nonobviousness requirement. Gene and protein-related patents are certainly not specific to synthetic biology, but emerging problems are aggravated by the complexity and interdisciplinarity of synthetic biology. A product generated by synthetic biology – for instance, a bacteria producing biofuel – can involve hundreds of different standardized parts that, in the extreme, might all be protected by different patents that are probably held by several rights holders.[104] Preliminary patent mapping also reveals a significant number of patents highly relevant to synthetic biology in particular.[105] Moreover, synthetic biology involves two areas, biotechnology and computing, both of which are at the center of the public debate about patents.[106] Some commentators have therefore warned of a 'perfect storm' with regard to patents in synthetic biology.[107] Last but not least, patents and patent-related rights will probably not be the only IPRs that can become relevant for synthetic biology. Regulatory exclusivities and alternative forms of protection, such as copyrights, trade secrets, and even trademarks, could presumably also be claimed for SB-related inventions, as has been pointed out by, *inter alia*, Andrew W. Torrance and Linda J. Kahl.[108]

The patent and IPR situation is therefore very hard to oversee, and there is a serious risk of so-called IPR or patent 'thickets'. So

---

[103]   See *Association for Molecular Pathology* v. *Myriad Genetics, Inc.*, 133 S Ct 2107 (2013) and *Mayo Collaborative Services* v. *Prometheus Laboratories, Inc.*, 132 S Ct 1289 (2102). See recent CJEU cases such as C-428/08 *Monsanto Technology* v. *Cefetra BV and others* [2010] ECR I-06765 (July 2010).

[104]   Rutz, n. 3 above, p. 551.

[105]   Rai, n. 42 above, p. 39.

[106]   *Ibid.* p. 38.

[107]   A. Rai and J. Boyle, 'Synthetic Biology: Caught Between Property Rights, the Public Domain, and the Commons' (2007) 5 *PLoS Biol.* 58.

[108]   A.W. Torrance and L.J. Kahl, *Synthetic Biology Standards and Intellectual Property*, Report commissioned by the National Academies (2012), available at http://sites.nationalacademies.org/PGA/step/PGA_070838. See also Torrance, n. 4 above, p. 629.

far, the SB community using BioBricks and the Registry of Standard Biological Parts appears to have been 'happily unconcerned' with patent rights, treating the Registry as a community source and putting the results into the public domain with a friendly request to contribute to the community by returning research data and results in order to improve the Registry. Potential background patents were often not considered to be a problem, since the risk to be sued for patent infringement was considered to be minimal due to the mere academic use and the arguably not very sophisticated applications. So far the industry seems indeed to rely on curtailed solutions rather than standardized bricks.

However, as the quality of the biological standards increases, the Registry will probably attract more users from the industry in the near future. Since it would be difficult to keep the use of the Registry secret, all of these industrial users will surely be very careful in considering potential patents directed to the key standards and conduct a 'freedom to operate' assessment. The publication of a draft contributor agreement for submitting parts to the Registry[109] can therefore only be welcomed as a first step. But further steps need to be taken.

As is pointed out by Arti Rai, the situation faced by the Registry is thus arguably rather similar to that faced by standards developers for the Web in its early days:

> For example, in the case of the XML standard for structured data presentation, the critical early work was done by developers from academic and commercial organizations, as well as independent contributors, without any significant thought being given to patents. As the Web matured, however, the issue of background patents on core technical standards had to be addressed. By 1999, the World Wide Web Consortium had created a patent policy working group. Participants in that group included representatives from the major software, hardware, and telecommunications firms.[110]

Unfortunately, however, many researchers, in particular in the academic environment, are not adequately trained in the basic

---

[109] D. Endy and D. Grewal, *The BioBrick Public Agreement DRAFT Version 1a* (2010), available at http://dspace.mit.edu/bitstream/handle/1721.1/50999/BPA_draft_v1a.pdf.

[110] Rai, n. 42 above, p. 39.

patentability rules, and without access to highly specialized IPR experts are often not sufficiently aware of the patent environment and how it could be monitored. In light of the above, it appears to be of particular significance for biobanks and international Bio-Bricks, Protein, and DNA repositories distributing and collecting community-supplied material to sufficiently consider legal frameworks, strategies, and choices on how to address, *inter alia*, IPR-related questions.[111]

3.3 DISCUSSION AND CONCLUSIONS

The enormous potential and characteristics of synthetic biology provide many new possibilities for the development of improved applications to solve pressing problems. But the technology also entails considerable safety risks that will need to be addressed. In addition, SB offers an exciting and challenging playground for the discussion of the current IPR-based innovation system and for the testing of new innovation models, including various open innovations scenarios.

In this context standardization represents without doubt one of the key issues. It can be hoped that current attempts to develop a robust technical standards framework will serve as the driver and promoter of a high-quality technical standards process for synthetic biology. Ideally, this would reduce the complexity and cost of activities in synthetic biology by leveraging cost-effective engineering principles of abstraction and standardization.

While the standardization activities of the SB are continuing on a very broad basis, many IPR-related questions have not been sufficiently addressed. Considering the broad scope of standards that could become applicable, as well as the great variety of standard-relevant IPRs that could be claimed for SB-related inventions, it would certainly make sense to cautiously scrutinize both successful and unsuccessful user-generated mechanisms and strategies previously devised in the ICT sector to address patent issues. However,

---

[111] See T. Minssen and J. Schovsbo, *Legal Aspects of Biobanking as Key Issues for Personalized Medicine and Translational Exploitation* (16 January 2014), available at http://ssrn.com/abstract=2380224 or http://dx.doi.org/10.2139/ssrn.2380224; see also Müller and Arndt, n. 34 above, p. 40.

at this early stage in the evolution of SB, it appears a little too early to clearly identify fundamental standards on which the SB community will finally agree.[112]

Besides that, it seems – at least so far – rather difficult to simply transform the (arguably much debated and litigated) strategies that have been applied in the ICT sector. This relates, among other things, to the different business environment in the field of biotechnology with a different regulatory framework, a different lifecycle management of the relevant products, a greater variety of different IPRs becoming relevant at the various stages, and more diverse actors and stakeholders. But it also relates to various scientific and technical problems that synthetic biology would still need to solve. These problems range from a great number of still undefined and incompatible biological parts, to the (despite recent scientific advances) persisting unpredictability and unreliability of how assembled parts behave in increasingly complex biological systems.[113]

These fundamental technical challenges are accompanied by a variety of crucial legal challenges. There is a pressing need to address these problems proactively if SB is ever to reach its expressed goals of an effective translational exploitation, in a reasonably open, standardized, and safe innovation system. The greatest legal challenges lie probably in devising effective legal strategies and regulations to control the immense security risks that this new technology creates.

But we consider an effective, sustainable, just, and controllable innovation system also to be important aspects, which might (for example, in terms of patent disclosures and governing open innovation environment) also relate to security considerations.[114]

Taking patents as an example, some of the problems envisaged in this chapter could be tackled both at the patent prosecution stage (in other words, *pre* grant), and during patent litigation and technology transfer (in other words, *post* grant). To tackle, or at least mitigate,

---

[112]   See also Rai, n. 42 above, p. 39.
[113]   R. Kwok, 'Five Hard Truths for Synthetic Biology' (2010) 463 *Nature* 288–90, available at www.nature.com/news/2010/100120/pdf/463288a.pdf.
[114]   F. Frischknecht, 'The History of Biological Warfare' (2003) 4 *EMBO Rep.* 547–52.

potential patent-related problems on the pre-grant level we see five major areas that deserve special attention:

First of all, patent offices and regulators should maintain or even raise the bar of patentability in order to guarantee a high quality of the granted patents. A rigorous application of the patentability requirements should guarantee that no patents are granted for obvious or trivial subject matter so that the current state of the art is surrounded by a sufficiently broad patent-free 'zone'.

Related to patent quality is also a second response that might prove to be very effective, and that is to collaborate with the scientific SB community in prior art searches during the granting procedure. This could be achieved for example, in the context of the so-called 'peer-to-patent' (P2P) or crowd-sourcing patent examination. One of the more recent reports evaluating these peer-to-patent programs was published by the UK Intellectual Property Office in September 2012.[115] The reports states, *inter alia*, that:

> In summary, the UK pilot, operating in the context of the UK system, and with an approach geared to all patent applications, not just those volunteered for the system, has demonstrated, in line with experiences elsewhere, that Peer To Patent can make an effective contribution to uncovering relevant documents which can help examiners to determine if an invention claimed in a patent application is new and inventive. The pilot has also shown the effectiveness of the use of social media technologies in this context, and the importance of building online communities to sustain a commitment to the programme over the long-term, if Peer To Patent is to be taken forward on a larger scale.[116]

These pilot programs were arguably mainly concerned with software-related inventions and it would still need to be explored to what extent such mechanisms would work for the biotech and pharma area. However, in general it appears as if the careful exploitation of such mechanisms can promote patent quality and the effectiveness of the system. It might also provide further democratic

---

[115]   See the 28-page final report on the experiences of the UKIPO in this experiment, 'Peer to Patent Pilot', available at www.ipo.gov.uk/p2p-report.pdf.
[116]   *Ibid.* p. 6.

justification for the patent system and might help to avoid expensive court litigation at a later stage.[117]

A third response is to make sure that the metes and bounds of what is claimed and protected by a patent are clearly defined and that the actual scope of the patent corresponds to the inventor's actual contribution to the state of the art.

Moreover, as a fourth and fifth response, patents should be examined without too much delay to provide legal certainty, and patent offices should ensure that patents and the patenting process are as transparent and understandable as possible. This entails investing in personnel, office internal and external educational training in patent searches, and technical solutions that make patents more easily detectable and retrievable by everybody working in the field, including small and medium-sized companies.[118] Recent US patent reform efforts, for example, would include a number of reforms designed to streamline patent enforcement, provide transparency of ownership, and force more targeted early disclosures in patent cases.[119] It seems important to us that other jurisdiction follow these examples as well.

Irrespective of the importance of these pre-grant factors, however, we see a particularly great potential in the further investigation of various post-grant solution-mechanisms that could facilitate collaborative research and open innovation in SB. These entail the consideration of patent pools, clearing houses,[120] liability regimes,[121]

---

[117]   From a broader innovation perspective, potential negative 'side-effects' could of course also be discussed, such as the risk of prior art avalanches, vexatious misuse of the P2P system by competitors, and a nonobviousness gap in the biopharmaceutical industry, see B.N. Roin, 'Unpatentable Drugs and the Standards of Patentability' (2009) 87 *Tex. L Rev.* 503, 542; see also T. Minssen, n. 7 above pp. 311–20.

[118]   Minssen, n. 7 above, p. 400 *et seq.* See also Rutz, n. 3 above, p. 516.

[119]   These include the so-called Goodlatte Innovation Act (HR 3309), which has already been passed in the House of Representatives; and in the Senate, Judiciary Committee Chair Leahy has proposed the Patent Transparency and Improvement Act (S 1720).

[120]   E. van Zimmeren *et al.*, 'Patent Pools and Clearing Houses in the Life Sciences' (2011) 29(11) *Trends in Biotechnology* 569–76.

[121]   G. van Overwalle (ed.), *Gene Patents and Collaborative Licensing Models: Patent Pools, Clearinghouses, Open Source Models and Liability Regimes* (Cambridge, Cambridge University Press, 2009).

fair use defences for diagnostic testing,[122] non-exclusive licensing, or the return of certain research results.[123] But once again, any debate of these often user-generated mechanisms in SB and the development of a framework exploiting them would have to carefully analyze their feasibility for the particular environment of biotechnological innovation and business.[124] Moreover, it should be realized that the necessary responses on the pre- and post-grant levels are interrelated and the feasibility and effectiveness of a user-generated solution on the post-grant level might also depend on the transparency and quality of the assets that are to be shared, for example, patents. All of these issues therefore require further careful examinations that recognize the peculiarities of SB.

In view of the major technical and legal challenges to standardization presented above, we fully agree with Martin Fussenegger, a synthetic biologist at the Swiss Federal Institute of Technology (ETH) in Zürich, who has stated:

> The field has had its hype phase. Now it needs to deliver.[125]

And so does the law!

---

[122]   See R.C. Dreyfuss, 'The Patentability of Genetic Diagnostics in US Law and Policy' in J. Drexl and N. Lee (eds.), *Pharmaceutical Innovation, Competition and Patent Law* (Cheltenham (UK)/Northampton, MA, Edward Elgar, 2013), pp. 41–50.

[123]   See Minssen and Schovsbo, n. 111 above.

[124]   Dreyfuss, n. 122 above, pp. 41–50 (providing a more detailed discussion of the differences between the ICT sector and life science with regard to patent pools and clearing houses).

[125]   *Ibid.* p. 290.

PART II

Private ordering in a shared knowledge environment

4. Openness in trademark law: a viable paradigm?

Annette Kur

4.1 INTRODUCTION

Most people will agree to the statement that, at least in principle, open access to subject matter covered by copyright or patents enhances public welfare – the availability of valuable achievements to many serves the common benefit. That effect is basically independent of whether or not the right-holder has consented to such use. Of course, on the other hand, it is commonly acknowledged that beyond a certain tipping point, unauthorized and unrestricted use is likely to jeopardize the incentives for bringing forth innovative achievements and creative works, ultimately resulting in market failure. It is the genuine task of intellectual property right (IPR) policy to consciously balance the beneficial effects of openness (as compelled for example, through statutory limitations or by principles of antitrust law) against the risk of impairing the market for innovation and creation.[1] However, that does not detract from the general observation that, at least in principle, openness in the sense of participation by others is likely to yield beneficial societal effects and, under the aspect of public welfare, also positive economic results.

Trademarks, on the other hand, present a different picture. As a matter of principle, marks must be *unique* in the sense that they

---

[1] The basic scheme of IPR law alternating between openness and exclusivity has often been described; see for example, H. Ullrich, 'The Interaction between Competition Law and Intellectual Property Law: An Overview' in C.-D. Ehlerman and I. Atanasiu (eds.), *The Interaction between Intellectual Property and Competition Law* (Oxford, Hart Publishing, 2007), pp. 28–75.

indicate a single commercial source. When third parties get access to using the mark without being authorized by the trademark holder, the mark fails to meet its purpose; it no longer constitutes a trademark in the legal sense. This rule is fundamentally important and of basically universal validity. Its universal character is confirmed, *inter alia*, by the fact that in trademark law, compulsory licenses are expressly banned by Article 21 of the Agreement on Trade-Related Aspects of Intellectual Property Rights (TRIPS),[2] while they are commonly accepted, if only under certain conditions, in patent law (Article 31 TRIPS; see also Article 5 of the Paris Convention) and also in copyright (Articles 11*bis*, 13 of the Berne Convention).[3]

Nevertheless, some forms of openness in the meaning of shared use also exist in trademark law.[4] In particular, the principle of uniqueness does not preclude voluntary licensing;[5] in that regard, trademark law does not differ substantially from other forms of IPR

---

[2]   'Members may determine conditions on the licensing and assignment of trademarks, *it being understood that the compulsory licensing of trademarks shall not be permitted* and that the owner of a registered trademark shall have the right to assign the trademark with or without the transfer of the business to which the trademark belongs' (emphasis added).

[3]   The fact that trademark, unlike other IPRs, cannot be subject to compulsory licenses makes it all the more urgent that competition concerns are fully taken into account for assessing the protectability as for measuring the scope of trademarks. European trademark law has some deficiencies in that regard; see A. Kur, 'Strategic Branding: Does Trade Mark Law Provide for Sufficient Self Help and Self Healing Forces?' in I. Govaere and H. Ullrich (eds.), *Intellectual Property, Market Power and the Public Interest*, College of Europe Studies No. 8 (Brussels, P.I.E. Peter Lang, 2008), pp. 191–217.

[4]   In this chapter, the term 'trademark law' generally refers to European trademark law, as regulated in Community Trade Mark Regulation (EC) 207/2009 (CTMR), and Trade Mark Directive 95/2008/EC ('TM Directive'). In Germany, the TM Directive was transposed in the Act on Trade Marks (Markengesetz, MarkenG) of 1994, in force since 1 January 1995.

[5]   However, for instance in Germany, it took some time before legal doctrine was ready to embrace trademark licensing as a legitimate concept that could be reconciled with the basic notions of trademark law. The key for acceptance was found in the fact that it is ultimately the trademark holder himself who controls the use of the mark, meaning that the principle of uniqueness – the mark indicating one particular source – was not disrupted. For a more extensive account see A. Kur, 'Die gemeinschaftliche Markenbenutzung – Markenlizenzen und verwandte Tatbestände' GRUR Int. 1990, 1.

law. Also, non-authorized use by others is allowed to a certain
extent (and under certain qualifications) on the basis of statutory
limitations, in particular regarding use for descriptive purposes,[6] in
comparative advertising,[7] or to indicate compatibility with other
goods.[8] More problematic, however, are instances where basically
independent companies use the same or similar signs not in a
descriptive or otherwise indicative manner, but to designate the
origin of their products, without the conditions for such use being
fixed by formal license agreements.

This chapter addresses a number of those more unusual constellations. In 4.2, the structural exception from the general concept of
trademark law that applies with regard to collective and certification
marks is briefly considered, with some remarks being added on the
'Green Dot' case, where the General Court (then: Court of First
Instance, CFI) went close to granting a compulsory license. In 4.3,
delimitation covenants are addressed under the aspects of competition law, contract law (termination), and consumer protection.
4.4 turns briefly to coexistence in the form of 'honest concurrent
use'. Finally, in 4.5 some conclusions will be drawn, *inter alia*, in
the light of the current European Commission proposals for reform
of European trademark law.[9]

4.2 COLLECTIVE MARKS AND (EXCEPTIONAL) ANTITRUST CONCERNS

The statement made above that trademarks need to be unique in the
sense that they must be able to indicate a single commercial source
must be qualified insofar as it only applies to ordinary, individual
marks. Different rules apply to collective marks and certification
marks: instead of indicating a specific commercial source, they are

---

[6]   TM Directive, art. 6(1)(a); see C-100/02 *Gerolsteiner Brunnen* v. *Putsch*
(Geri/Kerry Springs) [2006] ECR I-691, CJEU.
[7]   Comparative Advertising Directive 114/2006/EC, art. 4; see C-533/06
O2 v. *Hutchinson* [2008] ECR I-4231.
[8]   TM Directive, art. 6(1)(c); see C-228/03 *Gillette* v. *LA Laboratories*
[2005] ECR I-2337.
[9]   Commission Proposals of 27 March 2013, COM(2013)161 final (proposal for amendment of the CTMR); COM(2013)162 final (proposal for a
recast of the TM Directive).

typically meant to signify a particular quality or compliance with other, specific conditions.[10] Due to their objectives and character, such marks cannot be exclusive in the sense that their use is restricted to the owner and persons authorized by him at will; the system must remain accessible in principle for every person fulfilling the objective standards that the mark is intended to indicate. In case of collective marks, those standards are regularly stipulated in the statutes that the association applying for such marks must file with the application[11] and which are published together with the registration. The law usually sets forth that the association must accept as a member (subject to certain eligibility criteria) every person offering standard-compliant goods or services.[12] The rules are normally even stricter for certification marks: such marks can only be registered for institutions (or other legal persons) assuming a neutral, impartial position *vis-à-vis* stakeholders, with sufficient expertise and technical capacities to examine whether the required standards are fulfilled by companies requesting access to the sign, and to monitor compliance with those standards as long as the sign is used. Whatever the regulatory details may be, providing for openness in the sense that access is regulated under objective, non-discriminatory terms is a *sine qua non* for the legal acceptance of any form of collective signs.

---

[10]   In their basic form, collective marks merely signify membership of the association or other collective body who figures as the holder of the registration, without implying specific quality aspects. However, most collective marks (and, by definition, all certification and guarantee marks) are meant to indicate compliance with certain standards (material like 'pure wool'; handicraft items made by examined or otherwise qualified manufacturers; eco-friendliness; specific geographical origin). Under Community law, collective marks are regulated by CTMR, arts 66–74; according to the proposal for amendment of the CTMR (COM(2013)161 final), the current provisions will be complemented with a system of Community certification marks (arts 74b–74k of the Proposal). On the national level, all Member States have established schemes of collective mark protection, and most also provide for some kind of certification marks. In the current TM Directive, collective and certification marks are only foreseen as a voluntary option (TM Directive, art. 15; according to the pending proposal for amendment of the TM Directive (COM(2013)162) final), harmonized protection of collective marks will become mandatory.

[11]   For Germany see MarkenG, s. 102.

[12]   See MarkenG, s. 102(3), where that requirement is stipulated (only) where the collective mark consists of a geographical indication.

In contrast to that, the owner of an individual mark is basically free to determine whether and under which conditions the sign may be used. This may have questionable consequences when a sign is registered as an individual mark, but is used in practice rather in the manner of a collective mark. That aspect played a role in the 'Green Dot' case.[13] The sign consists of a Yin and Yang-shaped emblem signaling that companies whose products bear the sign have obtained a license from its owner, the Duales System Deutschland (DSD). The economic background is as follows: companies in Germany are obliged by law to recover the used packages of consumer goods sold by them. That obligation can be skipped, however, if the company joins a private waste disposal system. During the relevant time, DSD was the only system offering such services on a Germany-wide basis; the few existing competitors were only active in particular regions. Companies using those regional services needed an additional license from DSD, due to DSD's broader geographical coverage and also because consumers preferred products with the 'Green Dot', which they regarded as a stamp of ecology-friendliness.[14] As DSD calculated its license fees in proportion to the packages on which the Green Dot appeared, this meant that the companies had to pay twice, which they refused; they argued that DSD should be obliged to reduce the fee, considering that they did not use DSD's services to the full extent. The European Commission agreed with that view and issued an order against DSD; upon appeal, the order was (in most parts)

---

[13]   T-151/01 *Duales System Deutschland* v. *European Commission* [2007] ECR II-1607, General Court. For procedural issues on which an appeal was filed in this case see C-385/07P *Der Grüne Punkt–DS* v. *European Commission* [2009] ECR I-6155.

[14]   More specifically, it was generally assumed that the Green Dot signaled that the packages were recycled (at least to a substantial degree). As that was not the case – the waste was just collected and disposed of – a consumer association filed a claim for misleading advertisement, based on unfair competition law. The claim was dismissed by the Berlin court of first instance and the court of appeal; further appeal on points of law was denied by the German Federal Supreme Court. The main argument for rejecting the claim was that likelihood of deception of the public had not been sufficiently established. See *Der Grüne Punkt*, KG (Berlin Court of Appeal), WRP 1994, 625; for a comprehensive overview on the issue see H. Hartwig, 'Die lauterkeitsrechtliche Beurteilung der Werbung mit dem "Grünen Punkt" (§ 3 UWG)' GRUR 1997, 560.

upheld by the General Court.[15] As a result, DSD could neither require the full license fee, nor was it free to refuse 'Green Dot' licenses to companies using other services as well.

Arguably the case comes as close to granting a compulsory license for use of an individual mark as one may get without openly clashing with Article 21 TRIPS. Nevertheless the result seems justified: the deeper reason for the Commission's demarche and its confirmation by the General Court lies in the fact that although the Green Dot was registered as an individual mark, the way in which it was used in practice and also its perception by consumers was rather akin to a certification mark. The competition authorities' interference with the conditions for use of the sign, as well as with the structure of license fees, must be understood in reaction to that particular feature.

4.3   DELIMITATION AGREEMENTS[16]

4.3.1   Concept and General Remarks

According to the general doctrine any use of the same as well as of a (conspicuously) similar sign for identical or similar goods or services by third parties is likely to cause consumer confusion. From that it seems to follow that the scope of protection accorded to a mark is not at the disposal of private parties to be moderated or molded by contract. In principle, it is solely the public's perception and the public's interests that govern the question as to what extent a trademark is protected against a potentially conflicting sign.

However, it is well known among practitioners that the reality differs widely from that basic assumption.[17] Very frequently, parties

---

[15]   See n. 13 above.

[16]   In Germany, such agreements are uniformly referred to as Abgrenzungs-vereinbarungen. It is not clear whether a term with exactly the same meaning exists in English.

[17]   Though there is general agreement on this point, there are no statistical data available on the frequency of such agreements. Some authors (who are also practitioners) claim that about half of all trademark applications are somehow connected to delimitation agreements (Abgrenzungsvereinbarungen und Gemeinschaftsmkarken, H. Harte-Bavendamm and V. v. Bomhard in GRUR 1998, 531).

conclude covenants delimiting the scope of protection of two signs that are supposed to be in conflict with each other. In order to preserve and secure for both trademark holders their own place in the market, such agreements demarcate the mutual areas of exclusivity, by limiting the use of the respective signs to particular product sectors, geographic areas, target groups, get-ups, and so on. Given the frequency of such agreements it can be assumed that below the visible surface of registered marks whose scope according to the general rule should be fixed by the law and the law only, there exists a dense pattern of individual contracts moderating the scope of actual protection of those marks in relation to each other. In spite of its huge practical importance, the issue does not figure under the 'big' topics in scholarly writing,[18] and court decisions are relatively scarce. That does not mean, however, that delimitation agreements are legally uninteresting. On the contrary, there are a number of questions to be posed, of which only a few can be addressed in the following.

4.3.2   Antitrust Concerns

If competitors conclude an agreement by which they mutually limit the use of their signs to specific areas or modes of use, this obviously raises concerns under antitrust law – after all, it restricts competition in the sectors from which the respective parties commit to withdraw. From that perspective, such contracts only appear as unproblematic if they are concluded for the purpose of solving an

---

[18]   Though in recent years (probably triggered by the lawsuit leading to the *Jette Joop* decision by the BGH; see n. 24 below), a certain increase in books (dissertations) written on the issue can be observed in Germany; for example, K. Rissmann, *Die kartellrechtliche Beurteilung der Markenabgrenzung* (2008); D. Althaus, *Markenrechtliche Abgrenzungsvereinbarungen* (2010); S. Müller, *Abgrenzungsvereinbarungen im Markenrecht* (2011). The latest effort in that regard is the dissertation by G. Barros-Grasbon, *Marken- und wettbewerbsrechtliche Probleme von Abgrenzungsvereinbarungen* (unpublished manuscript on file with the author). A (still) informative, comprehensive account on the issue is given by H. Neubauer, *Markenrechtliche Abgrenzungsvereinbarungen aus rechtsvergleichender* (Köln, Sicht, 1983). For legal articles see in particular R. Knaak, 'Zur Wirksamkeit und Kündbarkeit von zeichenrechtlichen Abgrenzungsvereinbarungen' GRUR 1981, 386.

actual conflict, and not with a view to partitioning the market, or for gagging a potential competitor.

The last-mentioned constellation was at stake in an early case decided by the Court of Justice of the European Union.[19] The trademarks concerned were 'Toltecs Special' and 'Dorcet', both designating tobacco products. Dorcet was registered in Germany for BAT, whereas Toltecs was previously protected and sold in the Netherlands by its owner, Mr Segers, mainly for loose tobacco used for rolling cigarettes. When Segers obtained an international registration, with the intention, *inter alia*, to expand his business to Germany, BAT, upon the threat of challenging the validity of Segers' IR-mark extension to Germany, managed to conclude an agreement that restricted Segers' use and marketing of the mark to 'curly fine tobacco' made him refrain from publicizing in any description of the tobacco that it was suitable or recommended for rolling cigarettes; proscribed any steps being taken against BAT's Dorcet mark even if it was not used for more than five years; and obliged him to distribute the product only through retailers approved by BAT. The latter clause was used by BAT in the following years to interfere repeatedly with business relationships Segers tried to establish with German retailers. In the end, Segers gave up, terminated his business on the German market and alerted the European Commission. The Commission found that the agreement violated Article 85 of the EC Treaty (now: Article 101 of the Treaty on the Functioning of the European Union (TFEU)), and upon appeal, the CJEU agreed. It was held that although it must be acknowledged that:

> agreements known as 'delimitation agreements' are lawful and useful if they serve to delimit, in the mutual interest of the parties, the spheres within which their respective trademarks may be used, and are intended to avoid confusion or conflict between them ... such agreements are [not] excluded from the application of Article 85 of the Treaty if they also have the aim of dividing up the market or restricting competition in other ways.[20]

---

[19]   35/83 *BAT* v. *European Commission* (Toltecs/Dorcet) [1985] ECR 363.
[20]   *Ibid*. para. 33.

Examining the contents of the contract, the CJEU found that Segers' use of the mark was subject to far-reaching restrictions in the use of his mark whereas:

> BAT assumes a single obligation which proves, upon examination, to be purely fictitious. It agrees to withdraw its opposition to the grant of protection for the Toltecs trademark for the German market. Without its being necessary to resolve the question of which criteria must be used for assessing the risk of confusion between the two trademarks, it is sufficient to state that since, on the one hand, Segers is the proprietor of a trademark legally acquired and used in a Member State and BAT, on the other, is the proprietor of an unused, dormant, trademark which is liable to be removed from the register upon application by any interested party, BAT's opposition, as part of its efforts to control the distribution of Segers' products, *constitutes an abuse of the rights* conferred upon it by its trademark ownership. (emphasis added)

Taking these and other elements together, the CJEU found that this:

> leaves no room for doubt as to BAT's real purpose; this was not by any means to protect its interest in the dormant trademark, which had no economic significance whatsoever, but to prevent the marketing of Segers' product on the German market.[21]

The case was indeed a rather clear example of 'trademark bullying'. Nevertheless, the CJEU's decision met with reserved reactions in the German literature.[22] It was emphasized that although the bargaining power of the companies involved appeared uneven – the tobacco giant BAT posed against a small Dutch company – it should not be forgotten that the situation is different from consumer protection or similar areas characterized by clear structural imbalance. In trademark negotiations, even small traders are regularly represented by lawyers or agents who should be able to assess the legal implications of a conflict and advise their client accordingly. Also, it was criticized that the CJEU had not been more explicit with regard to the underlying issue of infringement, either by stating its own opinion on this point or by accepting that on the

---

[21] *Ibid.* para. 36.
[22] See in particular H. Schwanhäusser, 'Die Auswirkungen der Toltecs-Entscheidung des Europäischen Gerichtshofs auf Abgrenzungsvereinbarungen' GRUR Int. 1985, 816.

basis of German law with its (then) particularly low threshold for finding likelihood of confusion, the conflict between the two signs could actually be considered as 'genuine'. It is unclear whether the decision had any major impact on practice. No further cases were brought before the CJEU, and also in Germany, case law remained scarce. Nevertheless, it is a basically plausible assumption that parties in the aftermath of *Toltecs/ Dorcet* have become somewhat more cautious regarding the acuteness of the conflict to be solved, and were more concerned about the even distribution of rights and obligations.

4.3.3   Changed Circumstances; Termination of Agreements

Whereas it is a generally accepted rule after *Toltecs/Dorcet* that in order to avoid adverse consequences under competition law limitation agreements should not be unfounded and grossly imbalanced,[23] even diligent parties cannot guarantee that a balance once achieved will be maintained in the longer run. As the terms of contract necessarily reflect the parties' assessment at the time when the agreement is concluded, the question remains open as to how they can or must react when in light of changed conditions the obligations once accepted appear tilted towards one side. A solution to the issue will seldom be found in the contract itself. Though empirical evidence is lacking on that point (limitation agreements are usually confidential), it seems to be the exception rather than the rule that the contract explicitly provides for a termination or adaptation right to be invoked under certain conditions, or that it expires at a fixed date. On the other hand, being bound to an 'eternal' obligation to tailor one's business activities according to restrictions that may have seemed appropriate once is hardly satisfactory, if under current conditions the deal no longer appears as fair and reasonable.

The issue was of relevance in a case decided by the German Federal Supreme Court (BGH) concerning the trademarks 'JOOP!' and 'JETTE JOOP'.[24] 'Joop' is the last name of the German fashion designer Wolfgang Joop; Jette Joop is his daughter. The word/ devicemark 'JOOP!' is registered in class 25 (apparel) for a firm

---

23   See in particular Rissmann, n. 18 above, p. 39 *et seq.*
24   *Jette Joop*, BGH, GRUR 2011, 641.

originally founded by Wolfgang Joop. Jette Joop first started out as a designer of jewelry; later on she extended her activities, *inter alia*, to fashion articles including apparel. After negotiations with the owners of the trademark 'JOOP!' (subsequently appearing as plaintiffs in the lawsuit) she signed a contract in 1995 that restricted the use of her name to jewelry and costume jewelry. She confirmed that obligation in 1998, when the plaintiffs protested against her registration of the wordmark 'JETTE JOOP' for, *inter alia*, apparel. In 2003, Jette Joop launched a knitwear collection under her mark. The plaintiffs filed a claim against her, based on trademark infringement and on the limitation agreement. The appeal court dismissed the claim, arguing that in view of pertinent jurisprudence Jette Joop's use of her name did not give rise to a likelihood of confusion and therefore did not constitute trademark infringement.[25] Accordingly, it was held that the limitation agreement was not underpinned by a genuine conflict existing between the marks, and that it must therefore be considered as null and void under competition (antitrust) law.

The BGH, however, affirmed the validity of the agreement. It was stated that the appeal court erred when it considered the relationship between the parties in the light of jurisprudence on likelihood of confusion between personal names that had been developed only rather recently, whereas the validity of the contract had to be assessed on the basis of what the parties could have assumed in 1995, when the agreement was concluded. At the relevant time, the only decision by the BGH addressing a similar constellation could indeed be understood as indicating that using the mark 'Jette Joop' in connection with apparel would lead to infringement.[26] In the light of that decision the BGH concluded that the restriction Jette Joop had accepted to observe had appeared as justified.

---

[25] OLG Hamburg (Hamburg Appeal Court), BeckRS 2011, 8185. In the jurisprudence referred to by the appeal court, the BGH had emphasized that if the first name is added to a family name, this may be sufficient to rule out likelihood of confusion; *Carl Link*, BGH, GRUR 2000, 1032; *MEY/Ella May*, BGH, GRUR 2005, 514; similarly *Lions*, BGH, GRUR 1999, 241.

[26] In the relevant decision (*Caren Pfleger*, BGH, GRUR 1991, 477) it had been pointed out that first names are usually non-distinctive and will therefore regularly not exclude likelihood of confusion if they are added to a family name.

Neither the BGH nor the court of appeal embarked on a discussion of the question whether Jette Joop was entitled to terminate the contract irrespective of its validity,[27] now that the line of jurisprudence had changed so that using her own name could no longer be prohibited. There is indeed some uncertainty surrounding the issue of termination. In the literature, it is regularly pointed out that even if nothing is stipulated in the contract, it is accepted under general principles of contract law that it is always possible in a long-term contract relationship to give notice for 'important reasons',[28] in particular if the basis for mutual trust has been irreparably damaged. Furthermore, in case of changes impacting the very foundations on which the agreement was built, its termination may be requested in severe cases; however, primarily parties should seek to adapt the contract to the changed circumstances.[29] Arguably, the latter solution is also the most suitable when changes occur in jurisprudence by which the assessment of a conflict, once considered as genuine, now rather appears as unfounded.

4.3.4   Unclear Impact of *Martin Y Paz/Gauquie*

In a CJEU decision of September 2013, a situation closely resembling a limitation agreement was addressed in a manner which might have rather far-reaching consequences.[30] The underlying conflict had a rather complicated background: two firms, Martin Y Paz and Gauquie, had acquired, independently and at different times, rights in the trademark 'Nathan'. Martin Y Paz and committed himself to using the mark only for small leather goods, whereas Gauquie acquired the right to use the mark for handbags and shoes. Subsequently (with the details being unclear) both firms ceased using the mark 'Nathan' and instead used a picture mark consisting of an elongated 'N' and the wordmark 'Nathan Baume', each for

---

[27]   The BGH only refers to the fact that the parties had agreed in their contract to a termination right (for both sides) in the event of 'important reasons' ('Kündigung aus wichtigem Grund'; see also n. 28 below); as the defendant had not invoked that right, its justification under the pertinent circumstances remained untested.

[28]   Under German Civil Code (BGB), art. 314: 'Kündigung von Dauerschuldverhältnissen aus wichtigem Grund'.

[29]   BGB, art. 313: 'Wegfall der Geschäftsgrundlage'.

[30]   C-661/11 *Martin Y Paz* v. *Gauquie*, CJEU (not yet reported).

their respective products. In 1998 and 2002, Martin Y Paz, allegedly without informing Gauquie, registered both marks for itself. In 2005, Gauquie filed for cancellation based on bad faith insofar as the registration covered shoes and handbags; however, the claim was dismissed as time-barred.[31] Allegedly motivated by revenge, Martin Y Paz filed a claim for permanent injunction against Gauquie, whereupon Gauquie counterclaimed, asking to prohibit any use by Martin Y Paz of the registered marks except for the small leather goods for which the marks had been originally used. The appeal court granted Martin Y Paz's injunction except for shoes and handbags, holding that with regard to those products, the claim constituted an abuse of rights. Gauquie's counterclaim was granted, with the court arguing that use of the marks for shoes and handbags by Martin Y Paz would amount to unfair competition, as it served the aim of benefiting from the goodwill that Gauquie's investments had gained for those products. Upon further appeal against the decision, the Belgian Supreme Court referred the case to the CJEU, basically asking whether the reliance of the appeal court on national unfair competition law was compatible with the provisions of Trademark Directive 95/2008/EC ('TM Directive').

The CJEU denied the question. Whether or not a trademark can be enforced against third parties and whether the use of a mark can be prohibited can only be decided, according to the CJEU, on the basis of trademark law.[32] Apart from that, the CJEU says, all a national court may do is to:

> impose a penalty on the proprietor of a trademark or order it to pay compensation for the damage suffered if it finds that that proprietor has unlawfully withdrawn the consent by which it allowed a third party to use signs which are identical to its marks.[33]

---

[31]   No further information is given about the particular reasons leading to prescription of the claim. That the law imposes such time-bars appears somewhat odd: such limits usually serve to protect the bona fide interests of the party whose position is challenged; however, in a case like this where the challenged party allegedly acted in bad faith, no such protection is called for.

[32]   For a more comprehensive discussion of that point see A. Kur, 'Trademarks Function, Don't They?' *EIPR* 45 IIC, 434 (2014).

[33]   *Martin Y Paz* v. *Gauquie*, n. 30 above, para. 61.

If the same logic were applied to delimitation agreements – conflicts are only to be solved on the basis of trademark law, at least insofar as permanent injunctions are concerned – this would have a quite dramatic impact on the enforceability of such contracts. If one of the parties decides that it is better off by disregarding the contractual restrictions once accepted regarding the use of its mark, courts in a lawsuit eventually filed by the other party would be confined to assessing whether the unrestricted use objectively infringes the other sign. If that is the case, an injunction will ensue; if not, all the other party can ask for (at best) is some amount of damages. However, as always with CJEU decisions, one needs to be careful about drawing too far-reaching conclusions from a decision which, after all, concerned a very peculiar situation.

4.3.5   Consumer Protection

Last but not least in this context, it must be considered whether limitation agreements constitute a risk for consumer protection. Theoretically such a risk can hardly be denied: as pointed out in the context of antitrust concerns (4.3.2), the genuine character of the conflict between the marks involved is an important factor for assessing the validity of the contract. As genuine conflicts regularly invoke the risk of consumer confusion it appears to follow that they can only be solved by the prior right taking precedence and use of the later right being prohibited, as prescribed by law; from that perspective, middling solutions espoused by the parties are not 'safe' enough. However, that simple logic neglects the fact that the paper size of a trademark law and its actual use may be two very different things; accordingly, rights that conflict on paper may perfectly coexist on the market without confusing anyone as to the origin of the goods or services designated by one and the other mark. To underpin that view, it is often emphasized that the companies concluding limitation agreements have the strongest interest in avoiding anything that might lead to their own goodwill being diverted to the other party.[34]

---

[34]   The aspect is addressed, *inter alia*, by Althaus, n. 18 above, p. 119; comprehensively also Barros-Grasbon, n. 18 above, ch. 2 C III.

This is certainly true. Nevertheless, it is not completely excluded that the contracting parties overestimate the sophistication of consumers, while underestimating the risk of confusion. Also, the circumstances may be such that keeping a meaningful distance between the parties becomes difficult to impossible. The conflict between Martin Y Paz and Gauquie[35] provides an example for such a situation: the problems in that convoluted case started when the previous owner of the trademark 'Nathan' decided to divide and transfer the mark in two different segments. With handbags and small leather goods such as wallets and manicure cases being very similar goods, it is nearly inevitable that consumers are confused as to the origin of the respective products, even if each firm observes the boundaries of the right as originally accorded to it.

The law does provide certain safeguards against such risks, although they are rarely applied in practice. In a case like *Martin Y Paz/Gauquie*, where the root of the problem lies in the division and subsequent transfer of one mark in segments that are (too) close to each other to allow for a non-ambiguous identification of source, the trademark registry might deny recording the transfer on the basis of provisions that make such recording dependent on absence of the transfer giving rise to a likelihood of confusion of the public. However, such a provision exists only in the Community Trademark Regulation (CTMR),[36] where it is practically moot. Very few national laws take similar precautions,[37] whereas most legal systems do not consider the monitoring of such risks a meaningful exercise to be undertaken by public authorities. If the risk then materializes – if the mark actually leads to a confusion or misconception of the commercial source(s) on the market – its use can amount to a 'misleading action' in the meaning of article 6(2)(a) of Directive 29/2005/EC on Unfair Commercial Practices ('UCP Directive'). Consequently, persons and institutions entitled under national law to raise claims for violation of the consumer protection

---

[35] See n. 30 above and accompanying text.
[36] CTMR, art. 17(4).
[37] For instance in Italy, see Codice de la proprietà industriale, art. 23(4). In Hungary, trademark transfers are considered as null and void if they result in a likelihood of confusion to the public; see Hungarian Trademark Act, art. 14(4).

standards enshrined in the UCP Directive are entitled to file for an injunction and possibly claim damages.[38] The existence of such options is still a rather new phenomenon for German law. Previously, application of consumer protection norms such as article 3 of the old Act against Unfair Competition (UWG) in order to enjoin or modify the use of marks by their proprietors was severely limited due to the (rather dubious) doctrine developed by jurisprudence that consumer interests are only concerned by such uses if the mark at stake is a 'qualified indicator of commercial origin', in other words, a kind of mark ranging somewhere between a mark having reputation and a famous mark.[39] That doctrine had to be discarded after enactment of the UCP Directive.[40] However, the possibility to file for injunctions in case of trademarks being used in a misleading manner by their proprietor(s) at least until now remains a merely theoretical scheme: no such claims have been brought so far.

4.4 CONCURRENT USE

European trademark law does not embrace 'honest concurrent use' as a general concept. Nevertheless, in certain constellations[41] co-existence of basically conflicting signs will result. Contrary to the

---

[38]   See for example, Müller, n. 18 above, p. 100, possibly overestimating the practical relevance of that point.

[39]   The doctrine had been developed already by the German Imperial Court (Reichsgericht) and was later on adopted and confirmed by the BGH in *Zwilling*, BGH, GRUR 1952, 577; *Raiffeisen*, GRUR 1957, 351; *Triumph*, GRUR 1959, 29; *Nevada*, GRUR 1965, 676; *White Horse*, GRUR 1966, 270; *Grau/magenta*, GRUR 1997, 755; see critical remarks by A. Kur, 'Verwechslungsgefahr und Irreführung. Zum Verhältnis von Markenrecht und § 3 UWG' GRUR 1989, 242 *et seq.*

[40]   See in particular J. Bornkamm, 'Die Schnittstellen zwischen gewerblichem Rechtsschutz und UWG – Grenzen des lauterkeitsrechtlichen Verwechslungsschutzes' GRUR 2011, 2.

[41]   In addition to the cases addressed below, coexistence may also result in case of conflict between a sign not having more than local significance and a younger CTM: while the sign is not a prior right on which opposition or nullity requests can be based (CTMR, art. 8(4)), CTMR, art. 11 leaves it to Member States to protect the prior right within its local confines, either by granting

situation considered under 4.3, the conditions of coexistence in such cases are usually not moderated by party agreements; also, the conflict is typically not one existing merely (or primarily) on paper. The most important group of such cases concerns homonyms: marks registered and used by the descendants of one family, or their successors in title.[42] The basic rule governing such conflicts is set out in article 6(1)(a) of the TM Directive (accordingly: article 12(a) of the CTMR): both parties are allowed to use their name, if and to the extent that the use complies with honest business practices. In practice this means that although the marks can coexist, care must be taken to distinguish the commercial sources as appropriate; also, both parties must avoid taking unfair advantage of the reputation the other name holder may have acquired in commerce. How this is achieved – which kind of uses must be tolerated, and who has to do what in order to avoid serious confusion – has been the object in Germany of a rather comprehensive body of case law (*Recht der Gleichnamigen*) that cannot be presented here in detail.[43]

Apart from homonyms and similar constellations,[44] coexistence can also occur in consequence of acquiescence: if the proprietor

---

exclusivity (with the consequence that the CTM may not be used within the protected area), or, more realistically, by letting both rights coexist.

[42] An example of that is provided in Germany by the lawsuits filed between two firms acting under the names of the previous owners Peek & Cloppenburg; see *Peek & Cloppenburg I*, BGH, GRUR 2010, 738; *Peek & Cloppenburg II*, GRUR 2011, 623 and GRUR 2013, 397; for a case with a similar background see also *Gartencenter Pötschke*, BGH, GRUR 2011, 835.

[43] A brief account of the principle and its many facets is given by G. Schmitt-Gaedke and M. Arz, 'Das Recht der Gleichnamigen und seine Grenzen' GRUR 2012, 565; see also R. Knaak, 'Störungen kennzeichenrechtlicher Gleichgewichtslagen: Was ist hinzunehmen?' GRUR-Prax 2013, 171.

[44] Although not strictly being homonyms, coexistence may also govern the relationship between trademarks and trade names, even where the latter are used 'as a mark', in other words, in relation to goods and services. This results from the CJEU's interpretation of TM Directive, art. 6(1)(a): whereas according to a Common Statement formulated by the Commission and the Council when the TM Directive was enacted the limitation for use of one's own name was only meant to apply to personal names with regard to trade names, the CJEU went further than that and extended it to all kind of trade names (C-245/02 *Anheuser Busch* v. *Budejovicky Budvar* [2004] ECR I-10989, CJEU, at para. 80). According to the pending proposals for reform of the TM Directive and the CTMR, n. 9 above, this will be changed so that the original

fails to take steps against a conflicting sign within five years from having become aware of the conflict, further use of the sign can no longer be prohibited.[45] The same consequence ensues if a mark is registered at a time when a prior conflicting sign would be liable to revocation for non-use. If the use is resumed thereafter, the prior sign remains valid, but cannot be enforced against the younger mark, and vice versa: both signs must henceforth coexist.[46]

By contrast to homonyms, jurisprudence and legal literature until now have not considered the consequences of such other instances of 'forced coexistence' to any larger extent. Nevertheless, it is clear in principle that the situation deviates from the basic paradigms of exclusivity and uniqueness of trademarks, and must therefore be subject to precautions ensuring that no serious confusion will result. In practice, however, there seems to be a lack of legal principles guiding the analysis of whether, and if so which, additional measures must be taken to avoid detrimental effects. The indifference may be due to the relative scarcity of such cases; however, it may also result from the experience that the effect on consumer decisions of marks being conflicting in a legal sense is far less substantial in practice than it may seem in theory.

4.5 CONCLUSIONS

This brief review of non-exclusive uses of the same or similar trademarks has addressed a number of situations in which, for different reasons, the basic principle of uniqueness is to some extent qualified. The most common and legally interesting aspect of non-exclusive use (apart from licenses that were not the focus of this chapter) is presented by delimitation agreements which form an

---

intention of the legislature to restrict the privilege to personal names will be re-instated.

[45]   TM Directive, art. 9; CTMR, art. 54. The current provisions in the TM Directive and the CTMR are rather sparse and are usually complemented by more explicit provisions (or by general legal principles) in national law. For Germany see MarkenG, s. 22.

[46]   For Germany see MarkenG, s. 22. Until now the issue has not been explicitly regulated in European law; however, that would change under the Commission's reform proposals, see n. 9 above; CTMR Proposal, art. 13a; TM Directive Proposal, art. 18.

important though rarely highlighted part of market reality. From a legal as well as from an economic perspective there is little doubt that contracting out of trademark conflicts is a good way of avoiding situations that otherwise would burden the courts and impose costs on all parties involved. On the other hand, there is also reason for concern.

For one, this regards the parties' relationship in the twilight area between full contractual freedom and cogent legal rules, where the underdevelopment of legal doctrine creates uncertainties with regard to the foundations of such agreements and their legal effects as well as their duration. Is it so, as the *Joop* case seems to indicate, that the contract freezes a particular situation in time, even under changed circumstances? Or will CJEU jurisprudence rather lead to the situation that delimitation covenants are mere 'gentleman agreements' that cannot be enforced except (eventually) regarding damages? Those problems are likely to augment through the increasing number of cases when limitation agreements are not confined to one state but assume international or even global dimensions.

Furthermore, from a general point of view it could be asked whether the omnipresence of limitation agreements has an impact on the trademark system as a whole. Is trademark law still what it is generally declared to be – a system whose conditions are defined by the interests of the public at large – given that it apparently leaves much room for private bargaining? Does the leeway left for private arrangements indicate that trademark protection is oversized? Furthermore, what about the transparency that the registration system is supposed to offer? As the CJEU stated in *Sieckmann* (concerning the registration of smell marks), it is the purpose of registration to inform competent authorities and economic operators with 'clarity and precision' about the protected subject matter.[47] How does that fit with the fact that trademark holders often commit to narrow the space actually occupied by their mark, without that being visible to outsiders? For the 'economic operators' apostrophized by the CJEU in *Sieckmann*, especially for new market entrants, it would without doubt constitute a valuable piece of

---

[47] C-273/00 *Sieckmann*, CJEU, [2002] ECR I-11737, at para. 50 *et seq.*

information that the actual space occupied by a mark is substantially modified by private agreements in comparison to its appearance in the register.[48] Is denying such information detrimental to the dynamism of the market and to the equality of conditions for market actors?

Another point of the matter concerns the fact that companies owning multiple (unused) trademarks generally have a better bargaining position when limitations agreements are negotiated. That aspect tends to favor bigger companies *vis-à-vis* SMEs. Furthermore, it might motivate companies to adopt multiple filings as a general strategy, thereby enhancing the phenomenon usually referred to as cluttering: the registers becoming so full of 'deadwood' that access to new marks becomes severely hampered.[49]

All of this must be seen in the context of the European Commission's proposals for trademark reform that were published in March 2013 and are currently under consideration.[50] On the one hand, the Commission takes steps to ease concerns about cluttering by changing the previous rules so that only one class of goods or services is covered by the basic registration fee, instead of, as at present, (up to) three classes.[51] Furthermore, according to the proposals, but also due to a judgment of the CJEU that must already be implemented under the current legislation,[52] the specification of goods and services to which a trademark shall apply must become more precise than under the previous practice in particular of the Community registry (Office for Harmonization in the Internal Market, OHIM).[53] On the other hand, the proposals herald a

---

[48]   Although, of course, the delimitation agreement does not 'reduce' the legal scope of protection with effect *erga omnes*. Nevertheless, getting information about voluntary restrictions in the use of a sign may have certain strategic advantages for third parties operating in the same sector.

[49]   Whether that concern is justified or not is contentious, with both sides proffering (ultimately inconclusive) evidence; see Die Studie des Max-Planck-Instituts für Immaterialgüter- und Wettbewerbsrecht zum Funktionieren des europäischen Markensystems, R. Knaak, A. Kur and A. v. Mühlendahl in GRUR Int. 2012, 198.

[50]   COM(2013)161 and COM(2013)162; see n. 9 above.

[51]   TM Directive Proposal, art. 44.

[52]   C-307/10 *IP Translator*, CJEU.

[53]   According to Communication 4/03 from the President of OHIM, it was considered sufficient for purposes of classification that the so-called 'class

complete withdrawal of public authorities from precautionary conflict monitoring at the registration and pre-registration stage. National trademark offices will be prohibited from offering *ex officio* examination of the so-called relative grounds for refusal,[54] and neither OHIM nor the national offices will engage in *ex officio* searches for prior rights.[55] Consequently, the process will become increasingly privatized and, most likely, the disposition of trademark owners to regulate conflicts among themselves by concluding limitation covenants will increase in proportion.

A number of Member States, in particular those that currently conduct *ex officio* examinations and consider that to be an important pillar of the domestic trademark regime, have already signaled their opposition to the proposal, making it likely that some compromise solution will ensue. However, the general tendency seems to be geared towards restricting, for efficiency purposes, the role of registration authorities to assessing conflicts *ex post*, when an opposition or cancellation request is filed.

Time will tell whether that has detrimental effects, especially for the 'small guys' who may be less comfortable with having to search for potential conflicts and solving them through private agreements than bigger companies engaging in such activities on a routine basis. Furthermore, lack of transparency remains a concern that should be addressed at least in the longer run, especially if the problem of cluttering[56] should become worse.

Lastly, an important lesson appears to follow both from delimitation agreements and from the instances of 'forced coexistence' considered under 4.4. Likelihood of confusion is not an absolute

---

headings' set out in the Nice Agreement concerning the International Classification of Goods and Services for the Purposes of the Registration of Marks 1957 are indicated in the application; furthermore, it was declared that if all class headings listed in one class were indicated, this must be understood as meaning that all goods or services contained in that class were covered. That practice was considered as too vague and insecure by the CJEU.

[54]   TM Directive Proposal, art. 41.

[55]   Currently, the search for prior marks or applications forms a mandatory part of the application procedure at OHIM (CTMR, art. 38(1)). Searches in national registries are optional for a CTM application (CTMR, art. 38(2)), but Member States are free to make such procedures a mandatory part of their national systems.

[56]   See n. 49 above and accompanying text.

concept; it comes in different shades and degrees. Marks may be conflicting and still be able to stay on the market without actually hurting each other. Therefore the general axiom that trademark law is a no-go area for coexistence should be modified. For jurisprudence as well as for scholarly efforts, this poses the task to be more articulate than heretofore about the conditions under which coexistence can be tolerated without additional safeguards being taken to avoid actual confusion, where confusion becomes serious, and which measures are apt to provide appropriate and sufficient means to rule out pertinent risks for the public at large.

5. Managing the risks of intellectual property interdependence in the age of open innovation

Jacques de Werra

5.1 INTRODUCTION

Our globalized flat world[1] tends to intensify the exchanges and interactions between the market players. It mirrors the movement of open innovation which is characterized by the increased use of third party knowledge for the purpose of enriching a company's internal innovation (*inbound open innovation*), and by the continuing search for new markets and channels of distribution for the company's own innovation (*outbound open innovation*).[2]

In a world of open innovation, innovation does not result from the internal efforts of companies, but from the network.[3] Today's networked and interconnected economy therefore perfectly expresses the paradigm of open innovation.[4]

---

[1] By reference to the celebrated book of T.L. Friedman, *The World is Flat* (3rd edn, 2007).

[2] See the classic work of H.W. Chesbrough, *Open Innovation: The New Imperative for Creating and Profiting from Technology* (Cambridge, MA, 2003) (and its numerous subsequent publications); see http://openinnovation. berkeley.edu/.

[3] H.W. Chesbrough and W. Vanhaverbeke, 'Open Innovation and Public Policy in Europe' (2011) *Science Business* (December) 20, available at www.sciencebusiness.net/Assets/27d0282a-3275-4f02-8a3c-b93c2815208c.pdf: 'The locus of innovation is no longer in the firm but in the network'.

[4] It is consequently not surprising that the European Union treats open innovation in its 'Digital Agenda' program, see http://ec.europa.eu/digital-agenda/en/entrepreneurship-innovation/open-innovation; see the report of J. Vallat, *Intellectual Property and Legal Issues in Open Innovation in Services*

The intensive interactions between the market players which are at the core of the open innovation ecosystem generally materialize in a multiplication of contractual relationships by which companies integrate in their products and services the intellectual assets (and intellectual property rights) of third parties and also offer their own intellectual assets to the market according to (contractual) rules and principles that they choose.[5] This system makes it possible to capitalize on and benefit from the expert knowledge and experience of other entities, and can therefore contribute to an optimal allocation of corporate and societal activities and resources. These interactions can, however, generate risks which result from the interdependence that such interactions generate. The goal of this chapter is to explore some of the consequences of this network of intellectual property interdependence in the *creation* and in the *use* of innovation and to assess how the risks could be managed.

5.2 RISKS OF INTELLECTUAL PROPERTY INTERDEPENDENCE IN THE ERA OF OPEN INNOVATION

While open innovation networks obviously create promising opportunities, they can also generate risks which can be quite diverse.[6]

(European Commission Information Society and Media, 2009), available at http://ec.europa.eu/digital-agenda/en/news/intellectual-property-and-legal-issues-open-innovation-services.

[5] One avenue for fostering accessibility and sharing opportunities is to adopt an open licensing (open content / open source) strategy; open innovation however does not necessarily mean that the knowledge which is generated is offered for free to third parties under open licensing terms; two categories of open innovation have thus been identified: open boundary innovation which is designed to source new technology and concepts broadly without surrendering control of the innovation process; and open source innovation which is a more radical model that views the source of much innovation as originating in the collective knowledge and motivation of anonymous users; see J. Euchner, 'The Uses and Risks of Open Innovation' (2013) 56(3) *Research-Technology Management Journal* 49.

[6] See J. de Werra, 'Keeping the Genie of Licensing Out of the Bottle: Managing Inter-Dependence in Licensing Transactions' (2014) *IIC* 253 (from which some developments addressed in this chapter are derived); on open innovation from an intellectual property perspective, see generally J. Brand and S.

From an intellectual property perspective (on which this chapter will focus), risks generally result from the interdependence that open innovation can generate. The focus will here be on outsourcing of research and development (R&D) activities (see 5.2.1), joint generation of innovation (5.2.2) and the use of third party's intellectual property assets (5.2.3).

5.2.1   Interdependence from Outsourcing R&D

One aspect of open innovation is to outsource R&D.[7] This contributes to the creation of niche markets of highly specialized companies and service providers which offer their creativity (and R&D expertise) to the market and to their clients. Depending on the structure of the relevant market, clients operating in the same industry and market – who are thus direct competitors – can (or sometimes even have to) turn to the same provider of R&D services because of their unique expertise. This can raise difficult issues of intellectual property dependence, also because the allocation of intellectual property rights (IPRs) between the service provider and its client may be complex (if not adequately regulated by contract).[8] It is indeed established that clients are also the source of quite valuable innovation.[9] This complexity can be illustrated by reference to the dispute which arose between two Formula One teams and the company which provided them highly specialized services,[10] in other words, wind tunnel aerodynamic testing and development.

Lohse, The Open Innovation Model (2014), International Chamber of Commerce, Innovation and Intellectual Property Series, available at: http://www.iccwbo.org/Data/Documents/Intellectual-property/THE-OPEN-INNOVATION-MODEL/.

[7]   O. Gassmann, 'Opening up the Innovation Process: Towards an Agenda' (2006) 36(3) *R&D Management* 224: 'Technical service providers such as engineering firms and high-tech institutions have become more important in the innovation process'.

[8]   For an example, see C-32/08 *FEIA* v. *Cul de Sac Espacio Creativo SL*, CJEU [2009] ECR I-05611.

[9]   As admirably demonstrated by E. von Hippel in his (numerous) publications on user innovation and, more generally, on the sources of innovation, see E. von Hippel, *The Sources of Innovation* (Oxford, Oxford University Press, 1988), available at: http://web.mit.edu/evhippel/www/sources.htm.

[10]   *Force India Formula One Team Ltd* v. *1 Malaysia Racing Team SDN BHD and others* [2012] EWHC 616 (Ch) (21 March 2012); *Force India*

One of the issues in this case was to distinguish between the personal skill and knowledge of the employees of the service provider and the corporate trade secrets of its clients. The concern was expressed that the development contract should not 'unduly restrict the ability of Aerolab's employees from making use of their skill and knowledge, even if that skill and knowledge had been enhanced by information that they had acquired in the course of working on the Force India project'.[11] This dispute shows the difficulties in defining the scope of protection of trade secrets in an era characterized by employee mobility and by open innovation models. This is a challenge that will also have to be faced and solved in the European Union which is about to harmonize the protection of trade secrets as resulting from the Proposal that was submitted in November 2013.[12]

5.2.2 Dependence from Joint R&D

Open innovation networks also imply an intensification of the cooperation between entities in joint research and development activities. Joint innovation activities are likely[13] to lead to joint ownership of the intellectual property rights on the results which would be generated in the course of the joint research project. While joint ownership of intellectual property rights is anything but a new phenomenon in the intellectual property landscape, its lack of harmonization at the international level, and even at the national

---

Formula One Team Ltd v. *Aerolab SRL and others* [2013] EWCA Civ 780 (July 2013).

[11]   *Force India Formula One Team Ltd* v. *Aerolab* [2013] EWCA CIV 780, para. 61.

[12]   Proposal for a Directive of the European Parliament and of the Council on the protection of undisclosed know-how and business information (trade secrets) against their unlawful acquisition, use and disclosure, COM/2013/0813 final; 2013/0402 (COD) (28 November 2013); this project is still on-going as of the time of this chapter.

[13]   This will depend on contractual solutions and on the applicable regulatory framework (particularly if the cooperation is between private and public institutions).

level,[14] remains highly problematic.[15] The constraints and specificities of national intellectual property regimes are numerous and clearly do not meet the legitimate expectations of global innovation networks where innovation is shared and also co-owned.[16]

On this basis, it is clear that joint ownership of traditional categories of IPRs (particularly copyrights and patents) may already be difficult to manage, particularly in a transnational perspective. The management can become even more complex when dealing with more evanescent forms of intangible assets, and particularly with trade secrets. What rules shall apply in the case of jointly generated trade secrets, which is presented as a potential new business model in the draft Directive on the protection of trade secrets?[17] What shall each co-owner be in a position to do with its share of the joint knowledge? Shall each of the co-owners be in a position to independently transfer its share of the joint knowledge to a third party or license it out to a third party? Shall each of the joint owners be in a position to initiate judicial action against a third party for misappropriation of trade secrets? Ideally these issues should also be regulated in order to create an adequate legal regime of protection of trade secrets, knowing that trade secrets, similarly to other types of IPRs, are frequently the product of joint efforts made by several (generally many) individuals and are no longer the creation of an individual (and lone) creator.

---

[14]   It is not infrequent that the legal regime of co-ownership of intellectual property rights differs from one type of intellectual property right to another within one national legal system.

[15]   As evidenced by the special issue of the LES journal *Les Nouvelles* on joint ownership (December 2012), see the introduction to this special issue by S. Kim and V. Lipton, 'Joint Ownership of IP Around the World', at 250 (who indicate (251) that 'the effects of joint ownership differ significantly across different IP rights and across different jurisdictions').

[16]   By way of example, reference can be made to *Minden Pictures, Inc.* v. *Pearson Education, Inc.*, No. C 11-05385 WHA (ND Calif. 5 March 2013) in which the court invalidated over 4,000 identical copyright assignment agreements that had purported to grant co-ownership rights because such assignments did not transfer more than the bare right to litigate the copyright, which was not valid (as a result of previous case law: see *Silvers* v. *Sony Pictures Entertainment, Inc.*, 402 F.3d 881, 896 (9th Cir. 2005)).

[17]   The explanatory memorandum relating to the Proposal for a Directive, n. 12 above, p. 2, refers to 'new business models for using co-created knowledge'.

5.2.3 Dependence from Uses of Innovation by Third Parties (Licensing In/Out)

Open innovation means that companies frequently use intangible assets owned by other market players in their own business activities (particularly of technological solutions protected by IPRs).

It is obvious that such users (licensees or sublicensees) rely on their continued ability to use the IPRs owned by third parties on which they depend and which can be put at risk in case of early termination of the license from which they benefit or from bankruptcy proceedings that could be initiated against their licensor. From this perspective, the dependence of licensees and sublicensees is a common phenomenon. What is of relevance and of interest is to note a certain shift of power, which is perceivable in different countries and legal systems, that reflects the acknowledgment of the risks assumed by licensees and sublicensees which therefore call for some additional protection.

This is particularly reflected in two recent German decisions which protected sublicensees in case of termination of the main license. The German Bundesgerichtshof indeed held in two parallel decisions rendered on the same day in July 2012 that a copyright sublicensee could continue to benefit from its right to use the relevant work (a musical work and a software product, respectively) in spite of the termination of the main license.[18] The important lesson of these cases is that the termination of a main license does not necessarily affect the continuation of a sublicense. This consequently means that even if it validly terminated its license agreement with its licensee, a licensor can still face the risks of having to tolerate the existence of sublicensees (from which he could nevertheless still derive income). This does not appear as a natural and expected result in the light of fundamental principles of private law (particularly of the principles of privity of contract and the relativeness of contractual relationships: *res inter alios acta nec prodest nec nocet*) knowing that a licensor can end up being forced to tolerate (in a quasi-contractual relationship) the use of its IPRs by a third party with which it did not enter into direct contractual relationships. The solution developed by the German courts in these

---

[18]   *Take Five*, BGH, *GRUR* 2012, 914; *M2Trade*, BGH, *GRUR* 2012, 916.

parallel cases raises a number of complex questions and has unsurprisingly triggered many comments in the legal literature.[19] Viewed from the outside, these decisions are of key importance and trigger many questions: shall these cases also apply to other types of IPRs beyond copyright? Shall a sublicensee be protected only with respect to a use in Germany (in the affirmative, what would happen in case of multiterritorial sublicenses?)? How can the licensor terminate the license with the ex-sublicensee (in one of the two cases – *Take 5* – the exclusive license will expire in 2047)? On what legal basis can the royalties unduly paid by the ex-sublicensee to the ex-licensee be reimbursed to the licensor? These issues can become quite complex in an international setting because it will require to define the law that shall govern that (unjust enrichment) claim. Under Rome II,[20] this will be the law governing the former license agreement (now terminated) between the licensor and the ex-licensee (which was '[US law]' in the *Take 5* case).

Situations of interdependence can also occur in the classical scenario of bankruptcy of the licensor or of the licensee, as confirmed by recent case law. In a decision of 3 December 2013, the US Court of Appeals for the Fourth Circuit affirmed a decision of the lower court (the United States Bankruptcy Court, ED of Virginia) which held that licensees could continue to benefit from their licenses under US patents that were granted by a foreign licensor (German-based Qimonda AG) over which bankruptcy proceedings had been initiated in Germany. By doing so, the US

---

[19]   See, under German law, M. Dammler and K.-J. Melullis, 'Störung in der patentrechtlichen Lizenzkette – Folgen für die Unterlizenz im Patentrecht', *GRUR* 2013, 781; A. Heidenhain and K. Reus, 'Möglichkeiten der vertraglichen Bindung von Unterlizenzen an den Bestand der Hauptlizenz' (2013) *Computer und Recht* 273; see the analysis under Swiss law, M. Iskic and E.-M. Strobel, 'Lang lebe die Unterlizenz!?! Gedanken zum Schicksal von Unterlizenzen bei Wegfall der Hauptlizenz nach deutschem und nach schweizerischem Recht', (2013) *sic!*, p. 682.

[20]   Regulation (EC) 864/2007 of the European Parliament and of the Council of 11 July 2007 on the law applicable to non-contractual obligations ('Rome II'), art. 10(1), which provides that '[i]f a non-contractual obligation arising out of unjust enrichment, including payment of amounts wrongly received, concerns a relationship existing between the parties, such as one arising out of a contract or a tort/delict, that is closely connected with that unjust enrichment, it shall be governed by the law that governs that relationship'.

court essentially held that the interests of the licensees should prevail over those of the licensor (in other words, the German company holding the patents) thereby recognizing 'that licensees have a strong interest in maintaining their right to use intellectual property following the licensor's bankruptcy'[21] and that failing to do so would 'slow the pace of innovation'[22] in the United States. The Court noted that, even if the licensor (represented by the administrator of the bankruptcy in Germany) had committed to re-license the patents to the licensee on reasonable and non-discriminatory terms (RAND), this was not sufficient to eliminate the risk of dependence to which the licensees were exposed because it was 'far from clear whether, having once facilitated the termination of license rights in a foreign insolvency proceeding, the genie could ever be put back into the bottle'.[23]

These various decisions confirm that courts feel the need to intervene in order to protect licensees against (foreign) licensors in view of the dependence of the licensees, whereby courts sometimes rely on fundamental legal instruments, such as local public policy, in order to justify their decision. In *In re Qimonda*, the lower court held that not protecting licensees of the US patents in the bankruptcy of the foreign licensor 'undermine[s] a fundamental [US] public policy promoting technological innovation. For that reason, the court holds that deferring to German law, to the extent it allows cancellation of the US patent licenses, would be manifestly contrary to US public policy'.[24] This consequently shows that courts tend to

---

[21]   *Jaffe* v. *Samsung Electrics Co., Ltd*, 737 F.3d 14, 32 (4th Cir. 2013) (which refers to the Senate Report accompanying the Bill that became § 365(n) of the US Bankruptcy Code – which is the provision which grants a specific protection to licensees in case of bankruptcy of the licensor).

[22]   *Jaffe* v. *Samsung Electrics Co., Ltd*, 737 F.3d 14, 32 (4th Cir. 2013) (which quotes the expression used by the Bankruptcy Court, 462 B.R. 165, 185 (Bankr. ED Va. 2011)).

[23]   *Jaffe* v. *Samsung Electrics. Co., Ltd*, 737 F.3d 14, at 31.

[24]   *In re Qimonda AG*, Case no. 09-14766-SSM, United States Bankruptcy Court, ED of Virginia (28 October 2011), Bankruptcy Court, 462 B.R. 165, 167, it being noted that this finding of a conflict with US public policy was not expressly confirmed on appeal.

actively intervene in order to protect licensees who are confronted with the bankruptcy of their licensor.[25]

Court decisions rendered in other jurisdictions confirm this trend and show the complexities to find an adequate balance between the respective rights of the parties to an intellectual property contract. The High Court of Justice (Queen's Bench Division) of England and Wales recently had to decide whether to grant an injunction preventing the termination of a license agreement for which the ex-licensee had applied (pending the resolution of an arbitration which had just been initiated pursuant to the arbitration clause provided for in the license agreement). The licensee claimed that its business activities totally depended on the continuation of the license agreement (which related to the use of an 'eMarketplace', in other words, a commercial Internet-based electronic platform) because the termination of the license would 'permanently destroy' its business. The court ultimately refused to grant the injunction for the reason that the licensee had failed to show that damages were not an adequate remedy, but still admitted 'to a degree of unease at the result'.[26]

In Switzerland, the Swiss Supreme Court recently decided that a long-term contract entered into between graphic designers and a creative agency under which the designers assigned their copyrights in fictional graphical animals that they had created to the agency could not be terminated for just cause by the designers even if the animals had been slightly changed by the final client (a major Swiss food company) of the creative agency.[27] What is interesting in this case is that the Swiss Supreme Court essentially held that the agreement could not be terminated by the designers because the

[25] See also *Sunbeam Products, Inc.* v. *Chicago American Manufacturing, LLC*, 686 F.3d 372 (7th Cir. 2012), cert. denied, 133 S Ct. 790 (2012); for an analysis of this case, see R. Gabay, '*Sunbeam*: A Ray of Hope for Trademark Licensees' (2013) 82 *Fordham L Rev.* 245, available at http://ir.lawnet. fordham.edu/flr/vol82/iss1/6; see also M. Reutter, 'Intellectual Property Licensing Agreements and Bankruptcy' in J. de Werra (ed.), *Research Handbook on Intellectual Property Licensing* (Cheltenham (UK)/Northampton, MA, Edward Elgar, 2013), p. 281 *et seq.*
[26] *AB* v. *CD* (Rev. 2) [2014] EWHC 1 (QB) (3 January 2014), Stuart-Smith J (in a 'postscript' to the decision) para. 43.
[27] Decision of the Swiss Federal Supreme Court (4A_598/2012) of March 19, 2013, (2013) *sic!*, p. 600.

final client had made significant investments and should therefore be in a position to continue to use the animals in spite of the minor breaches of the agreement.[28] The Court thus implicitly admitted that the client's dependence over the use of the copyrighted works created by the designers should be protected.

What can we learn from these decisions? Beyond the complex legal issues that they raise under the relevant applicable laws[29] and even if at least some of the issues could adequately be addressed by contract,[30] these decisions fundamentally illustrate the growing awareness of the *dependence* which can be generated in intellectual property licensing transactions and which are particularly apparent and complex when these transactions have a transnational scope (as illustrated by the US decision in the *Qimonda* case).

They also demonstrate that courts increasingly perceive the need to protect licensees (or sublicensees) in certain circumstances, thereby reflecting the concern that licensees may sometimes be extremely (if and perhaps excessively) dependent on the use of the licensed IPRs which are owned by a third party.

5.3 CONCLUSION

In today's networks of (open) innovation, intellectual property interdependence is pervasive: individual companies can (heavily)

---

[28] Decision of the Swiss Federal Supreme Court (4A_598/2012) of March 19, 2013, (2013) *sic!*, p. 603 paragraph 5.5.: *The party which intervenes in these proceedings has acted as an advertising agency between the two parties. Given this situation, it was not only admissible, but it was even required for the previous court to include the interest of the defendant [in other words, the final client] to be able to continue the extensive and long term kids program in the general balance of interests in the overall assessment of all relevant circumstances* (original German text: 'Die Nebenintervenientin agierte als Werbeagentur zwischen den beiden Seiten. Bei dieser Sachlage war es daher nicht nur zulässig, sondern geboten, dass die Vorinstanz bei der Abwägung der Interessen auch das Interesse der Beschwerdegegnerin, dieses breit und langfristig angelegte Kinderprogramm fortführen zu können, in die Gesamtwürdigung aller Umstände einbezog').

[29] It is not the goal of this chapter to express an opinion on these decisions under the applicable local laws.

[30] Heidenhain and Reus, n. 19 above, p. 778; Iskic and Strobel, n. 19 above, p. 689.

depend on third parties with respect to their use of intellectual property for running their business activities. As discussed above, interdependence can arise in very diverse settings, and particularly between innovation generators (R&D entities) and their clients, between joint creators of innovation and between licensors and licensees (and sublicensees).

As we know, the entire intellectual property system is based on a balance of interests through which the existence and the scope of IPRs should carefully reflect the delicate and evolving balance between the respective interests of the stakeholders (specifically the owners and the users of the rights). Now, it is also important to make sure that this balance is equally reflected in intellectual property licensing transactions. While common wisdom may hold that licensors generally benefit from a privileged position because of the control they exercise over their intellectual assets, so that, as a result, licensees depend on their licensors, the recent case law discussed above suggests that licensees (and even sublicensees) have gained significant power: under certain circumstances, they can continue to benefit from a license or from a sublicense even if such possibility is not granted under the bankruptcy laws of the country where the licensor is based or even if the main license is terminated: licensors can therefore also depend on their licensees or even their sublicensees.

Even if this is obviously good news for the licensees/ sublicensees, this should not hide the fact that in a globalized world in which open innovation flourishes, almost every company is (or can quickly become) both a licensor (outbound open innovation) and a licensee (inbound open innovation). It would thus be clearly erroneous and risky for a local regulator or a local court to adopt or promote a legal regime which would tend to protect licensees in view of their dependence. While this may look attractive in the short run, such approach would ultimately affect negatively the ability of the (local) licensees to access and use (foreign) IPRs and their ability to operate as licensors.

What is consequently needed is a system which shall adequately manage the *interdependence* between the market players, and most particularly between the parties to licensing transactions. Such regime should equitably balance the respective interests of the stakeholders, and as regards licensing transactions, the regime should balance the interests of licensees in continuing to use the licensed rights and those of the licensors in keeping control over such rights.

In this respect, it is essential to realize that this growing interdependence is not limited to issues of substantive law, such as the regime of intellectual property co-ownership (*substantive* interdependence): interdependence also materializes in the way in which disputes arise and are solved (*procedural* interdependence).

As exposed in a recent survey conducted by the WIPO Arbitration and Mediation Center on technology disputes, today's business transactions are 'increasingly complex, with the contractual framework often involving multiple parties from different jurisdictions and different types of organizations', it being further stated that '[t]here is a trend away from one off licensing of A to B, and towards multi-party know-how and IP arrangements in the context of bigger projects' (IP Lawyer, France).[31] On this basis, the increased interactions between companies in the generation and use of innovation and of intellectual property assets increase the risks that complex multiparty disputes may arise and that stakeholders may face a situation of procedural interdependence.

Managing the risks of intellectual property interdependence therefore also means ensuring the efficiency of dispute mechanisms. This particularly implies being aware that different proceedings may increasingly need to be coordinated or that the outcome of certain proceedings may be dependent on the outcome of other preliminary proceedings.[32] The question therefore arises whether

---

[31] *International Survey on Dispute Resolution in Technology Transactions* (March 2013), p. 13, available at www.wipo.int/export/sites/www/amc/en/docs/surveyresults.pdf.

[32] This scenario is reflected in recent decisions rendered in Switzerland; see, for example, the recent decision of the Federal Patent Court which addressed the procedural issue of the fixing of filing fees for the proceedings (which depends on the determination of the amount in dispute), in which the court acknowledged the existence of previously filed arbitration proceedings in which the amount in dispute was much higher by comparison to the amount which was disclosed before the court; see decision of the Swiss Federal Patent Court of 28 October 2013 (ref. O2013_004); see also judgment of the Swiss Federal Supreme Court of 11 May 2010 (ref. 4A_616/2009) (proceedings based on a violation of Swiss unfair competition law for misappropriation of trade secrets, referring to an arbitration proceeding in which an ICC arbitral tribunal had already decided on a related breach of an obligation of confidentiality).

and how the parties can anticipate such scenarios and adopt – if possible and if felt appropriate – a dispute resolution system which may make it possible for them to solve the entirety of their dispute before one unique dispute resolution body (particularly an arbitral tribunal).

In short, there is a need to conceptualize a framework that shall address these situations of intellectual property interdependence. If this is not done, the risk is that this may hamper the future development of cooperative open innovation networks which characterize our connected network economy.

6. Expressive dimensions of design: a question of incentive?

Dana Beldiman

6.1 INTRODUCTION

Design plays a significant role in modern culture. Intellectual property (IP) protection of industrial design, however, remains a challenge to scholars and policy-makers. This chapter considers two attributes of product design[1] and explores their relevance in terms of IP law. These attributes – capacity for information spillover and expressive dimensions – will be discussed in turn.

The operation of these attributes is illustrated in the context of the fashion industry. This industry deviates from the standard exclusionary IP model, in that it functions largely on a shared knowledge basis and, at the same time, places little reliance on IP laws. This type of model would, according to classical IP theory, result in a lack of incentive to create. An explanation for the fact that this does not occur in the fashion industry is sought in the effect of self- and social expression, expressive dimensions which facilitate important processes relating to the consumption of goods.

---

[1] Product design will be used here in the sense of industrial design, a discipline concerned with 'creating and developing concepts and specifications that optimize the function, value and appearance of products and systems for the mutual benefit of both user and manufacturer'. See Industrial Design Society of America, www.idsa.org/what-is-industrial-design. This is to be differentiated from design engineering, which refers to transposing specifications provided by a customer into a product.

6.2 PRODUCT DESIGN IN MODERN SOCIETY

6.2.1 Importance of Design

Visual imagery has become predominant in modern culture.[2] One of the main reasons for this is that modern technology has provided tools that allow the handling of digital images with increasing ease. As never before in human history, visual images can be viewed, created, copied, manipulated, searched and broadcast. Ubiquity and widespread access to images and designs, in turn, spawns further creation. The twenty-first century has become a 'visual age', an age in which visual images have come to play a significant cultural and economic role.[3]

One burgeoning area of visual imagery is industrial product design, a discipline which synthesizes utilitarian and aesthetic components;[4] it combines innovative technological performance with a pleasing appearance. In addition, through its visual dimension, product design has the ability to communicate meaning,

---

[2] Graeme Dinwoodie and Mark Janis, *Trade Dress and Design Law* (Aspen Publishers, 2010), p. 3. See generally Orit Fischman Afori, 'Reconceptualizing Property in Designs' (2008) 25 *Cardozo Arts and Entertainment Law Journal* 1105. See also http://ssrn.com/abstract=1015212; Uma Suthersanaen, 'Function, Art and Fashion: Do We Need the EU Design Law?' in Christophe Geiger (ed.), *Constructing European Intellectual Property* (Edward Elgar, 2013), p. 357; Alice Rawsthorn, 'The shape of things to come', *International Herald Tribune*, 19 August 2008.

[3] See Dana Beldiman, 'Protecting the Form but Not the Function: Is U.S. Law Ready for a New Model High Tech?' (2004) 20 *Santa Clara High Tech. LJ* 529, 541. This is evidenced by the popularity of image-based online communication devices such as Instagram, Flickr and Pinterest, increased use of YouTube and Facebook for commercial advertising, as well as the new wave of design museums. See Alice Rawsthorn, 'Design museums pay homage to digital revolution', *New York Times*, 4 February 2014, and design schools and institutes all over the world; see also Alice Rawsthorn, 'What defies defining but exists everywhere', *International Herald Tribune*, 19 August 2008.

[4] Design 'is the merger of aesthetic and utilitarian concerns. It is the influence of non-aesthetic factors, the nexus between what the product must do and how it must look, that distinguishes true industrial design from other artistic endeavors': Robert Denicola, 'Applied Art and Industrial Design: A Suggested Approach to Copyright in Useful Articles' (1983) 67 *Minn. L Rev.* 707.

because a picture 'is worth a thousand words'.[5] This latter attribute makes product design valuable from a commercial standpoint. At a visceral level, superior design renders products appealing to consumers. Between two products equal in price, function and quality, consumers will prefer the one that is more pleasing to the eye.[6] As consumers are faced with a wide selection of functionally similar products, differentiation among these products is largely determined by the emotional response to pleasing visual images.[7] Product design, through its combined utility, aesthetic appeal and communication attributes, thus has the ability to impact consumers' purchasing behavior.[8]

From an IP law perspective, the field of design has long intrigued scholars,[9] because it does not fit neatly into the traditional

---

[5]   The phrase 'One picture worth a thousand words', attributed to Confucius, is frequently used to denote the superiority of graphically presented information over verbal explanations.

[6]   '[B]etween two products equal in prices, function and quality, the better looking will outsell the other': Dinwoodie and Janis, n. 2 above, p. 8 n. 46, quoting Raymond Loewy, *Industrial Design* (1979), p. 13. Superior design is one of the primary means by which consumers will differentiate among products. Dinwoodie and Janis, n. 2 above, p. 8 n. 49.

[7]   Fischman Afori, n. 2 above, p. 1113; 'The developed world is embracing design as a killer weapon in the battle against low cost competition from China, which, like other developing countries, is building new design schools to fight back in the future'. Alice Rawsthorn, 'Design 2006: a year of innovation and utility', *New York Times*, 17 December 2006.

[8]   This accounts for the increasing commercial importance of design and its use as a branding tool and the increasing amount of investment that goes into the design aspect of product development. The commercial effect of design as product differentiator is particularly strong in products that are technologically mature, because in such cases, the product's appeal is based in increased measure on its visual component. Maybe the best-known example is the aesthetic redirection of computer equipment by Steve Jobs. While some view Apple as having built exclusively on existing technology with its contribution consisting solely of design, it indisputably has had a powerful effect on the market.

[9]   Denicola, n. 4 above; Jerome H. Reichman, 'Design Protection After the Copyright Act of 1976: A Comparative View of the Emerging Interim Models' (1984) 31 *Journal of the Copyright Society of the USA* 267; Jerome H. Reichman, 'Legal Hybrids Between the Patent and Copyright Paradigms' (1994) 94 *Columbia Law Review* 2432; Jerome H. Reichman, 'Past and Current Trends in the Evolution of Design Protection Law: A Comment' (1993–1994) 4 *Fordham Intell. Prop. Media and Ent. LJ* 387.

categories of IP law.[10] Situated on the crossroads between two forms of intellectual property, the economically important utilitarian innovation and the culturally exalted artistic creativity, design has always been treated as a stepchild. However, the ubiquity of visual imagery in recent years is bringing to the forefront of attention certain of its attributes, which, particularly in a digitally enabled consumption-focused culture, have the power to affect the market-place.[11] To the extent that they impact the supply and demand of design products, these attributes may impact the incentive structure provided by IP law.[12]

The first of the two attributes is the fact that design bears its know-how on its face, in other words, its IP content is readily apparent. This facilitates spillover. In turn, this easy dissemination of a design's IP content leads to emulation and imitation of original designs. The second attribute relates to the capacity of visual images to express and carry meaning. Product design, as a form of visual imagery, can function as a communication mechanism. It can act as a differentiator in the market and, thereby, impact consumption behavior.[13]

6.2.2   Knowledge Spillover[14]

One of the main attributes of product design is the fact that its knowledge content is readily apparent. This means that its

---

[10]   Suthersanen, n. 2 above, p. 356.

[11]   See generally, Fischman Afori, n. 2 above, p. 1114, referring to the dimension of design that has social cultural and political effects of consumption on self-conception and cultural identity. These in turn further affect market efficiency. See also, Barton Beebe, 'Intellectual Property and the Sumptuary Code' (2010) 123 *Harvard Law Review* 809.

[12]   Design lies between 'the value- and emotion-laden sentiments of beauty, aesthetic and pleasure [and] … design leads and is lead by market conditions, including consumer perception, product identity and competitive edge': Suthersanen, n. 10 above, p. 356.

[13]   *Ibid.* See also Rawsthorn, n. 2 above.

[14]   At issue here is intra-market spillovers whose benefits accrue to firms competing in the same product market, as opposed to inter-market spillover, which benefits other industries. Adam Jaffe, *Economic Analysis of Research Spillovers: Implications for the Advanced Technology Program*, Advanced Technology Program (Washington, DC, Economic Assessment Office, National Institutes of Standards and Technology, US Department of Commerce, 1996).

intellectual property becomes public knowledge, once the product is publicly displayed and is subject to copying by third parties.[15] One effect of this attribute is that the knowledge thus disseminated benefits firms competing in the same market.[16] The ease of capturing a design product's IP content all too readily leads to its replication. The more interesting and distinctive the design, the more likely it will generate 'progeny' in the form of imitations, emulations or interpretations.[17] This phenomenon leads to an increase in the supply of goods and thus benefits consumers, but is detrimental to creators of original products because lower-priced goods compete in the market.

Effects of spillovers: copying, counterfeiting and non-original products
Copying, imitation and emulation have, of course, existed since the very beginnings of cultural expression. In the past decades, however, these phenomena have gained an entirely new magnitude. Advances in communications,[18] transportation and manufacturing technologies,[19] and enhanced know-how and production facilities in emerging economies with low wage structures, have all contributed to reducing production costs and enabling mass production and

---

[15]　This is in contrast, for instance, with products involving complex engineering, whose IP content can only be identified through laborious reverse engineering, and which, consequently, are less readily duplicated.

[16]　Jaffe, n. 14 above; Brett M. Frischmann and Mark A. Lemley, 'Spillovers' (2007) 107 *Columbia Law Review* 257, 268: 'spillovers also benefit third parties, including competitors and potential competitors … Industries with significant spillovers generally experience more and faster innovation than industries with fewer spillovers'.

[17]　For instance, design products such as the iconic quilted Chanel bag, Charles Eames Lounge Chair, Ligne Roset's Togo sofa, and many others, have spawned numerous look-alikes of varying degrees of similarity.

[18]　Rawsthorn, n. 7 above.

[19]　Technology allows production of counterfeits that are indistinguishable from genuine products. For instance, even holograms can be perfectly imitated, a fact which renders counterfeits virtually impossible to detect. See www. iprcenter.gov/reports/ipr-center-reports/IPR%20Center%20Threat%20Report% 20and%20Survey.pdf/view.

reproduction of virtually any design.[20] This has led to an increase in the supply of non-original[21] products of all kinds, ranging from apparel to electronics, sporting goods, all types of machinery, food, medicines, and even store décor.[22]

A further effect of technological advances is the fact that the speed with which non-original products reach the market has sharply increased the economic impact on original producers. In the past, the arrival of non-original products in the market was delayed by slow communications, transportation and the overall difficulties of trading internationally. The original producer thus had a lead-time over low-cost competitors, which gave it the ability to monetize its IP without being undercut in the market.[23] At present, a non-original product can reach the market in a matter of weeks, maybe even days, after the launch of the original.[24] As a result, the original producer's lead-time is reduced or even eliminated and, with it, its prime mover advantage and opportunity for economic gain. To a large extent, spillover of IP content therefore operates as

---

[20]   See generally, Beebe, n. 11 above. See also 'Britain flooded with fake goods', *Daily Telegraph*, 16 July 2011, available at www.telegraph.co.uk/news/8641018/Britain-flooded-with-fake-goods-EU-figures-show.html.

[21]   These products are also referred to as look-alikes, knock-offs, copies, and so on. This chapter will use the neutral term 'non-original', reflecting the absence of a conclusion on infringement.

[22]   See generally, David Wall and J. Large, 'Jailhouse Frocks: Locating the Public Interest in Policing Counterfeit Luxury Fashion Goods' (2010) 50(6) *British Journal of Criminology* 1094, available at http://papers.ssrn.com/sol3/papers.cfm?abstract_id=1649773. But note that as a result of new technologies and the drop in production costs, changes similar to the ones the Internet has wrought in digital content are poised to sweep through the economy of goods and services placing counterfeiting as a business in just as much jeopardy as record labels due to download technology. Mark Lemley, *IP in a World Without Scarcity*, Stanford Public Law Working Paper No. 2413974 (2014), available at http://papers.ssrn.com/sol3/papers.cfm?abstract_id=2413974.

[23]   Stephen Breyer, 'The Uneasy Case for Copyright: A Study of Copyright in Books, Photocopies and Computer Programs' (1970) 84 *Harvard Law Review* 281, illustrating the concept of lead-time in the context of software programs.

[24]   For instance, companies such as Zara and H&M are able to place non-original products on the market within just two weeks from the date the product was originally placed on the market.

a facilitator of the present-day proliferation of non-original design products in the market.[25]

6.2.3 Communicative Dimensions of Design: Self-expression and Social Expression

If spillover affects the supply with non-original goods, the second attribute of design at issue here, its expressive dimension, impacts the demand side.

As a form of visual imagery, the design of a product can 'speak' a thousand words. An individual's selection of a design product with a specific appearance can therefore also speak. It can convey certain information about the individual who makes the choice.[26] This function is referred to as self-expression.[27] Upon receiving self-expressive information, third parties may act upon it by mimicking the choices made, a function referred to as social expression.

Self-expression and social expression operate as follows. By purchasing, using or publicly displaying a distinctive design product, such as clothing, electronics, sports equipment or vehicles, an individual paints a certain image about himself or herself.[28] This image signals to third parties specific information, such as the individual's identity, preferences, adherence to certain beliefs and aspirations, socio-economic status, appurtenance to certain groups or desire to differentiate themselves within a certain group, and so on.[29] In other words, an individual's consumption behavior, with reference to a particular design, acts as a means for expressing and communicating to others certain preferences about the individual's social and cultural values, taste, style, and so on. Self-expression is most frequently observed in connection with goods that impact a person's appearance, such as clothing and accessories.

---

[25]   For the overall effect of this dynamic, see Lemley, n. 22 above.

[26]   See generally, Fischman Afori, n. 2 above.

[27]   Also referred to as self-identification.

[28]   'A producer sells a good which is used by consumers as a signaling device': Giacomo Corneo and Olivier Jeanne, 'Segmented Communication and Fashionable Behavior' (1999) 39 *J Econ. Behav. and Org.* 371.

[29]   Consumers strive to attain 'optimal distinctiveness', Beebe, n. 11 above, p. 819.

Its counterpart, social expression, occurs when an individual's self-expression induces action by third parties.[30] The fact that an individual stands for particular values, or pertains to a particular cultural, social, economic or professional group, may engender certain types of emotions. The individual may command admiration or respect, appear to be 'in', 'cool' or 'trendy' or, alternatively, rebellious or non-conformist, and thus becomes a 'model'. Third parties, aspiring to emulate the 'model', would mimic its behavior and become followers.

Because these signals communicate to the outside world the choices made by particular individuals and then influence purchasers' buying behavior, they act as a form of secondary advertising and affect consumption behavior.[31] In the present consumption-oriented society, their economic role is becoming increasingly important. This, however, is of relatively recent date.

Impact of communication dimensions on consumer behavior
Historically, the consumption paradigm for most goods was primarily utilitarian: an item was purchased for its utility, used and disposed of, once it ceased to be useful. Consumption was usually limited to a single copy of the product necessary for fulfillment of a particular function, in other words, one article of clothing or pair of shoes for a specific purpose, one bottle-opener, and so on. In other words, self-expression played virtually no role in consumption. Consumption for purposes of expressing preferences or conferring status was limited to a small social and economic elite, whose

---

[30] 'Consumption of certain goods symbolizes a certain socio-economic status, but also serves goals such as social equalization, self-identification, and so on': Fischman Afori, n. 2 above, p. 1112. Product branding makes heavy use of the social expression function of visual images. See for example, Hamish Pringle, 'How Brands Should Use Celebrities to Build Their Business' (1 September 2014), www.thedrum.com/opinion/2014/09/01/how-brands-should-use-celebrities-build-their-business.

[31] Fischman Afori, n. 2 above, p. 1114. This dynamic gives rise to trends prompted by the operation of self-expression and social expression. C. Scott Hemphill and Jeannie Suk, 'The Law, Culture, and Economics of Fashion' (2009) *Stanford Law Review* 1147, 1153. A creative industry that 'combines self-expression with social expression' is determining of consumer behavior: Gene M. Grossman and Carl Shapiro, 'Foreign Counterfeiting of Status Goods' (1988) 103 *QJ Econ.* 79, 82.

needs were generally supplied by small-scale, custom-manufactured handicraft production. In the 1920s, however, production of consumer goods, including apparel, evolved into an industry. This resulted in a drop in manufacturing costs, the advent of mass retail in large department stores and an unprecedented diversity of products available to the public. The increased purchasing power of the middle class, fuelled by advertising, moved the markets of industrialized countries from scarcity to abundance[32] and thus made room for the exercise of subjective considerations in purchasing.

The widespread availability of affordably priced products from different producers induced a tendency to make purchases for other than primarily utilitarian reasons. Subjective purchase motivations, such as satisfaction of individual preferences, signaling information about one's economic and social status, beliefs, appurtenance to groups, and so on, which had always existed, could now be acted upon and began to emerge as an important means of self-expression.

Certain products are particularly well suited to serve a self-expressive function. In such products, the purely utilitarian consumption motivation has become largely eroded and is replaced by subjective considerations.[33] Clothing, for instance, has the capacity to become part of the general appearance of an individual's persona, not unlike speech, demeanor or actions. Selection of a fashion product therefore primarily serves the need for personal expression of individuality, the desire to fit in or to stand out. The utility of a clothing article, namely covering the body and providing warmth, then comes to play largely a collateral role. Erosion of the purely functional purchase motivation occurs in almost all consumer goods, such as gadgetry or vehicles, albeit in a less extreme manner than in fashion, clothing and accessories.

Subjective purchasing considerations also impact a product's life-span. A primarily utilitarian product's life-span is mostly a function of its performance from a functional standpoint. The

---

[32] See generally, Lemley, n. 22 above.

[33] See generally, Kal Raustiala and Christopher Sprigman, 'The Piracy Paradox: Innovation and Intellectual Property in Fashion Design' (2006) 92 *Virginia Law Review* 1687; Christopher Sprigman and Kal Raustiala, 'The Piracy Paradox Revisited' (2009) 61 *Stanford Law Review* 1201.

life-span of products whose value lies largely in subjective considerations ends when the product no longer satisfies the consumer's need for self-expression. Usually that occurs due to mass proliferation of a particular style, which leads to loss of distinctiveness and an inability to meet consumer expressive needs. The product's life-cycle will then end regardless of its functional life.

Having determined that on the supply side, information spillover contributes to increased supply with non-original goods, while on the demand side, the expressive dimensions of goods accelerate consumption, we now turn to the effect of this dynamic on producers of original goods and the harm it causes.

6.3 HARM

6.3.1 Substitutive Harm

If an unauthorized third party places large quantities of lower-priced identical or similar products on the market, the products tend to substitute for the original and can easily eviscerate the original producer's economic advantage and its ability to recover its investment.[34]

The impact of this 'substitutive' harm varies depending on whether the product is purchased for purely utilitarian reasons or whether subjective considerations play a role in its purchase. The harm tends to be strongest in products purchased primarily based on a product's utilitarian value, because purchasers are more likely to opt for a lower-priced product of comparable functionality and characteristics.[35]

---

[34] For instance, in the fashion industry, an emerging talented designer may easily be undercut in the market by unauthorized mass production of the same product. Alternatively, a season's key design in haute couture might be replicated by a competitor and diminish the original producer's sales.

[35] By way of illustration: in dealing with a claim relating to the sale of knock-off clothing a court concluded that no substitutive harm occurred. The court 'could not conclude that it was probable that a consumer who bought the [defendant's] dress would, if that dress had been unavailable, have bought the [plaintiff's] dress instead': *Review Australia Pty Ltd* v. *Innovative Lifestyle Investments Pty Ltd* (2008) 166 FCR 358, 365.

As additional non-objective concerns come into play, purchasers tend to focus less on the function of the product and more on the product's expressive aspect. In branded, primarily high-end products, purchasers are not satisfied with functionally equivalent products from a different, possibly less prestigious, source and will limit their purchases to the original product or style. A branded product is thus less vulnerable to substitutive harm; the stronger the brand, the more the products will be immune to substitutive harm.

6.3.2   Reputational Harm

A second type of harm an original producer may be subject to is harm to its commercial reputation. The nature of reputational harm to the original producer depends to some extent on the information asymmetry in the initial purchase, in other words, on whether the initial purchaser was deceived as to the source of the product.

If a product is deceptively passed off as being from the original source, the information available to the parties is asymmetrical, in that the purchaser is ignorant of the product's origin. If the non-original product's quality is poor and its purchaser may believe it derives from the original producer, the purchaser will think less of the original producer and its products. This type of harm is typically covered by anti-counterfeit laws.

On the other hand, the transaction may be such that the purchaser receives clues to suggest that the product does not derive from the original producer. These clues may take the form of a product's appearance, price, channel of distribution, or other circumstance of the sale. The information asymmetry is thus lessened or eliminated, the transaction is reputationally neutral and less likely to cause direct harm to the original producer. The majority of non-original products found in the market fall into this category and are therefore not necessarily captured by trademark law.[36]

---

[36]   The situation differs slightly at the level of subsequent purchasers or secondary markets. Because the secondary purchaser is ignorant of the source and circumstances of the original sale, it is likely to judge the product simply based on its quality and appearance. In this case, the information asymmetry is greater and reputational harm is more likely to occur, even though the initial sale was non-deceptive. Furthermore, reputational harm may result from physical injury to people and property as a result of, for example, health

6.3.3 Dilutive Harm[37]

A third type of harm is also reputational in nature, but operates more indirectly. It differs from simple loss of reputation, in that it is based less on the quality of a product and more on the proliferation of similar or identical products in the market. The presence in commerce and in everyday use of non-original products may have a dilutive impact on a particular product's or style's reputation. Even remote or imperfect similarity, which would ordinarily fall below the infringement threshold, may contribute to a consumer's perception of proliferation. This is so, because often original and non-original products are not perceived in a side-by-side setting and similarity is evaluated based on memory. A non-original product, which displays even few, but distinctive, similarities to the original, may be substituted for the original in the purchaser's mind. The more distinctive the product, its design or style, the more easily it will be remembered (even though possibly inaccurately).

Proliferation tends to diminish a design's ability for self-expression. An observer may perceive it as a signal that the design loses its distinctiveness. This, in turn, will erode the design's ability to fulfill the desired self-expressive function. The resulting harm can be twofold. First, the design's reputation may be lessened as a result of proliferation of similar non-original designs, because its distinctiveness is lost. Loss of distinctiveness means loss of self-expressive capacities.[38] Second, it may reduce existing customers'

---

damaging materials, poor materials or workmanship in food, car parts, airplane non-original parts, and so on. Due to information asymmetry the secondary purchaser is often unable to take adequate precautions, the purchaser remains defenseless and the producer's reputation is impacted.

[37] The term 'dilutive' is used here simply in its lay meaning of causing something to become thinner or weaker. In this case it refers to the weakening of a particular design's ability to provide the requisite amount of individuality to its user. As used here the term should not be confused with the legal doctrine of dilution, see for example, *Moseley* v. *V Secret Catalogue, Inc.*, 537 US 418 (2003); US Trademark Dilution Revision Act of 2006; EU Trademark Directive 2008/95/EC, art. 4(3) *et seq.*

[38] The social expression function would be at play here signaling, for example, that the exclusive club of quilted Chanel bag wearers might be diluted by the proliferation of similar looking handbags in the market. Potential

sense of value of the investment already made into specific design products. In other words, products owned by a consumer, deemed to be in scarce supply, would become less scarce and therefore less valuable.[39] This brings about a loss of the customer's personal individuality and status.[40] Both types cause the interest in the original producer's products or brand to diminish.

So far we have seen that, on the one hand, information spillover contributes to increased supply, and on the other, that expressive attributes give rise to subjective purchase considerations that increase demand. Furthermore, the presence or absence of expressive dimensions correlates with a certain type of harm. The more a good is purchased for self-expressive reasons, the more likely it is to suffer reputation-related harm, whereas the more it is purchased for utilitarian reasons, the more likely it is to suffer substitutive harm.

The following section will look at the types of protection that are available in this context to original producers affected by the proliferation of non-original goods.

---

purchasers seeking distinctiveness would be deterred from making further purchases.

[39]   '[T]he purchaser of an original [luxury good] is harmed by the widespread existence of knockoffs because the high value of originals, which derives in part from their scarcity, is lessened': *Hermes International* v. *Lederer de Paris Fifth Avenue*, 219 F.3d 104, 108 (2d Cir. 2000). See also, Beebe, n. 11 above.

[40]   '"[S]nob effects" tend to reduce the value of goods to existing users, in the hands of existing users and would-be new users': Hemphill and Suk, n. 31 above, p. 129; consumers simply note the fact that the good is being consumed, lacking the ability to determine whether it is original or not. Gene M. Grossman and Carl Shapiro, 'Foreign Counterfeiting of Status Goods' (1988) 103 *QJ Econ.* 79, 82. In *Mastercrafters Clock and Radio Co.* v. *Vacheron and Constantin-Le Coultre Watches, Inc.*, 221 F.2d 464, 466 (2d Cir. 1955), the Second Circuit shaped the doctrine of 'post-sale confusion' on the basis of the loss of reputation to original producers due to purchases of a cheaper non-original clock to acquire prestige by displaying the article in their home.

6.4 LEGAL THEORIES ADDRESSING SUBSTITUTIVE AND REPUTATIONAL HARM

6.4.1 Substitutive Harm

International IP law[41] and the laws of most jurisdictions provide for protection against substitutive harm under the doctrines of copyright,[42] design patent[43] and *sui generis* design protection (in the European Union).[44] As discussed above, goods for which purchase considerations are based on subjective criteria, such as self-expression and social expression, are probably less vulnerable to substitutive copying. Therefore doctrines which protect against substitutive copying tend to be applied with less frequency.[45] Even if a producer of original goods would wish to rely on these doctrines, certain challenges arise. A common issue is that these doctrines are intended to protect either utilitarian or aesthetic features, but not both.[46] Design, however, is a synthesis of aesthetic and utilitarian features. Its essence is 'the nexus between what the product must do and how it must look',[47] and its value resides in the fact that the two are inseparably intertwined. Because it is often impossible to separate utilitarian from aesthetic features, in many instances it is hard to meet the separability requirements of the applicable doctrines.

---

[41] The Paris Convention protects industrial designs in Art. 4; and so does Agreement on Trade-Related Aspects of Intellectual Property Rights (TRIPS) in Art. 25.

[42] See for example, 17 USC s. 101 *et seq.*; French Code of Intellectual Property, art. L.112-2; Italian Copyright Law No. 633/41.

[43] 35 USC s. 171 *et seq.*

[44] Council Regulation (EC) 6/2002 of 12 December 2001 on Community designs, amended by Council Regulation (EC) 1891/2006; Directive 98/71/EC of the European Parliament and of the Council of 13 October 1998 on the legal protection of designs.

[45] Fridolin Fischer, 'Design Law in the European Fashion Sector' *WIPO Magazine* (February 2008), noting that fashion houses tend rarely to register clothing, compared to accessories, see www.wipo.int/wipo_magazine/en/2008/01/article_0006.html. Similarly, there is a dearth of litigation involving IP issues relating to clothing items involving the fashion industry.

[46] Utilitarian features are generally deemed more appropriately protectable under patent laws.

[47] Denicola, n. 4 above.

Copyright is intended to protect an author's original expression. Policy-makers fear that utilitarian features, which are properly the domain of patent law, will become subject to copyright, a doctrine that lacks the anticompetitive safeguards of patent law. For this reason, copyright law separates utilitarian features from aesthetic ones, and limits protection to the latter.[48] Long-standing doctrinal tradition supports this method, but in practice it is difficult to apply. US copyright law, for instance, protects 'useful articles'[49] only to the extent that their aesthetic features are physically or conceptually separable from the utilitarian ones.[50] This rule results in the fact that clothing articles and other designs of manifest utility generally remain unprotectable. Italian author's rights law, which had been subject to similar restrictions, is now adopting a more attenuated version.[51] The most generous copyright protection for design is offered by French author's right, which under the principle of 'l'unite de l'art' grants full protection to all works featuring an aesthetic component.[52]

The European Union has implemented one of the most advanced design laws in its *sui generis* Community Design as a single,

---

[48]   See *Kieselstein-Cord* v. *Accessories by Pearl*, 632 F.2d 989 (2d Cir. 1980); *Inhale, Inc.* v. *Starbuzz Tobacco, Inc.* (Case no. 12-56331) (9th Cir. 2014).

[49]   A useful article is copyrightable 'only if, and only to the extent that, [it] incorporates … sculptural features that can be identified separately from, and are capable of existing independently of, the utilitarian aspects of the' article. See 17 USC s. 101.

[50]   *Kieselstein-Cord* v. *Accessories by Pearl*, n. 48 above; *Brandir Int'l, Inc.* v. *Cascade Pacific Lumber Co.*, 834 F.2d 1142 (2d Cir. 1987); *Inhale* v. *Starbuzz Tobacco*, n. 48 above.

[51]   Italy's strict adherence to separability seems to become more attenuated as (effective 2001) the Italian design law now grants protection to 'works of industrial design having creative character and artistic value' (Italian Copyright Law, art. 2(1)(10)), replacing the requirement that works of industrial design be 'severable from the industrial nature of the product' under art. 2(1)(4). For details on the Italian doctrine and the concept of 'scindibilita' see Reichman, 'Design Protection After the Copyright Act of 1976', n. 9 above; Reichman, 'Legal Hybrids Between the Patent and Copyright Paradigms', n. 9 above; Reichman, 'Past and Current Trends in the Evolution of Design Protection Law', n. 9 above.

[52]   Code de la Propriete Intellectuelle, art. L-112-2 (France). See also Sam Ricketson and Uma Suthersanen, *The Design/Copyright Overlap: Is there a Resolution?* (2012).

unitary design right,[53] which provides registered and unregistered protection throughout the territory of the European Union.[54] Its explicit intent was to shape the protection of design to the needs of the industry and to avoid some of the doctrinal legacies, which made them impractical for businesses to use.[55] The unregistered protection is geared specifically to seasonal industries, such as fashion and textiles, which typically develop a large number of designs with short, single-season commercial life. The separation of aesthetic from functional features is de-emphasized, in that the exclusion is limited to those features 'solely dictated' by the function of the product, in recognition of the fact that design is intended to be a hybrid of functional and aesthetic features.

In the United States, design is protected by the US design patent, which extends protection to new, non-obvious and ornamental, in other words, non-functional, designs of articles of manufacture. Again the separation of ornamental from functional features is fraught with difficulties.[56]

A significant hurdle in using these doctrines in the context of a global market is the fragmentation of national design laws. National design laws, with the exception of the ones in the European Union, lack harmonization, with the result that requirements for protection vary widely. Furthermore, the international Convention for facilitating filing of applications in multiple countries has not been joined by some of the key jurisdictions relevant in terms of manufacturing

---

[53] This protection exists as a result of the adoption of Directive 98/71/EC of the European Parliament and of the Council of 13 October 1998 and Council Regulation (EC) 6/2002 on Community Designs. The effect is that European legislation coexists with national copyright laws.

[54] Council Regulation (EC) 6/2002 on Community Designs protects designs which display novelty and individual character against unauthorized use/copying of designs which do not create a different overall impression, for up to 25 years, if registered, and up to three years if unregistered, see www.ohim.eu.int/en/design/. See also Beldiman, n. 3 above.

[55] Possibly the most significant advancement is that applications are not subject to substantive examination. Rather, the role of challenging validity is left to competitors by way of invalidity and infringement proceedings. In effect, the validity evaluation is thus outsourced to the market. The speedy issuance of protection certificates has made this a highly popular device.

[56] The US design patent provides protection, upon registration, of new non-obvious and non-functional ornamental designs for articles of manufacture against unauthorized use, for a period of 15 years. 35 USC s. 171.

locations and markets for design products.[57] Overall, the laws available are not a comfortable fit for a producer of original goods seeking remedies against substitutive harm from the mass presence of non-original goods.

6.4.2 Reputational Harm

Reputational harm is primarily addressed by trademark type doctrines, such as trademarks, registered and unregistered, protection of trade dress or get-up and dilution.[58] Classic trademark doctrines generally protect the ability of a trademark or trade dress to signal the fact that a product derives from a certain source. The presence in the market of non-original products may cause the signal that serves as identifier of source to lose its uniqueness. In that case, consumers may be confused and their search costs in identifying the correct product may increase. Brand value decreases and brand owners may be unwilling to further invest into maintaining the brand's quality.[59]

Trademark protection is subject to similar limitations as design laws. Utilitarian features are generally not protectable, as their removal from the public domain for an indeterminate period of time would adversely impact competition.[60] Furthermore, many jurisdictions view product design as incapable of being inherently distinctive. In other words, a design would have to acquire secondary meaning before it can be registered or enforced.[61]

---

[57] Hague System for the International Registration of Industrial Designs, available at www.wipo.int/hague/en/. Countries such as China, Japan and the Republic of Korea have not joined the Convention to date.

[58] See Trademark Directive, art. 5; 15 USC s. 1125(c); TRIPS, Arts 16.2 and 16.3.

[59] Giving rise to a 'market for lemons'. See generally George Akerlof, 'The Market for Lemons: Quality Uncertainty and the Market Mechanism' (1970) *Quarterly Journal of Economics*.

[60] Trademark protection of three-dimensional shapes and trade dress doctrines are subject to the functionality doctrine, which seeks to separate a design's functionality from its role as indicator of source. For instance, US law precludes protection of designs which are essential to the purpose and use and affect the cost and quality of a feature, *TrafFix Devices, Inc.* v. *Marketing Displays, Inc.*, 532 US 23 (2001); *In Re Becton Dickinson & Co.*, 675 F.3d 1368, 1376 (Fed. Cir. 2012).

[61] See for example, *Wal-Mart Stores* v. *Samara Bros.*, 529 US 205 (2000).

Complementing classical, confusion-based trademark law, many jurisdictions have also recognized the doctrine of dilution, which protects famous marks (marks with a reputation) from harm against a 'likelihood of dilution' arising from unauthorized use of the mark in the context of goods that are different from the original producer's goods.[62]

Under either the classical trademark or dilution theory, however, there is little that takes into account the effect on reputation of the subjective consumption preferences, which result from the expressive attributes of design. The doctrine that comes closest to this concept is 'post-sale confusion', which seeks to remedy reputation-related harm caused by copies of a 'rare' product.[63] The operation of self- and social expression creates the perception that a formerly rare product has become commonplace. This affects a consumer's subjective sense of individual distinctiveness and outward status. However, this doctrine requires a showing of consumer confusion, which may constitute a hurdle in many cases.

This brief review shows that traditional IP doctrines do not provide easy protection to design products against either substitutive or reputational harm. Furthermore, none of the doctrines factors in the expressive dimensions of design. All of this leads to the question how the presence of a high degree of expressive dimensions in design products plays into the existing IP laws.[64]

---

[62]   15 USC s. 1125(c). This doctrine comes closer to the harm described above in that it protects against the risk of the brand name, or in this case, the design becoming capable of a multiplicity of meanings. See *Visa International Service Association* v. *JSL Corporation*, 610 F.3d 1088 (9th Cir. 2010).

[63]   *Mastercrafters Clock and Radio Co.* v. *Vacheron and Constantin-Le Coultre Watches, Inc.*, 221 F.2d 464, 465 (2d Cir. 1955); see also Beebe, n. 11 above, p. 845.

[64]   Beebe, n. 11 above, p. 864 *et seq.* proposes that, in general, IP laws have evolved into mechanisms for protecting the individual ability of differentiation (creation of status) and to preserve cultural values and 'rarity'. This occurs by preventing excessive replication and 'competitive consumption' which does not result in differentiation, just in noise and inconclusiveness. IP laws therefore take on the role of sumptuary laws.

6.5 A DIFFERENT PARADIGM WHERE SUBJECTIVE CONSIDERATIONS ARE INVOLVED?

Neoclassical economic theory teaches that the exclusionary nature of IP laws is dictated by the need to avoid undersupply of knowledge products, which arises from a market failure associated with the non-rivalry and non-excludability characteristics of IP goods.[65] Undersupply is avoided by creating a temporary competition-free market environment which provides a creator/inventor with the opportunity for economic gain. The exclusivity in the market is generally thought to act as an incentive for further creation and innovation.[66]

This system works well for products whose value resides primarily in their utility and where the invasion of rights consists of substitution. However, in products where the self-expressive and social expressive dimensions are major components of a product's value, the dynamics may be different.[67]

The question then becomes to what extent this dynamic may affect inventors'/creators' incentive to create. In other words, can the subjective dimensions of design products independently serve to stimulate creation in a way that is comparable or complementary to the incentive provided by IP law?

This area remains largely unexplored, however some clues on how creativity is impacted by the subjective dimensions of design can be gleaned from the fashion industry.[68]

---

[65]   See generally, William M. Landes and Richard A. Posner, 'An Economic Analysis of Copyright Law' (1989) 18 *J Leg. Stud.* 325; William Landes and Richard Posner, *The Economic Structure of Intellectual Property Law* (Harvard University Press, 2003); Mark A. Lemley, 'Property, Intellectual Property, and Free Riding (2005) 83 *Tex. L Rev.* 1031.

[66]   Landes and Posner, *The Economic Structure of Intellectual Property Law*, n. 65 above.

[67]   Possible additional criteria of differentiation are the fact that design products generally involve a low IP content, that is necessarily disclosed because it resides in the product's appearance, resulting in a low barrier to entry.

[68]   See for example, Hemphill and Suk, n. 31 above, p. 1149 n. 4 and authorities cited therein.

6.6 CONSUMER PREFERENCES IN THE FASHION INDUSTRY

The fashion industry places particularly heavy reliance on the self- and social expression of visual images, because of all design products, fashion can most closely impact an individual's appearance and outward image. Studies have established that consumer choices in the fashion industry are characterized by two simultaneous, but opposing tendencies.[69]

The first of these tendencies involves the need for differentiation. It reflects the desire for self-identification and for defining one's individuality *vis-à-vis* or within a specific group.[70] It is an instance of self-expression. The second of these tendencies results from the fact that individuals also tend to exercise a certain amount of conformity in their choices, in a desire to 'move in step' with others,[71] not to stand out or to be singled out or possibly made subject to ridicule.[72] This is an instance of social expression.

As will be discussed in the next section, the interaction of these opposing tendencies results in a dynamic that recurs in cycles. It affects the consumption patterns and the life-span of products[73] and, as a result, impacts the demand for products.

---

[69]   Where innovation involves both self-expression and social expression, producers and consumers flock to these in common; then differentiating themselves within the flocking. Hemphill and Suk, n 31 above, p. 1153. Profs Hemphill and Suk have called these two coexisting opposing preferences 'differentiation' and 'flocking'. Hemphill and Suk, n. 31 above, pp. 1152–3, 1164.

[70]   This occurs as a result of the desire to attain what has been referred to as the 'optimal distinctiveness' or 'rarity'. See Beebe, n. 11 above, pp. 821–2.

[71]   Hemphill and Suk, n. 31 above, p. 1152.

[72]   *Ibid.* p. 1152.

[73]   '[I]n fashion we observe the interaction of the tastes for differentiation and for flocking, or more precisely, differentiation within flocking': Hemphill and Suk, n. 31 above, p. 1165. Individual behavior naturally differs; some consumers are more oriented towards differentiation, such as early adopters; others to conformity, depending on age, status, education, cultural background, personal preferences, social and economic circumstances. 'Consumers have a taste for trends – that is, for goods that enable them to move in step with other people. But even in fulfilling that taste, they desire goods that differentiate them from other individuals. Fashion goods tend to share a trend component, and also to have features that differentiate them from other goods within the trend': Hemphill and Suk, n. 31 above, p. 1152.

6.6.1   The Cycle

The literature describes the life-cycle of any given style as unfolding in a four-phase sequence of introduction, emulation, mass conformity, and decline.[74] The phases succeed each other and recur cyclically, as illustrated graphically in Figure 6.1.

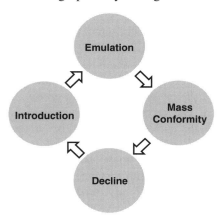

Figure 6.1   The cyclical nature of styles

(a) *Introduction.* Prior to the launch of a new style, fashion designers usually share a common corpus of information, which establishes a common style direction or trend. Within the industry a new style is 'in the air' as a result of extensive preparation of a fashion season for up to 24 months in advance.[75] This results in a 'buzz' among all players in the fashion industry: manufacturers, designers, purchasers, retailers, models, consultants, the press, marketers, social media, and so on.[76] The launch, usually in the form of fashion shows, introduces the style.

---

[74]   Corneo and Jeanne, n. 28 above.

[75]   This preparation covers topics such as color and fabric ranges, fashion shows, and so on.

[76]   For the sake of accuracy, it must be noted that designers closely protect the specifics of their individual designs prior to launch. Still, because so much preparation goes into the launch of the season and because so many industry players are involved, the industry operates even pre-launch in an environment of a generally shared knowledge base relating to the coming season.

(b) *Emulation*. Once the new style has been launched, it is communicated to the market. This process has been described as 'anchoring' the trend,[77] and is intended to position the new style so it starts driving consumption.[78] Emulations, interpretations and re-workings of the original style are sold under different high end and luxury brand names, at substantially equivalent quality and price levels, supplying the upper segment of the market.[79] Consumption at this level is often motivated by social and economic aspirations, 'status seeking' or conspicuous consumption preferences.[80]

(c) *Mass conformity*. Once the style has become a trend, it moves into mass production. The style is produced for progressively declining market segments under different brand names at progressively lower, and at various quality grades and price levels, differentiated in a variety of ways such as quality of material, minor cost-saving shortcuts, workmanship, and so on.[81] 'Fast fashion', low price style imitators such as Zara and H&M contribute to the proliferation of the design. At this point, the style has lost its

---

[77] Individual preferences exercised collectively by a large number of people result in trends which reflect the social and cultural context of the times, in other words which express the 'Zeitgeist': Hemphill and Suk, n. 31 above, p. 1159; see also, Sprigman and Raustiala, 'Paradox Revisited', n. 33 above, pp. 1207–8.

[78] Yi Qian, 'Impacts of Entry by Counterfeiters' (2008) 123(4) *Quarterly Journal of Economics* 1577 (November)8, cited in *World Intellectual Property Report 2013*, available at www.wipo.int/econ_stat/en/economics/wipr/; Sprigman and Raustiala, 'Paradox Revisited', n. 33 above, pp. 1207–8; Jonathan Barnett, Gilles Grolleau, and Sana El Harbi, 'The Fashion Lottery: Cooperative Innovation in Stochastic Markets' (2010) 39 *J Legal Stud.* 159, 165–6.

[79] Following the launch of the new season, further targeted disclosures of designs early on in the life of a style serve the purpose of 'anchoring', in other words, communicating styles to selected public in order to get public acceptance of this particular style, by allowing wide-spread copying to set the trend. Barnett *et al.*, n. 78 above, p. 166. This is meant to familiarize customers with styles that are to be subsequently commodified in the form of lower cost merchandise. Beebe, n. 11 above, p. 866.

[80] 'The motive is emulation – the stimulus of an invidious comparison which prompts us to outdo those with whom we are in the habit of classing ourselves': Thorstein Veblen, *The Theory of the Leisure Class* (Bremen, Outlook Verlagsgesellschaft, 2001 (1899)), p. 72. In part this behavior is motivated by what Veblen termed 'conspicuous consumption'.

[81] See generally, Sprigman and Raustiala, 'Piracy Paradox', n. 33 above.

distinctiveness and ability to satisfy the need for self-expression. Its mass presence brings with it the seeds of decline.
(d) *Decline.* With diminishing distinctiveness,[82] the style becomes commonplace and no longer provides the desired individuality.[83] The style goes into decline; it loses appeal because the market is saturated with mass copies. Its formerly expressive value lessens, leaving the merely utilitarian one.

At this point, the quest for new forms of distinction start over and consumers seeking differentiation will look for new products with a fresh capability to meet that need.[84] This allows a new style to rise and starts a new cycle.

6.7 DECONSTRUCTING THE FASHION INDUSTRY MODEL FROM AN IP PERSPECTIVE

The fashion industry model highlights the role of knowledge spillover and self- and social expression in driving consumption. Here is how these two dynamics work together.
(a) *Self- and social expression.* When a style is freshly launched, it is at the height of distinctiveness and, at that point, has the greatest strength of self-expression. Social expression then prompts a following by consumers who seek to emulate. Distribution in increasingly larger quantities and at lower price levels causes the style to lose distinctiveness and, with it, its ability to self-express. In turn, the social expression function slows down.[85] Both functions essentially cease once the style has become commonplace.[86]

---

[82]   See Beebe, n. 11 above, p. 819.
[83]   Sprigman and Raustiala, 'Paradox Revisited', n. 33 above, p. 1218.
[84]   See Wall and Large, n. 22 above, pp. 6 and 19. Basically, consumers who buy luxury branded products do so to position themselves in order to stay ahead of others in the fashion game. This is described as the 'snob effect'. Once the market has become saturated by a particular design or branded product, the (snob) consumer group quickly moves on to buy other elite products. See also Jonathan Barnett, 'Shopping for Gucci on Canal Street: Status Consumption, Intellectual Property and the Incentive Thesis' (2005) 91 *Virginia Law Review* 1381, 1387; Sprigman and Raustiala, 'Piracy Paradox', n. 33 above.
[85]   Wall and Large, n. 22 above, p. 19.
[86]   Counterfeits also operate as a contributing factors in accelerating the consumption cycle. Qian, n. 78 above.

Still, the need for self-expression persists. New styles will emerge season after season and will follow the same pattern. And so, in an ongoing repetition of cycles, the alternating effect of self-expression and social expression drives consumption behavior and, with it, generates constantly renewed demand.[87]

(b) *Information disclosure.*[88] In the course of a design's life-cycle, successive information disclosures are made. The first such disclosure occurs prior to the launch of a style, during the preparation of the season's release, and ensures that releases by all fashion houses are within the parameters which define the new season.[89] Next, a series of targeted communications follows early on in a style's life-cycle, meant to 'anchor' the style. Finally, at later stages, design information is publicly available to third parties.

Significantly, this review reveals that the effect of these information disclosures is not only to stimulate supply as a result of easy availability of information, but also to accelerate consumption, and thereby demand. This is why the more information is disseminated, the more a style will proliferate and the faster the style's expressive attributes will cause it to lose distinctiveness.

This means that the information spillover, in this context, has two different effects. On the one hand, broad availability of design

---

[87]   This dynamic has been referred to as 'induced obsolescence': Sprigman and Raustiala, 'Paradox Revisited', n. 33 above, p. 1206. Apparel firms 'themselves manage and profit from the staged dilution of their designs' distinctiveness by gradually trickling down their haute couture designs – or perhaps more accurately, the brand built up by those designs – to various levels of ready to wear': Beebe, n. 11 above, p. 867.

[88]   One explanation for these disclosures lies in the economics of the fashion industry. Fashion is a high risk business, characterized by extreme demand uncertainty, short product life, long production lead-time, virtually unlimited range of combinations of fabrics, colors and styles, where only a small number of designs succeed. As investment is required at a time when the outcome of a season is unpredictable, companies seek to neutralize this risk by sharing information in a type of cooperative regime among participating producers. This model operates as a form of insurance that mitigates losses from seasonal product failure. See generally, Barnett *et al.*, n. 78 above, p. 167. From an IP standpoint, one possible rationalization of early disclosures within the fashion industry is that they transform a potential 'winner takes all, loser takes nothing' scenario into an 'all take some' model. Unlike the 'winner takes all' model, the latter preserves a second comer's incentive to create.

[89]   Barnett *et al.*, n. 78 above, pp. 165–6.

information within the industry allows competitors to increase the production of non-original products. On the other hand, dissemination of information also accelerates the effect of self-expression and social expression and thus stimulates demand.

6.7.1 Substitutive Harm

This review allows us to draw the following conclusions from the fashion industry's business model. The fashion industry has established a model of monetization of its IP content that deviates from the proprietary model common in most industries. According to classical IP theory, the multiple levels of disclosure, described above, would result in inability to recoup investment and constitute a disincentive to further creation. This would cause the undersupply that IP laws are designed to prevent.

The fashion industry has avoided this outcome. To the contrary, empiric observation supports the notion that the fashion industry is thriving[90] and there is no evidence of risk of undersupply or lack of investment in the industry.

Based on these facts, we return to the question posed earlier regarding the role of the combined effect of knowledge spillover and self- and social expression in providing an incentive to create. Had there been a serious threat to the incentive to create, as contemplated by IP law,[91] this would have been manifest in a heightened use of the legal tools made available by the IP system. This is not the case. The fashion industry displays broad tolerance and even, to some extent, encouragement of imitation and reuse of designs by third parties,[92] as well as generally limited reliance on the instruments offered by IP law.[93] All of this suggests that, from

---

[90]   See generally, Michael Jeffrey and Natalie Evans, *Costing for the Fashion Industry* (Berg Publishers, 2011).
[91]   Without taking into account possible other harm which might occur outside the realm contemplated by IP laws.
[92]   Barnett *et al.*, n. 78, p. 185; Sprigman and Raustiala, 'Piracy Paradox', n. 33 above, p. 1718.
[93]   '[W]ith fashion seasons lasting only a few months, the five-year minimum protection period offered by these registration systems is not appropriate for often ephemeral fashion designs, and ... their time and money would therefore be better spent on creating new designs than on registration': Fischer, n. 45 above.

an IP standpoint, and as regards the effect of substitutive copies, the fashion industry appears to be fairly well balanced.

In conclusion, it appears that a strong presence of expressive attributes in a design product has the ability to accelerate consumption to create ongoing renewed demand. The resulting opportunity for economic gain could be seen to operate as an incentive, sufficient to overcome the risk of undersupply in the industry.[94]

6.7.2 Reputational Harm

In terms of reputation, review of the fashion industry model reveals an impact on two levels: the reputational degradation suffered by designs and that suffered by the brand. Both are the product of self- and social expression.

The former is one of the drivers and an intrinsic part of the fashion cycle, a dilution of the design's distinctiveness.[95] It helps stimulate demand in the manner described above and thus has an overall beneficial effect. The latter consists of a reputational degradation that may affect the brand. A proliferation of non-original products may both adversely impact the brand perception, to the extent it relies on 'rarity',[96] as well as the existing consumers' sense that their investment into an item of value is diminished in reputation because the item is in common use. This type of harm affects the entire brand and therefore its impact is more significant in terms of scope and of duration.[97]

---

[94] This hypothesis of course raises many questions, including, importantly, whether this observation is limited to the fashion industry. In this context, see also Eric E. Johnson, 'Intellectual Property and the Incentive Fallacy' (2011) 39 *Florida State University Law Review* 623, questioning the incentive theory.

[95] 'This is that such industries benefit from dilutive copying – indeed, they encourage it – but only if they can plan and control the process of dilution. In apparel design firms' traditional business model, they themselves manage and profit from the staged dilution of their designs' distinctiveness by gradually trickling down their haute couture designs – or perhaps more accurately, the brand built up by those designs – to various levels of ready-to-wear and merchandise': Beebe, n. 11 above, p. 867.

[96] The term in this context is borrowed from Beebe, n. 11 above, p. 864 *et seq.*

[97] Were one to visualize a brand as a building and individual designs and products as its individual bricks, a sufficiently well-built structure can tolerate the loss of individual bricks. However, erosion of reputation may lead to a

In short, the reputational effect can either be positive and production-stimulating, or negative, in that it erodes the brand. Whether these effects, both deriving from self- and social expression, are different in nature, is a question that needs to be answered, but is beyond the scope of this chapter.[98]

Overall, it can be concluded that to the extent reputational harm occurs from the proliferation of non-original products, the most significant risk to the producer of original products lies in the erosion of the brand itself. IP law, however, provides no effective remedy for it.

6.8 CONCLUSION

This chapter seeks to draw a link between the expressive dimensions of industrial product design and intellectual property law.

Product design, as all visual images, is capable of carrying meaning. This feature brings about two expressive dimensions: first, that an individual's choice of a specific design can convey 'self-expressive' information about the individual making the choice, and second, that self-expressive information may induce third parties to act upon it, by mimicking the choices made, in an exercise of 'social expression'. Combined, these expressive functions of design facilitate processes relating to the consumption of goods; a product with strong expressive dimensions is subject to an accelerated consumption cycle, as is well illustrated by the fashion industry.

In the fashion industry, a further element is at play, namely an unusually open treatment of IP content, which results in spillover of the design content within the industry, and is characterized by a high tolerance toward imitation. The interaction between readily available design information and the expressive dimensions of design brings about a specific consumption model, that recurs

---

downward spiral of consumers diminishing loyalty, resulting in the producer's diminishing investment in the brand, eventual loss of customers and ultimate collapse.

[98]   One possible differentiator could be the longevity of the brand compared to the extremely short life-cycle of the style. It is possible that, given greater longevity of products, the reputational degradation of an individual style could impact the brand image. Quaere whether this observation is limited to the fashion industry, where the turnover of styles is particularly rapid.

cyclically: a newly launched design will initially satisfy a consumer's self-expressive needs. Social expression then prompts emulation of the original use and dissemination of the design. As a design gains traction and moves into mass use, it loses its distinctiveness as a result, and with it, its ability to self-express and its continuing commercial viability. However, continuing need for self-expression will prompt another style to emerge and follow the same pattern, creating constantly renewed demand in the market.

According to classical IP theory, an open treatment of IP content, combined with tolerance for massive imitation, would cause harm by substitutive copying and result in an inability to recoup investment. Yet this is not the case in the fashion industry. This fact supports the theory that strong expressive dimensions of design, coupled with information spillover, stimulate consumption and fuel ongoing demand. Predictably renewed demand may therefore operate as an incentive to create, and complement the incentive provided by IP laws. The stronger the impact of the expressive dimension, the lower the need for protection against substitutive copying.

PART III

Allowing for creative space towards an open environment

7. A positive status for the public domain

Séverine Dusollier

> The existence of a robust, constantly enriched public domain of material not subject for copyright (or other intellectual property protection) is a good in its own right, which our laws should promote at the same time as they provide incentives or reward creativity.[1]

The public domain is generally defined as encompassing intellectual elements that are not protected by copyright or whose protection has lapsed, due to the expiration of the duration for protection. Sometimes the definition is stricter, focusing only on works whose copyright has ended, or broader, welcoming in its ambit uses of works still protected by copyright, but legitimized through the operation of an exception or of a license.

When considering the substance of the public domain, one is immediately confronted with the strong rhetoric that has unfolded around that notion. The public domain is a very abstract idea shaped in a very concrete territorial metaphor. The 'domain' evokes a particular place, a territory where no intellectual property rights apply, a domain where anybody is free to enter and to help herself. The private domain of intellectual property, characterized by exclusive rights, monopolies, and authorization/prohibition schemes, looks as if it was fenced off from the public domain, as if both domains were contiguous, though separate, as if the domain of commoditized and privatized assets faces the domain of freely available resources, with no connection or relation between them. On one side, there would be the perimeter of intellectual property

---

[1] D. Lange, 'Recognizing the Public Domain' (1981) 44 *Law and Contemp. Probs* 147.

protections, where copyright exclusive rights would be the sole area for commodification process and action, whereas, on the other and opposite side, the public domain, where the unprotected elements would lie, would be the only place where artistic or scientific creation could take place without infringing the right held by an author.

This metaphorically-driven vision is both mistaken and fallacious.

It is mistaken to the extent it is inapt to embrace the full reality of the public domain, conceived as freely available resources for intellectual production, as demonstrated by Julie Cohen[2] who points out the inconsistency of considering the public domain as a separate place and argues for a new metaphor, that of the cultural landscape. Cohen alleges that the fact that the opponents of the increasing encroachment of the public domain are using the same metaphor that helps the proponents of a rising commodification in intellectual property to deny that threat, makes it impossible to reach an effective solution for the preservation of the public domain.[3]

But the domanial metaphor is also fallacious as it pretends to shape the substance of the public domain. The public domain seen as a separate place and the ensuing binary rhetoric of 'intellectual property versus the public domain'[4] is the metaphor that hides the real epistemology of the public domain where private and public are much more intertwined.

As it is conceived in copyright law, the public domain does not create at all a separate site immune from any privatization,[5] as the terminology of the public domain inclines to signify. Defined by the lack or expiration of copyright protection, the public domain is primarily a negative notion as its realm is the inverse of the scope of copyright protection. This negative approach of the public domain prevails in most copyright regimes. It entails that if

---

² J. Cohen, 'Copyright, Commodification, and Culture: Locating the Public Domain' in B. Hugenholtz and L. Guibault (eds), *The Public Domain of Information* (Alphen aan den Rijn, Kluwer Law International, 2006), p. 121.
³ Cohen, n. 2 above, p. 157.
⁴ A. Chander and M. Sunder, 'The Romance of the Public Domain' (2004) 92 *Cal. L Rev.* 1340.
⁵ C. Rose, 'Romans, Roads, and Romantic Creators: Traditions of Public Property in the Information Age' (2003) 66(89) *Law and Contemp. Probs* 96.

copyright is regulated and promoted, the elements of the public domain themselves are generally not subject to any rules or protection: the term 'public domain' rarely appears in the provisions of the law. It is even more rare that specific rules are attached to the public domain or to its elements.[6]

This lack of a positive legal definition or regime is crucial in any analysis of the public domain. It reveals the profound conception of the public domain the copyright laws have adopted and constitutes one of the first obstacles to its promotion and preservation.

This chapter aims at pleading the case for a positive public domain, one that would no longer be defined in the negative but would rely on a substantive notion, capable of ensuring some sustainability. The first part will explain the composition of the public domain, marked by this 'negativity', as it is merely a sum of what is not protected by copyright. It will also describe some difficult cases of identification of the public domain. The second part will then illustrate the instability and fragility of the public domain that is inapt to resist enclosure or recapture by reconstituted exclusivity, due to this negative definition. In the last part, this chapter will try to focus instead on what could positively define the public domain, in other words, the free use of the elements contained therein and the absence of any exclusivity in such elements.

7.1 COMPOSITION OF THE PUBLIC DOMAIN

The public domain is composed of elements that are by themselves unprotected, or are no longer protected after the expiration of copyright. That public domain is free to use by nature as it is premised on the absence of an exclusive right therein. The elements included in the public domain will then depend on the extent and conditions of copyright protection as to the protected subject matter; the conditions to get access to the protection; the possible exclusions from the protection; and the duration of the right. The reverse application of these parameters will draw the contours of the public domain. Before envisaging that reverse design of the

---

[6]   One notable exception is the Chile copyright law that prohibits the fraudulent claim of economic rights in a work belonging to the public domain.

public domain, one should first be reminded that the delineation of copyright subject matter and duration is governed by a territoriality principle which will accordingly make the public domain vary from one country to another.

7.1.1   Territoriality of the Public Domain

The status of an intellectual resource depends on the law applicable thereto. The Berne Convention, like many national laws or case law providing for a rule determining the applicable law in copyright, provides that the enjoyment and exercise of copyright 'shall be independent of the existence of protection in the country of origin of the work' and that 'the extent of protection, as well as the means of redress afforded to the author to protect his rights, shall be governed exclusively by the laws of the country where protection is claimed' (Article 5(2) of the Berne Convention). Where there is subject matter for the application of the Berne Convention, the law applicable to the existence of copyright is the *lex protectionis*. This rule of applicable law, that is inherent to the fundamental principle of territoriality in copyright, also applies to the duration of copyright protection, with some qualifications that will be addressed below.[7]

As a consequence, the status of a copyrighted work will vary according to the laws of the country in which protection is sought. Creative material is not henceforth in itself in the public domain or not, but will be considered as subject to copyright or not according to the law applicable thereto. A work can still be protected by copyright in one country but be considered as belonging to the

---

[7]   The only exception concerns expressions of folklore, by virtue of Art. 15(4)(a) of the Berne Convention: 'In the case of unpublished works where the identity of the author is unknown, but where there is every ground to presume that he is a national of a country of the Union, it shall be a matter for legislation in that country to designate the competent authority which shall represent the author and shall be entitled to protect and enforce his rights in the countries of the Union'. This provision deals more with the competent authority to enforce rights in folklore than with the determination of the applicable law, but its rationale at the time of its insertion in the Berne Convention was certainly to ensure that national folklore is protected according to the law of the country of their origin.

public domain in another, based on the different rules applicable to copyright protection or duration.

For instance, as originality might be defined differently depending on the country, a work can be protected or not. Duration will also diverge territorially. Works of Virginia Woolf, who killed herself in 1941, have been in the public domain in the European Union since 1 January 2012, but some of them might not be in the United States, where works published after 1923 will still be protected until 2019. Another example could be a US movie of the 1950s whose copyright owner failed to renew its copyright, which will be in the public domain in the United States, but not in the European Union, which will calculate the duration on the basis of the date of death of the film-maker and all co-authors.

This variability can greatly complicate the task of identifying the composition of the public domain, particularly when the exploitation or use of a public domain work is envisaged simultaneously in many countries, as is increasingly the case with the advent of online exploitation. This constitutes a key conundrum in the safeguarding and promotion of the public domain. If a work has no definitive and permanent status, how can one promote its free use beyond a national basis? How can the user be certain of the free use she is entitled to make of such work, wherever such use will occur?

7.1.2 Idea/Expression or the Ontological Public Domain

A key dividing line between the subject matter of copyright and the public domain resides in the so-called principle of the idea/ expression dichotomy. This principle means that only creative expressions deserve protection, leaving ideas or information themselves free for all to use or, as Desbois has famously written, 'de libre parcours'. Works are expressions and embodiments of ideas, facts, principles, methods. Actually, the idea/expression dichotomy is what constitutes the notion of the work,[8] even prior to the question of what is a literary and artistic work, or of what is an original work. Ideas, facts, style, methods, intrigue, mere information, concepts, are thus by nature unprotected and constitute

---

[8]   V.-L. Benabou, 'Pourquoi une œuvre de l'esprit est immatérielle' (2005) *Revue Lamy Droit de l'Immatériel* 53.

commons in the proper sense of the word. They can be said to form an *ontological* public domain.

Ideas can still be protected by secrecy and non-disclosure but 'once an author reveals his work to the public, therefore any *ideas* contained in the work are released into the public domain, and the author must be content to maintain control over only the *form* in which he first clothed those ideas'.[9] More than being a watershed dividing the protected copyright domain from the unprotected public domain, it also serves as a criterion for determining a possible copyright infringement, as only copying expression, and not idea, will amount to a copyright violation.

The Berne Convention does not explicitly state the principle of the idea/expression dichotomy. That has been completed by the WIPO Copyright Treaty in 1996, of which Article 2 provides that 'copyright protection extends to expressions and not to ideas, procedures, methods of operation or mathematical concepts as such'. This formulation has been borrowed from Article 9(2) of the Agreement on Trade-Related Aspects of Intellectual Property Rights (TRIPS).

The ideas, procedures, methods of operations or mathematical concepts can be considered as being only examples of what the general term 'ideas' encompasses.[10] Information as such, plain facts, raw data, functions, concepts or styles are not protected either. One could add thereto words, musical notes, colours, or any other basic elements serving to express oneself.

The rationale underlying this principle comes from the recognized assumption that ideas and information are the basic building blocks of innovation, creation, scientific research and education. Copyright cannot restrict the ability of users and creators to get access to and build on existing knowledge to enable creation to progress.[11]

---

[9]   C. Joyce, M. Leaffer, P. Jaszi and T. Ochoa, *Copyright Law* (7th edn, Dayton, OH, Lexis Nexis, 2006), p. 106.

[10]   J. Reinbothe and S. Von Lewinski, *The WIPO Treaties 1996* (London, Butterworths Lexis Nexis, 2002), p. 47.

[11]   See C-406/10 *SAS Institute*, CJEU, Judgment of 2 May 2012, ECLI: EU:C:2012:259, para. 40: 'to accept that the functionality of a computer program can be protected by copyright would amount to making it possible to

Ideas constitute the 'hard kernel' of the public domain, as being per se incapable of benefiting from copyright protection. Obviously, even when such ideas take the form of original expressions and leave the public domain, the object of protection is a new one, in other words, an original work, and leaves untouched the idea now contained in the work itself. In that sense the idea never really leaves the public domain and can be used again by anyone, anytime. Because of their ubiquity, ideas remain resistant to copyright protection focused on form and not on content.

7.1.3 Requirements for Protection or the Subject Matter Public Domain

7.1.3.1 Originality

The entrance to the copyright building is conditioned on a finding of some degree of originality in the work. Originality is, to borrow the words of R. Casas Valles, 'the evidence and materialization of authorship and what justifies the granting of copyright'.[12] All countries apply this principle. Originality is not explicitly mentioned in the Berne Convention, and rarely in national laws, even though one can probably infer it from the 'literary and artistic work' wording and find it in the intellectual creation condition that applies to the protection of collections (Article 2.5 of the Berne Convention).

The Berne Convention also leaves the contours of originality to national determination, which leads to differences between countries as to the definition and degree of originality required, even though the pretended radical distinction between the criteria used in countries of the *droit d'auteur* and copyright traditions has been often exaggerated and has been somewhat attenuated by case law.[13]

---

monopolise ideas, to the detriment of technological progress and industrial development'.

[12] R. Casas Valles, 'The Requirement of Originality' in E. Derclaye (ed.), *Research Handbook on the Future of EU Copyright* (Cheltenham (UK)/ Northampton, MA, Edward Elgar, 2008), p. 102.

[13] See on that difference A. Strowel, *Droit d'auteur et copyright: divergences et convergences* (Bruylant, 1993). As examples of case law bridging this pretended gap, see *Feist Publications Inc. v. Rural Telephone Service Co.*, 499 US 340 (1991), US Supreme Court; C-604/10 *Football Dataco*, CJEU, Judgment of 1 March 2012, ECLI:EU:C:2012:115.

But the touchstone of copyright protection is not a very selective tool for building the public domain. On one hand, in many countries, the threshold of originality is very low and is generally construed to encompass any intellectual involvement, any stamp of personality. Few intellectual creations will stay in the public domain by default of the required originality. In that sense, originality as a criterion for propelling a creation into copyright protection is very minimal. On the other hand, originality is difficult to determine with certainty and its final appreciation will often be left to the courts. In other words, the contours of that part of the public domain may be very uncertain and blurry.

This low level of originality also constitutes a threat to the public domain, as it leaves fewer and fewer works unprotected, extending to sometimes incongruous subject matter of which the creativity seems very minimal.

7.1.3.2 Fixation

Some countries require the work to be fixed in a tangible embodiment in order to benefit from copyright protection. This is the case in the United States where the fixation requirement is satisfied when the embodiment of the work 'in a copy or phonorecord, by or under the authority of the author, is sufficiently permanent or stable to permit it to be perceived, reproduced, or otherwise communicated for a period of more than transitory duration' (US Copyright Act, section 102(b)). In other countries, works are said to be protected as soon as they are created.

7.1.4 Term of Protection or the Temporal Public Domain

7.1.4.1 Determination of a limited duration

An essential feature in intellectual property, save for trademarks, geographical indications and, to some extent, the *sui generis* right conferred to databases, is its limitation in time. After a determined period of time has elapsed, the work or invention is said to fall into the public domain. This can be defined as a *temporal* public domain.

The importance of that limitation in time for the constitution of a public domain explains why, in many countries and for a long time, the expression 'public domain' itself essentially referred to works that were no longer protected. At the origin of copyright, a defined duration was also considered as being the main engine for ensuring access to literary and artistic production by society at large, and as the best evidence for a trade-off between protection and the public interest.

The debates that took place in many countries during the nineteenth century as to the extension of such duration fiercely insisted on that point. A limited duration aimed at achieving a balance between proprietary protection and public availability, thus creating two separate domains, constituted by the passing of time. The public domain was also recognized as being the principle and the copyright the exception, necessary but application of which should not be eternal, as is reflected in that oft-quoted declaration of Lord Macaulay, in a speech before the English House of Commons in 1841:

> It is good that authors should be remunerated; and the least exception-able way of remunerating them is by monopoly. Yet monopoly is an evil. For the sake of the good we must submit to the evil; but the evil ought not to last a day longer than is necessary for the purpose of securing the good.[14]

The erection of a private property right was only a limited intrusion into the public domain that should stay the rule. J. Ginsburg has shown that this predominance of the public domain was present in the early regimes of literary and artistic property both in France and in the United States.[15] In 1774, in *Donaldson* v. *Beckett*,[16] one of the seminal copyright cases in the United Kingdom, the House of Lords voted in favour of the principle that copyright should be limited in time, insisting on the public interest in preserving the public domain as the rule.

These days, all countries abide by the principle of limitation in time. The minimum duration for countries adhering to the Berne Convention or the TRIPS Agreement is 50 years after the death of the author. In addition, Article 7 of the Berne Convention provides for specific ways of calculating the duration in particular cases.

---

[14] T.B. Macaulay, *Macaulay Speeches and Poems* (1874), p. 285.
[15] J. Ginsburg, 'A Tale of Two Copyrights: Literary Property in Revolutionary France and America' (1991) *RIDA* (January) 144.
[16] Eng. Rep. 1, 837 (H.L. 1774).

But those terms are only minimal thresholds and nothing prevents states from extending the duration beyond the 50-year rule. Therefore the duration of a copyright in a work, and thus figuring out what is in the public domain and what is not, is left to national laws. The length of protection therefore varies greatly from one country to another, and can be difficult to ascertain, also due to the application of conflict of law principles to determine it.

In the European Union, the term of protection has been harmonized to 70 years after the death of the author. Some countries keep the rule of the Berne Convention, such as Canada, China, Japan and most African countries, while others employ a very long duration, such as Mexico, where copyright is protected for 100 years after the death of the author.

Different rules can also apply in some countries which will render the calculation more complicated. In the United States, the now abrogated formalities as a condition for copyright enjoyment still leave some traces in the computing of the copyright term, which has, however, aligned with the EU duration of 70 years. For US works created on or after 1 January 1978, copyright protection extends to the life of the author plus 70 years. When it is an anonymous or pseudonymous work, or a work made for hire, this duration extends to 95 years after first publication or 120 years after creation, whichever expires first. The same applies to works created but not published or registered before 1 January 1978, with one special rule in case of a subsequent publication before 2003, in other words, that the term will not expire before the end of 2047. For works created before 1978, the belonging or not to the public domain will still depend on the former accomplishment of formalities. Should the work be published at the time with a proper notice, the 28-year first term of protection is automatically renewed for a supplementary duration of 67 years (only if the renewal was properly obtained for works published between 1923 and 1963). Works published before 1923 are in the public domain. It should also be noted that these already complex rules only apply to works of US origin, foreign works being submitted to even more intricate provisions.[17]

---

[17]   For a complete overview of the way to calculate the copyright duration of work in the United States, see http://copyright.cornell.edu/resources/publicdomain.cfm.

The determination of the public domain status of a domestic work in the United States is thus based on many elements, such as the existence and date of publication, the compliance with the notice formality then applicable, the existence of a renewal of protection, all information that might be difficult to obtain by non-specialists.

The analysis of these national laws appears to contradict the automatic building of the temporal public domain, according to which once a certain period of time has passed, the work falls into the public domain. Many events can render uncertain the date when its entry into the public domain will effectively occur, possible legislative extension of the duration not being the least of these (see below).

7.1.4.2 Added difficulties

Comparison of terms In line with the territorial nature of copyright, Article 7(8) of the Berne Convention provides that the duration will be determined by the legislation of the country where the protection is claimed. However, the same provision attenuates somewhat this principle by stating that: 'unless the legislation of that country otherwise provides, the term shall not exceed the term fixed in the country of origin of the work'. This is one of the main exceptions to the general application of the lex loci protectionis, which will be mandatory if the state has not decided otherwise.[18]

The effect of this term comparison rule might further complicate the task of calculating the duration of copyright in a work and will give an unstable definition to the public domain. It implies a rule of 'material reciprocity',[19] favouring the application of a shorter term of protection as fixed in the country of origin of the work. For example, the duration of the works of the Nobel Prize winner Rabindranath Tagore, whose country of origin is India (where the term of protection is fixed to 60 years *post mortem auctoris* (*pma*)) will be considered in France or in the United Kingdom (both countries that apply the rule of the shorter term) to be 60 years after the death of the author, putting aside the application of the normal

---

[18] For a comprehensive explanation of the rule of term comparison, see S. Choisy, *Le domaine public en droit d'auteur* (Paris, Litec, 2002), pp. 117–42.
[19] Reinbothe and von Lewinski, n. 10 above, p. 117.

term of 70 years.[20] In the United States, though, where the comparison of terms is not applied, the works of Tagore will be subject to the same rules of duration as US works. As a consequence, computing the term of protection will first require knowledge as to whether the country has explicitly derogated from Article 7(8) of the Berne Convention, and secondly, determination of the country of origin of the work and the duration applicable in that country in order to compare it with the duration provided by the law of the country where the protection is sought.

Wartime extensions   The so-called wartime extensions purport to add some time to the normal duration of copyright in order to compensate the lack of exploitation suffered during the two World Wars. Such rule exists (or existed) in France, Belgium and Italy.[21] For instance, two French laws, in 1919 and 1951, added extra months of protection to works that were not in the public domain when the laws were enacted. The first law added six years and, depending on divergent computation, 83 or 152 days; the second one added eight years and 120 days.[22] Besides, if the author died fighting for France, his (or her) works enjoyed a supplementary term of protection of 30 years(!). The 'authors who died for France' are enumerated in an official list.[23]

This set of extensions has created much controversy in France, particularly as to whether it was compatible with the now harmonized term of protection throughout the European Union. The French Cour de Cassation has partially settled the controversy in 2007 in a

---

[20]   The French law reinforces the rule of shorter term by providing that the duration of a work whose author and country of origin is non-European, will be that granted in the country of origin without being superior to the term provided in France (see art. L.123-12 CPI).

[21]   Belgium only extended the protection by 10 years for the First World War and this law is considered to have been absorbed by the extension to 70 years *pma* by the Copyright Duration Directive. Italy's war extensions have been abrogated when transposing the Directive.

[22]   A. Lucas and H.J. Lucas, *Traité de la Propriété Littéraire et Artistique* (3rd edn, Paris, Litec, 2006), para. 513.

[23]   Including the authors whose certificate of death indicates that they died for France and authors similarly acknowledged as having died for France in a government decree.

case involving a painting by Monet who died in 1926.[24] The work would normally have entered into the public domain on 1 January 1997,[25] but the right owners claimed the benefit of the two wartime extensions and hence protection until 2011. The Supreme Court refused such extension on the ground that it was covered by the 70 years now imposed by the EU Copyright Duration Directive 93/98/EC. It read article 10(1) of the Copyright Duration Directive that states that 'Where a term of protection which is longer than the corresponding term provided for by this Directive was already running in a Member State on 1 July 1995, this Directive shall not have the effect of shortening that term of protection in that Member State', as meaning that on 1 July 1995, Monet's works should have still been protected in France, which was not the case as the duration then applicable was 50 years after the death of the author plus 14 years and 172 days of wartime extensions. The copyright expired in 1991, thus before the extension to 70 years. Monet benefited from this extension to 70 years but not from anything more, and his works went into the public domain in early 1997. This decision leaves open the possibility that a longer term has been running in France for some works, which should then be respected according to the Directive, which could make the French exception of wartime extensions still applicable in only rare cases.

One recent example is Apollinaire, who died in 1918 from the Spanish flu. But as he was wounded on the battlefield in 1916, which had weakened him when he got the flu, he was considered as 'mort pour la France'. Therefore, without considering the wartime extensions, the work of Apollinaire, published before the First World War, should have entered the public domain on 1 January 1969 (50 years after the death of the author, which was the duration at that time). Apollinaire benefited from an extension of 30 years (as having died for France), six years and 152 days (for the First World War) and eight years and 120 days (for the Second World War). His work actually fell in the public domain only on 29 September 2013, which is 95 years after the poet's death. In 1995, when the Copyright Duration Directive entered into force, this

---

[24]   Cass. D, 27 February 2007, 807.
[25]   The first term of 50 years *pma* being extended by the Copyright Duration Directive, the work still being protected in Germany at the date of entry into force of the Directive.

longer duration than the now applicable 70 years *post mortem auctoris* was already running, which allowed the subsistence of this extended term according to article 10(1) of the Directive. A similar situation relates to the works of Saint-Exupéry, the famous author of *The Little Prince*. Saint-Exupéry disappeared with his plane in the Mediterranean sea in 1944, while he was flying for the Allied forces. There was a great deal of controversy as to the circumstances of his death, some German soldiers claiming they had shot down a plane on that date approximately when he disappeared, but suicide was also sometimes advanced. In 1948, Saint-Exupéry was officially recognized as 'mort pour la France' even though his plane was only found and identified in 2000. His works having all been published between the First and Second World Wars (*The Little Prince* in 1943), he would enjoy only the second wartime extension (eight years and 120 days) plus the 30 years' extension for his honorable death, which would add 38 years and four months to the normal 70 years. As at 1 July 1995, when the Directive entered into force, this new period of 38 years had already started to prolong the then applicable 50 years' duration (ending on 1 January), this extension was maintained and the Little Prince bitten by the snake will still be alive on his planet until mid-2033 (and later in the hearts of all lovers of that book). But only on his French planet, as the work has fallen into the public domain in all countries applying a 50 years' *pma* copyright term and its copyright has expired in all other EU Member States from the beginning of 2015 (supposing that the duration of 70 years is there applied with no consideration of wartime extension).[26]

The perpetual Peter Pan   Another Little Prince is the marvellous character created by J.M. Barrie in the 1930s, Peter Pan. This child, who did not want to grow old, has seen his wish granted by the UK Copyright, Designs and Patents Act 1988. Its section 301 contains a

---

[26]   This interpretation is supported by the text of art. 10(1) of the Copyright Duration Directive which states that 'Where a term of protection which is longer than the corresponding term provided for by this Directive was already running in a Member State on 1 July 1995, this Directive shall not have the effect of shortening that term of protection in *that* Member State' (emphasis added).

very peculiar rule that says: 'The provisions of Schedule 6 have effect for conferring on trustees for the benefit of the Hospital for Sick Children, Great Ormond Street, London, a right to a royalty in respect of the public performance, commercial publication [or communication to the public] of the play "Peter Pan" by Sir James Matthew Barrie, or of any adaptation of that work, notwithstanding that copyright in the work expired on 31st December 1987'.

Technically speaking, one could say that this right to remuneration is not an extension of duration of copyright as the text itself states that the copyright has expired in 1987, in other words, 50 years after the death of J.M. Barrie (or rather in 2007 considering the application of the transitional rule of the Copyright Duration Directive), but is rather a specific right to remuneration that is not even conferred on the heirs of the author but on an institution that does not hold any copyright in the work. In any case, Peter Pan has not completely fallen into the public domain.

7.1.5 Excluded Creations or the Policy Public Domain

The public domain is also enriched by elements that are explicitly excluded from the field of protection. Those exclusions concern intellectual creations that could on their face qualify for the protection granted by copyright, but that the law-maker has decided to render ineligible for protection for reasons of the public or general interest. Such exclusions constitute what can be called the *policy* public domain.

The Berne Convention provides for two possible exclusions from copyright protection. One is mandatory and concerns news of the day and miscellaneous facts (Article 2(8)), the other is optional and covers official texts of a state (Article 2(4)). Many countries follow the Convention in providing both exclusions.

The first exclusion purports to leave documents such as laws, court decisions and other kinds of official documents available to all, to make effective the norm according to which 'ignorance of the law is no defence'. Another ground might be that, to the extent such official acts are enacted by elected representatives of the people, they cannot be appropriated and are held in common by all citizens.

The news-of-the-day exclusion feeds the public domain more on the grounds of the idea/expression dichotomy than on a public policy justification. It is by their very nature that information, mere facts and news are unworthy of copyright protection, which makes them belong to the *ontological* public domain we defined above.

7.1.6   Relinquishment of Copyright: the Voluntary Public Domain

A recent question about the composition of the public domain relates to the possibility that the public domain would incorporate works in which copyright has been relinquished. Works for which copyright protection has been abandoned by their owners would form a sort of *voluntary* public domain,[27] not through the effect of the law but by the mere will of the authors themselves.[28]

Unlike other intellectual property rights such as patent or trademark, copyright ownership is triggered by the sole act of creation (or fixation in some legal systems). One cannot refuse the 'title' once it has been granted, the 'authorship' being consubstantial with the phenomenon of creation. There are no registration formalities, fees, costs, conflict with public order, which could possibly deny the author protection under a monopoly. Had she wanted not to be protected as such, the creator has no way of escaping from the legal pattern of exclusive protection.

Relinquishing works into the public domain thus requires some formal act, a positive gesture of opting out from copyright. Such dedication of works to the public domain is increasingly occurring and takes part of a more general contestation of intellectual property. It is sometimes an offspring of movements that have experienced the licensing of copyright in open access schemes, such as Creative Commons, which now also proposes a complete renunciation of copyright in one's creation through a standard license called Creative Commons CC0.[29] The purpose of this standard license is to affirm that a copyright owner waives all her copyright and related rights in a work, to the fullest extent

---

27   Or 'domaine public consenti' to borrow the expression of Choisy, n. 18 above, p. 167; see also M. Clément-Fontaine, *Les oeuvres libres* (Thesis, Montpellier, University of Montpellier, 2006 (to be published soon by Larcier)), p. 281 *et seq.*
28   Clément-Fontaine, n. 27 above, p. 420.
29   See http://wiki.creativecommons.org/CC0_FAQ.

permitted by law. Other abandonment of copyright can take the form of a less formalised license or even a mere statement to that effect.

Some countries, like Chile or Kenya, include such renunciations of copyright protection in their definition of the public domain. Save for countries explicitly allowing and formalizing such dedication to the public domain, the legitimacy and validity of copyright relinquishments raise many questions.[30]

Under most legislation, it is not clear whether the right-holder can renounce the full exercise of his/her exclusive rights. From a perspective of economic rights only, renunciation thereof will beg the question of the nature of the copyright itself. Should it be considered as a fundamental right, as might be the case in some legal systems? Is it legally allowed to renounce such a right? Conversely, if copyright is considered as a property right, the matter is less complicated as such right contains the inherent attribute of renouncing property itself (right of abusus).

But the key and more intricate issue will be the moral right. Attached to the person of the creator, the moral protection is deemed inalienable in many countries, which automatically implies an impossibility to forsake one's moral interest in the creation. Consequently, even if economic rights can be lawfully surrendered, the work will still be protected by the moral right and the copyright owner could exercise it to retain some control over use of her work.

Another question, if one admits some validity of a total waiver of copyright, is the irrevocability thereof. Can the author change her mind and, at some point, exercise again her exclusive right in the work, negating then the placing of the work in the public domain? Here again, there is no certainty. Everything will depend on the revocable character of licenses or unilateral acts by which the author will in practice affirm the termination of any protection in his/her work. Responses can greatly vary from one legal system to another.

---

[30]   R. Burrell and E. Hudson, 'Property Concepts in European Copyright Law: The Case of Abandonment' in H. Howe and J. Griffiths (eds), *Concepts of Property in Intellectual Property* (Cambridge, Cambridge University Press, 2013).

7.2 RELATIVITY OF THE PUBLIC DOMAIN

7.2.1 Consequences of a Negative Delimitation

The main result of the lack or expiration of copyright in an element of the public domain is the absence of any exclusivity in the use of such element. Public domain material is said to be free for all to use. In other words, no one can control or prevent its reproduction, public communication or any other use that would be in the realm of the copyright prerogatives. However, as pointed out in the introduction, this reverse definition by what is left after copyright has taken its toll, does not favour a definite and closed public domain.

The public domain is *relative* in many respects. First, its composition will depend on the national law applicable to copyright, due to the principle of territoriality of intellectual property. The case of duration is particularly illustrative of the geographically shifting boundaries of the temporal public domain. Second, as it is subject to the contours of copyright, the oft-denounced increasing enclosure of public domain[31] is the logical effect of the ongoing extension of copyright in subject matter, scope and duration. This results in unsteadiness of the public domain, as the lack of definitive protection makes it incapable of resisting copyright regularly grabbing new pieces of land.

Finally, since the public domain is only the counterpart of copyright but does not have any status or regime of its own, it stands in a legal limbo.[32] As a result of its negative definition, elements belonging to the public domain will only be free from exclusivity by operation of copyright law. *De lege lata*, nothing prevents their reservation or privatization by other mechanisms, as the public domain so defined does not follow an absolute rule of non-exclusivity and is rather unequipped to resist any encroachments or regained exclusivity.

---

[31] J. Boyle, 'The Second Enclosure Movement and the Construction of the Public Domain' (2003) 66(89) *Law and Contemp. Probs* 33.

[32] J. Cahir, 'The Public Domain: Right or Liberty?' in Ch. Waelde and H. MacQueen (eds), *Intellectual Property: The Many Faces of the Public Domain* (Cheltenham (UK)/Northampton, MA, Edward Elgar, 2007), p. 39.

That means that some material that can be categorized as uncopyrighted, hence belonging to the public domain in copyright law, can be protected by other means, legal, contractual or technical. As a consequence, the contours of the public domain we have just drawn are only relative and do not result in an unquestionable status of non-protection or public property.

The relativity of the public domain could also explain why the freedom of use that is attached to the unprotected elements therein is only a description of the absence of exclusive rights of copyright. Using a public domain work will not be enforced under copyright, but such use will not be guaranteed as it will depend, first, on the possibility to gain access to the work which is not guaranteed by its 'public domainness' but depends on many factors. Beyond the possibility of regaining exclusivity by other means (other exclusive rights, contracts or technical lock-ups), getting access to the tangible embodiment of the work will depend on the property right therein, which can be more or less constraining depending on the number of copies in circulation and on the cost of such copies.

Another key factor in the effectiveness of access to works, closely related to the very regime of copyright, is the possible absence of divulgation or disclosure. Many works have been created without their author feeling the need to divulge them. Whether not original enough or after the term for their legal protection, they are technically in the public domain, but will remain unknown, hence unavailable to the public, as will undisclosed ideas. The effective public domain will then be reduced to the body of works and creations that have been published.[33] The same can be said of public domain works that have fallen into oblivion. No or few copies might still be available which renders their re-use illusory. An unknown symphony by Mozart will be in the public domain but will not enrich it in any way if that work is lost or no longer known. Lots of novels or writings published before the nineteenth century are not read or known any more, rare copies are covered with dust in libraries: they might belong to the public domain in theory but are not a very effective part thereof.

---

[33] R. Deazley, *Rethinking Copyright: History, Theory, Language* (Cheltenham (UK)/Northampton, MA, Edward Elgar, 2006), p. 111. It should be noted also that a revived copyright can vest in works unpublished during the normal term of copyright when subsequently published.

The relativity of the public domain will now be illustrated by several cases.

7.2.2   Repeated Term Extensions and Copyright Restorations

The duration of copyright is not irreversible and has been extended several times in history, hence postponing the entry of works into the public domain. Many reasons have been invoked to argue that repeated extensions are related to the protection of the creators and their heirs and their participation in the benefits from exploitation of the works, but most of the time, the demand for an extended protection comes from the industry, hence from the market, that would like to enjoy an unlimited monopoly over some works.

Everybody remembers the strong opposition to the US Copyright Extension Act of 1998 (known also as the Sony Bono Act) that extended the term of protection of copyrighted works to 70 years after the author's death, as in Europe. This extension was challenged before the Supreme Court on the basis of its unconstitutionality, the US Constitution providing that the Congress has the power 'to promote the Progress of Science and useful Arts, by securing *for limited Times* to Authors and Inventors the exclusive Right to their respective Writings and Discoveries'. In *Eldred* v. *Ashcroft*,[34] the Supreme Court upheld the law: a 'limited time' was thus not considered as a short time but only as a non-unlimited time, a subtle but meaningful difference.

Rather than adhering to a view of the term of protection that would draw a clear line between protected works and the public domain as in *Donaldson* v. *Beckett*, the US Supreme Court has admitted that the duration of copyright can be regularly extended as long as Congress can proffer a rational basis for that extension. Economic needs are then approved to be a particularly strong motive for extending the protection. As was the case in Europe at the time of adoption of the Copyright Duration Directive, the argument of increased human longevity was again raised: copyright should benefit the author and two successive generations of heirs, which, for demographic reasons, is not perfectly achieved with a 50-year rule. But what also counts as the 'necessary life of

---

[34]   537 US 186 (2003).

copyright' is the productive life of works, the period of time during which they are valuable in the market, again according to the US Supreme Court. In other words, if works can still have a commercial value, copyright should subsist in them and the duration be extended accordingly. Under that reasoning, the public domain is reduced to garbage of valueless (at least in economic terms) works and the copyright regime will only be for market failures that need not be cured. This illustrates that the temporal public domain is not the predominant principle and that the definition of the public domain in the copyright regime is not strong enough to resist such ongoing extension. The effect of a term extension on the public domain is rarely assessed in such legislative contexts.

When harmonizing the term of protection to 70 years *post mortem auctoris*, the European Union has opted for the restoration of copyright for works still protected in one country of the Union at the time of the entry into force of the Directive. Consequently, a work in the public domain in one state could see its copyright revived if it was still protected in another Member State.

The Court of Justice of the European Union (CJEU) had to deal with such copyright or related rights restorations in two cases. The first one related to rights in phonograms which were restored by the effect of the Copyright Duration Directive, their duration being extended from 30 to 50 years.[35] In its decision the Court clearly stated that 'application of the terms of protection laid down by the Directive may have the effect, in the Member States which had a shorter term of protection under their legislation, of protecting afresh works or subject-matter which had entered the public domain'.[36] Another case followed ten years afterwards, again with rights in phonograms that had the curious effect of granting a right in recordings that had at no time before been protected in the Member State concerned.[37] V.-L. Benabou called this 'renaissance' of rights in previously public domain works or subject matter, the

[35] C-60/98 *Butterfly Music*, CJEU, Judgment of 29 June 1999, ECR 1999 p. I-3939.
[36] *Ibid.* para. 18.
[37] C-240/07 *Sony Music Entertainment*, CJEU, Judgment of 20 January 2009, ECR 2009 p. I-263.

'zombies of copyright',[38] which perfectly describes the effect of a copyright restoration law that creates new living creatures amongst the dead.

This also implies that the public domain, once constituted by the rule of the term of protection, is only relative, or rather that the public domain does not take its definitive form once for all. To put it simply, we do not know now when existing works will fall into the public domain, we only know that all works will do so eventually. That does not confer much strength on the public domain.

In the same vein, a recent decision of the US Supreme Court refused to consider the public domain as immutable. Whereas one Court of Appeals had qualified the public domain as a 'bedrock principle of copyright law' with the consequence that 'what is in the public domain should remain there',[39] the Supreme Court held that 'Neither the Copyright and Patent Clause nor the First Amendment makes the public domain, in any and all cases, a territory that works may never exit'.[40]

This case challenged the constitutionality of a law restoring copyright in foreign works to comply with the adherence of the United States to the Berne Convention. Article 18(1) of the Berne Convention provides that 'This Convention shall apply to all works which, at the moment of its coming into force, have not yet fallen into the public domain in the country of origin through the expiry of the term of protection'. Many foreign works were not protected in the United States due either to lack of mutual recognition between the United States and their country of origin, or on the ground that they did not comply with the formalities required by the US Copyright Act. The application of Article 18(1) imposed a change of law to make those works benefit from the protection. The Uruguay Round Agreements Act (URRA), enacted in 1994, achieved that objective by restoring copyright in such works and providing some period of time during which the users of those formerly in-the-public-domain works could obtain the now-needed copyright clearance. One user, who managed a website playing

---

[38]   V.-L. Benabou, 'The Duration of Copyright', paper presented at ALAI Conference Vienna, September 2010.

[39]   *Golan* v. *Gonzales*, 501 F.3d 1179 (10th Cir. Colo., 4 September 2007).

[40]   *Golan* v. *Holder*, 132 S Ct 873 (2012), US Supreme Court.

versions of classical music tracks, including many foreign works, opposed that copyright restoration on the basis of freedom of expression and the limited constitutional mandate conferred to Congress with regard to copyright ('to promote the progress of science and the arts').

It is worthwhile to note that the Supreme Court validated the transitional regime that was imposed by that law to preserve some '*droits acquis*', at least for a limited period in time. The URRA laid down some protections for 'reliance parties', in other words, for persons who had, before the copyright restoration, used or acquired a foreign work in the public domain, in order to authorize some further exploitation for some time. Such protection, however, could not amount to 'vested rights' in works of the public domain.[41] The *Golan* decision rather stated that: 'the "vested rights" formulation might sound exactly backwards: rights typically vest at the *outset* of copyright protection, in an author or rightholder. Once the term of protection ends, the works do not revest in any rightholder. Instead, the works simply lapse into the public domain'.[42] This confirms the Supreme Court's view in the *Eldred* case, of a public domain only defined negatively and not granting anyone a fixed and enforceable privilege.

The same Article 18(1) of the Berne Convention was also invoked by the French Cour de cassation in a case involving the Howard Hawk movie, *His Girl Friday*. The film was in the public domain in the United States by default of renewal of its copyright. One company sold DVDs of the film in France, probably based on the conviction that it was also not protected in France through the application of the rule of the shorter term (see above). The court decided otherwise by applying together the Article 18(1) and Article 5(2) prohibiting formalities.[43] When the United States became a party to the Berne Convention, the film was in the public domain there not by the expiration of duration, but by the effect of unaccomplished formalities. Such formalities being outlawed by the Berne Convention, *His Girl Friday* would still have been protected by the-then applicable term of 56 years. This is another example of

---

[41] *Ibid.* 26–28.
[42] *Ibid.* 28.
[43] Cour de Cassation (1ère civ.), Judgment no. 1302 of 17 December 2009.

a 'copyright zombie', no longer protected in its country of origin but regaining a new life in other countries.

7.2.3 Reconstitution of Copyright in Some Works

Once a work has fallen into the public domain through the passing of time, no copyright should be vested again in such work. Yet some specific mechanisms can restore protection by copyright. The EU Copyright Duration Directive of 1993 provides for two mechanisms that can restore a copyright or a similar right in public domain works.

The Directive requires the Member States to confer protection of 25 years limited to the economic rights of copyright to 'any person who, after the expiry of copyright protection, for the first time lawfully publishes or lawfully communicates to the public a previously unpublished work'.[44] This protection of posthumous works, in other words, of works unpublished during the normal time of copyright based on the life of the author, purports to give an incentive to publishers to make available such public domain works. Its effect, however, is to remove these works from the public domain by restoring a limited copyright therein. Due to the absence of moral right protection and the grant of the economic right to the person investing in the publication (and not to the heirs of the deceased author), this copyright is more akin to a neighbouring right.

This protection of posthumous works in the European Union enhances the publication and making available of works that might otherwise stay undisclosed, making void and useless their public domain status. To that effect, the restriction it places on the public domain itself can be seen as a necessary evil.

The same Directive also allows (but not obliges) the Member States to provide for a limited protection of 30 years after publication for 'critical and scientific publications of works which have

---

Council Directive 93/98/EEC, art. 4 [1993] OJ L290/9) codified by Directive 2006/116/EC of the European Parliament and of the Council of 12 December 2006 on the term of protection of copyright and certain related rights (codified version).

come into the public domain'.[45] Italy has implemented such protection and grants a protection of 25 years to critical and scientific publications of works in the public domain (Italian Copyright Law, article 85-*quater*). Even in default of the originality required for the critical work to be protected by copyright, as any other adaptation of a public domain work, this special right (limited to economic exploitation) aims at providing incentives to the publisher of critical publications of unprotected works, as in the case of posthumous works. The Italian Court of Cassation has held that reconstituting the original work is not sufficient to be protected, but that the critical publisher has, for instance, to recreate a missing part of the work.[46]

The latter case creates less interference with the public domain than the regime for posthumous works, as only the critical publication will be protected, but not the original work on which it is based which is still in the public domain and free to use.

7.2.4   Other Intellectual Property Rights

The public domain in copyright can also be affected by other intellectual property rights that might subsist in public domain works. Consequently, the use of such material shall not be subject to copyright reservation but might well be covered by the exclusive rights granted by other systems of intellectual property.

The problem will not generally occur with design rights or patent rights. First, the duration of such rights being shorter than that of copyright, it will be rare, even impossible, that a work fallen into the public domain after the expiration of copyright might be re-appropriated by a patent or a design right. Previous disclosure of a work destroys its novelty, which prevents in most cases an extension of its protection by an adjunct of design or patent rights after the term of copyright. Besides, it is difficult to imagine that a

---

[45]   *Ibid.* art. 5.
[46]   *BMG Ricordi spa, Fondazione Gioacchino Rossini and Azio Corghi v. Ente Autonomo Teatro Regio di Torino*, Cass. 17 January 2001, no. 559, in *Giur. it.*, 2001, 1421, note M. Crosignani, 'Edizione critica e diritto d'autore: un'antitesi superata?'.

literary and artistic work that was eligible for copyright protection could qualify as a technical invention likely to be protected by patent.

As to the interface between copyright and design right, it is difficult to imagine that a work that lacks the originality to accede to copyright protection will be sufficiently new and have the required individual character to be protected as a design. Actually, the key issue for the public domain lies with trademark protection. The name or visual aspect of a character, a painting or the form of an object might be entitled to trademark registration, even after the copyright vesting in such works has expired. Through the trademark protection so granted, the owner of the mark could in theory prohibit the free use of such name, image or form. Imagine that the appearance of Mickey Mouse is registered as a visual trademark (it is in many countries). When the copyright in that little mouse will elapse (if ever!), Disney could still rely on its registered mark, being unlimited in time, to prevent some uses of its famous character.

As a matter of principle, a work that has fallen into the public domain is free for all to use. Therefore, this freedom to use also includes its registration as a trademark, the former copyright owner being no longer capable of preventing such registration[47] (save by a moral right, if perpetual, and if the registration could harm the integrity of the work). Many examples of public domain works registered as trademarks can be found in the trademarks registers, from cartoons or comic book heroes, to pieces of music[48] and famous paintings.

In the United States, the character of Peter the Rabbit by the English illustrator Beatrix Potter, albeit in the public domain under copyright, or more precisely the covers of some of her children's books, have been protected by trademarks.[49] The publication of a new version of the books using the same covers and illustrations was deemed to be an infringement of the trademark rights since

---

[47]   See for example, German Federal Patent Court, 25 November 1997, GRUR 1998, 1021 (concerning the registration as a trademark of 'Mona Lisa'); Benelux Court of Justice, 27 May 1999, BIE 1999, 248 (registration of the initial notes of 'Für Elise' of Beethoven).

[48]   At least in the countries admitting registration of sounds as trademarks.

[49]   *Frederick Warne & Co.* v. *Book Sales*, 481 F. Supp. 1191 (SDNY 1979).

they had acquired secondary meaning with consumers who could then mistakenly confuse the books with those of the original publisher.[50]

The threat of a reconstitution of an undue monopoly over a public domain work is, however, limited by the very principles of trademark law in many regards.

A first feature of trademark protection is the requirement of distinctiveness: the sign claiming the protection must be distinctive enough in the eyes of the consumer of the goods or services concerned. Popular images or sounds will probably lack inherent distinctiveness since the public will be more accustomed to see them as creative expressions and in cultural contexts, than to perceive through them the indication of a commercial origin of the goods on which they are affixed,[51] unless they can establish secondary meaning. In many cases, the primary value of creation pursued by the work, whether in the public domain or not, will stand in the way of a valid registration as a trademark. For instance the names 'Tarzan' or 'Harry Potter' have not been accepted as valid trademarks in the Benelux countries, since they referred mainly for the public to the character, the work and its author, but not to the provider of the goods related to the claimed trademark.[52]

This can particularly be so with trade dress or trademarks consisting of the shape of a product. One can imagine that the three-dimensional form of a product is original and as such protected by copyright. Registration as a trademark can then continue the protection once the term of copyright has ended. However, the registration of a form is even more limited. Beyond the requirement for distinctiveness and the intrinsic difficulty in establishing it for the shape of a product,[53] some exclusion might

---

[50] See the other cases of trademark in public domain works commented by J. Liu, 'The New Public Domain' (2013) *U Ill. L Rev.* 1395.

[51] A. Kur, 'General Report: Does/Should Trademark Law Prohibit Conduct to which Copyright Exceptions Apply?' in *Adjuncts and Alternatives to Copyright*, Proceedings of the ALAI 2001 (New York, 2001), p. 600.

[52] Gerechtshof Amsterdam, 26 July 2001 and 6 November 2003, both cited and discussed in V. Vanovermeire, 'Inschrijving als merk van een in het publiek domaingevallen werk' in A. Cruquenaire and S. Dusollier (eds), *Le Cumul des droits intellectuels* (Larcier, 2009), p. 185.

[53] See for example, German Supreme Court, GRUR 1952, 516, excluding the appearance of popular porcelain figurines, by lack of distinctiveness.

exist, as is the case in the European Union for shapes giving a substantial value to the product. Famous works of sculpture would certainly fall within that exclusion as their substantial value lies in the form itself. As to the shape of works of applied art, such as furniture having a recognized design, that specific design can arguably give a substantial value to the product itself, irrespective of its possible distinctiveness to the public.[54] Such exclusion will equally raise some obstacle to the registration of three-dimensional characters.

Besides, trademark law only allows the registration of a specific sign, which can limit the protection as a trademark of a character in itself.[55] In other words, Mickey Mouse himself cannot be registered, but only a specific graphic representation thereof (especially in the EU where a graphical representation is required). True, the protection will extend to signs similar to the registered mark if there is a risk of confusion for the public. But the argument will not operate for the registration of paintings as trademarks, that have a unique representation.

A final and essential limitation of trademark protection is its principle of speciality. The assessment of the necessary distinctiveness will be carried out in light of the products and services for which the mark is registered, and the protection granted will be limited to the products so defined. As a consequence, Mickey Mouse might well be registered as a trademark either as a name or as a visual sign, but must only be valid in respect of some limited products or services. The famous *Milkmaid* painting by Vermeer has, for example, been registered as a trademark and held valid for dairy products. Therefore, it does not unduly affect the public domain character of the work itself, which can still be free for all to use, reproduce and serve as a basis for derivative creation. The only limited use will be to affix it to milk products in the territory where the trademark is effective. The monopoly regained by the trademark registration, as demonstrated by that case, is hence rather narrow

---

[54]   Vanovermeire, n. 52 above, p. 190 *et seq.* See the recent decision of the CJEU, C-205/13, *Hauck v. Stokke*, Judgment of 18 September 2014.
[55]   A.V. Gaide, 'Copyright, Trademark and Trade Dress: Overlap or Conflict for Cartoon Characters' in *Adjuncts and Alternatives to Copyright*, Proceedings of the ALAI 2001 (New York, 2001), p. 557.

and only partially encroaches upon the public domain constituted by copyright principles.

Yet, this reassuring conclusion might prove untrue in some cases. On the one hand, in many countries, the protection will exceed the speciality realm for famous trademarks, upon some conditions, namely in the case of dilution or tarnishing of the mark. Courts should then be attentive not to apply too broadly the notion of dilution or tarnishing of a famous trademark when it is composed of a work fallen into the public domain and whose free use in creative expression is deemed to harm the goodwill of the mark by its trademark owner.

On the other hand, trademark owners will be tempted to register their signs for many classes of products that can in reality make void the principle of speciality. Even worse, a registration of a trademark in a class of products strongly related to the work itself and its creative value will likely undermine the free use pertaining to public domain work. As examples, one can cite the registration of the name 'Mickey Mouse' as a Community trademark for products and services of class 41, and particularly for 'education; providing of training; entertainment; sporting and cultural activities', or that of 'Tintin' in the same class for 'providing of education; training; teaching, entertainment; organization of events and exhibitions for cultural, teaching and educational purposes; amusement parks; production of films, live and animated; publication and dissemination of books, newspapers and periodicals'. Through such registration the owners of the rights in such popular cultural icons will be able, if the trademark is held valid and sufficiently distinctive (which might not be the case as seen above), to prevent the reproduction of the hero itself in books or films, after the copyright has expired.

This is where the actual risk to the public domain lies within the trademark monopoly. In order to immunize the public domain from such renewed commodification, the registration of a trademark should be denied when it would lead to the reconstitution of a monopoly akin to that provided formerly by copyright and preventing use of the work in creative expression. The public interest or general interest could be taken into account as a ground for such a refusal. It has sometimes been used in case law to prevent the overlapping of successive intellectual property rights when detrimental to the public domain.[56] In a European case brought before the CJEU, the Advocate-General has held that: 'the public interest should not have to tolerate even a slight risk that trademark rights unduly encroach on the field of other exclusive rights which are limited in time, whilst there are in fact other effective ways in which manufacturers may indicate the origin of a product'.[57] Here, the trademark was used to gain a new reservation over an invention whose patent has expired, but the affirmation was broad enough to be developed as a general principle applying also to the copyright public domain. In a recent trademark case, the Court itself reaffirmed 'the aim of preventing the exclusive and permanent right which a trade mark confers from serving to extend indefinitely the life of other rights which the EU legislature has sought to make subject to limited periods'.[58]

A similar rationale was used by the US Supreme Court in the *Dastar* case.[59] The plaintiff relied on the Lanham Act which was sometimes used to grant a form of moral right of attribution by a doctrine of passing off in trademark. A television series, fallen in the public domain by lack of renewal of its copyright, had been incorporated by Dastar in its own audiovisual works, without much change and notably without crediting the source of the footage or its former producer, Fox. The latter alleged that the lack of attribution amounted to a false designation of origin or a reverse passing off. The Supreme Court refused to follow that argument, as the misrepresentation of origin of the goods, which was prohibited under the Lanham Act, could not apply to the 'origin' of the creative material (the footage used to make the film of Dastar) but only to the origin of the physical product, which was not misleading as the DVD originated from Dastar. More fundamentally, the

---

[56]   See a recent Belgian decision refusing the registration of 'The Diary of Anne Frank' (in Dutch) as a trademark: Court of Appeal of Brussel, 3 October 2013, R.G. 2012/AR/2166.

[57]   C-53/01–C-55/01 *Linde AG, Winward Industries Inc. and Radio Uhren AG*, CJEU, 8 April 2003, Opinion of Advocate-General Ruiz-Jarabo Colomer delivered on 24 October 2002, ECR 2003 p. I-3161, at 29.

[58]   C-205/13, *Hauck*, CJEU, 18 September 2014, point 3.

[59]   *Dastar* v. *Twentieth Century Fox*, 539 US 23 (2003).

Court rejected an application of trademark law that could reconstitute some (moral) right in public domain work and impair the free use of such content. That would create, said the Court, 'a species of mutant copyright law'. It should be noted here that the work itself was not the subject matter of trademark protection, which makes it slightly different from what we have discussed above. But the buttress that the Court set up around the public domain to prevent some intrusion by trademark, albeit indirect in *Dastar*, was nevertheless remarkable.

7.3   A POSITIVE REGIME FOR THE PUBLIC DOMAIN

The request for positive protection of the public domain that could preserve it against privatization is an old demand. In his seminal article on the public domain, D. Lange asked for recognition and legal status of the public domain as early as 1981.[60] This legal status has not yet been created at the international or national level.

The reverse definition of the public domain and its negative approach are key obstacles to a genuine status of the public domain. As public domain is not a notion consecrated by copyright law but only a default position, attempts to regain exclusivity in its resources are difficult to counter. The case law analyzed above, such as the *Golan* case, underlines the fragility of the public domain.

One French court decision had tried to give more strength to the public domain.[61] Two authors had restored and added a contemporary work of art in a public and historical square, the Place des Terreaux in Lyon. They sued a company having reproduced the square in a postcard that included both the public domain buildings and the pavement, which was a protected work. The key argument of the decision was that the public domain status of the buildings necessarily constrained and limited the exercise of copyright held by the authors of a derivative work to the extent required by the free reproduction of the public domain. Otherwise, a copyright

---

[60]   Lange, n. 1 above.
[61]   TGI Lyon, 4 April 2001, RIDA, October 2001; Choisy, n. 18 above.

would be indirectly restored in the public domain work for the benefit of the authors of its restoration or modification. The decision was upheld on appeal, mainly on different grounds, even though the Court of Appeal stated that 'the protection granted to the authors of the new design of the square should not prejudice the common enjoyment',[62] which still recognizes a positive protection of the public domain and of its inherent collective use. The Cour de cassation set aside any reference to the public domain and opted to allow the reproduction on the ground of the exception for ancillary reproduction of a work.[63]

This example demonstrates the uneasy issue of the preservation of the public domain. Irrespective of the wish to protect it from new enclosure, no legal tool effectively helps to maintain its elements in the realm of free and unrestrained use against legitimate regained exclusivity claims.

Public domain deserves better. So far, copyright law has done nothing to preserve the public domain or to give it some consistence. Even worse, any extension of copyright, its scope or duration has been enacted with very little consideration for the resulting reduction of the public domain. Expanding the public domain can be achieved by curbing the ongoing enlargement of copyright, but it would not give it much more substance or solidity. One should rather look into the nature itself of the public domain and of the entitlements it confers to make it more sustainable.

A sound policy for the public domain would be first to help its identification and its inscription in a specific legal regime, in order to remove it from the garbage or fallow land of copyright protection where it mainly stands.

Being the reverse of copyright protection should not necessarily equate to being the valueless part of intellectual property. As intellectual property is characterized by exclusivity, the public domain should conversely operate on the ground of non-exclusivity.

---

[62] Lyon, 20 March 2003, Communications – Commerce Electronique, September 2003, note C. Caron. The Court of Cassation has confirmed the ruling on a very different justification, not making any mention of the public domain status of the underlying work. See Cass., 15 March 2005, available at www.courdecassation.fr/jurisprudence_2/premiere_chambre_civile_568/arret_no_632.html.

[63] Cour de cassation, Judgment no. 567 of 15 March 2005.

Such absence of exclusivity could be described positively, not as a lack but as a presence of something else, that one could call 'inclusivity'. Public domain could be characterized not only as being hollow, a deprivation of exclusivity, but also as being full of non-exclusivity. In other words, inclusivity would the positive reverse of exclusivity, and not its mere failure.[64] One could equate such inclusivity to the nature of commons, that have been defined by Benkler as situations where users benefit from equal, symmetric and non-exclusive entitlements to use a resource.[65] Public domain complies with such definition as it creates an equal privilege of everyone to use an unprotected element or a work whose term of protection has lapsed. In civil law, the notion of *choses communes* or commons, appearing in article 714 of the Civil Code, defining the commons as 'goods that are owned by nobody and whose use is common to all' could also be used to develop a positive protection for the public domain.[66]

Considering the public domain in copyright as a commons or *res communis* in the legal meaning of the term, is not very controversial. But what is rather new is the attempt to attach to such qualification a status that could immunize the public domain from any recapture or appropriation. The qualification of the public domain as a *res communis* would imply two consequences. The first one is the prohibition of a recapture of the work as a whole, even though partial recapture can be envisaged (as seen above with trademark registration of a work fallen into the public domain). The second one is to guarantee a collective use of the work: each member of the public should be entitled to use, modify, exploit, reproduce and create new works from public domain material. The collective nature of the commons further entails an obligation of preservation thereof, as is the case for environmental commons.

---

[64]   For further development of this notion of inclusivity, see S. Dusollier, 'The Commons as a Reverse Intellectual Property or the Model of Inclusivity', in G. Dinwoodie (ed.), *Intellectual Property and General Legal Principles – Is IP a* Lex Specialis?, Edward Elgar, 2015, forthcoming.
[65]   Y. Benkler, 'Between Spanish Huertas and the Open Road: A Tale of Two Commons?', paper presented at Convening Cultural Commons Conference, New York University, 2011.
[66]   Choisy, n. 18 above.

Whatever the legal tool, based on the existing notion of *choses communes* or to be developed around a new concept of inclusivity, a strong public domain should be anchored in normative rules rejecting any exclusive reservation. A principle of inclusivity could be endowed with two rules: a rule of enforceability enabling anyone to secure the free use of the public domain element, and a rule of sustainability preventing a recapture of elements in the public domain.

8. Why protecting Internet service providers from liability for users' copyright infringement has been a policy success

Michael W. Carroll[*]

8.1 INTRODUCTION

The character of Dr Pangloss is usually invoked in modern discourse as a means of expressing derision over the target's naivety, cynicism or self-delusion for expressing satisfaction with the status quo, or more colorfully, for holding the view that this is the best of all possible worlds. This is a particularly common use among scholars who study the ever-dynamic Internet or scholars with a progressive bent who can always find room for improvement in the law. This author is no Dr Pangloss, but this chapter largely defends the legal status quo against an increasingly loud chorus of calls for change because, for the most part, the fundamental policy decision discussed below has struck a reasonable balance of interests in the contexts of the United States and the European Union (an important qualification).

The policy decision is to shield providers of information society services from liability for copyright infringement for engaging in the necessary activities to provide these services or for infringing communications by users of the provider's services under circumstances. This decision was taken at the turn of the millennium,

* This chapter incorporates some material from M.W. Carroll, 'Pinterest and Copyright's Safe Harbors for Internet Providers' (2014) 68 *Miami L Rev.* 422. Thanks go to Alexandra El-Bayeh for research assistance. All errors remain mine.

when the legislators on both sides of the Atlantic amended copyright law to update its application to the digital environment and the information society through the Digital Millennium Copyright Act (1998) in the United States and the E-Commerce Directive (2000/31/EC) in the European Union. After more than a decade of experience with this provision, some influential voices are calling for a reassessment in light of the rapid growth of the Internet and the emergence of companies providing large social media platforms.[1] Of course there is room for improvement, but the basic balance of interests reflected in these laws is sound.

The original rationale for this policy decision focused on reducing legal responsibility to a reasonable level so that service providers could continue to provide their basic services of providing email, website hosting, and communications fora such as chatrooms. What has become clear in the intervening years is that this decision did more than secure the status quo for service providers. Instead, it has shown that limitations and exceptions to the exclusive rights under copyright often provide the necessary preconditions for innovation. In this case, the service provider limitations enabled a wave of innovation that has led to rapid growth of a vast array of social media companies whose services define what it means to use the Internet for a large number of Internet users.

---

[1] H. Comm. on the Judiciary, Press Release, 'Chairman Goodlatte Announces Comprehensive Review of Copyright Law', 24 April 2013, available at http://judiciary.house.gov/news/2013/04242013_2.html; M.A. Pallante, 'The Next Great Copyright Act' (2013) 36 *Colum. JL and Arts* 315, 320; The Register's Call for Updates to US Copyright Law: Hearing Before the Subcomm. on Courts, Intellectual Prop., and the Internet, 113th Cong., 2013, pp. 6–38 (statement of M.A. Pallante, Register of Copyrights, US Copyright Office); P. Samuelson *et al.*, 'The Copyright Principles Project: Directions for Reform' (2010) 25 *Berkeley Tech. LJ* 2010 1176; A Case Study for Consensus Building: The Copyright Principles Project: Hearing Before the Subcomm. on Courts, Intellectual Prop., and the Internet, 113th Cong., 2013 (statement of P. Samuelson, Professor, Berkeley Law School).

8.2 POLICY BACKGROUND

Limitations on legal responsibility for service providers were a compromise that emerged from an energetic and sometimes heated policy debate in both the United States and Europe. The rapid expansion of the Internet in the early- to mid-1990s raised a number of legal issues concerning whether existing principles might readily apply to new Internet services or whether new, Internet-specific, rules were in order. In particular, a pressing question was what the principles would be for determining the legal responsibility of service providers that enabled Internet communications for the harmful communications sent by their users. Analogies to these providers as newspapers, broadcasters, bookstores, and telephone companies were common. But, the scale of these services was unprecedented. Service providers enabled direct one-to-one and one-to-many communications without reviewing the content in ways that traditional content intermediaries had done. This communicative immediacy provided a number of benefits but also imposed the harms of dignitary injuries and infringement of intellectual property rights.

The policy conversations in Europe and in the United States about these issues had common themes but proceeded from different frameworks. In Europe, service provider responsibility was considered as a whole inside the larger framework of e-commerce. In the United States, service provider responsibility was treated contextually, dividing responsibility for dignitary harms as part of telecommunications policy and responsibility for infringement as part of copyright policy. This conversation produced Internet-specific legal rules first in the United States followed closely by Europe.

8.2.1 United States

What is now the provision for Internet service provider liability in the United States Copyright Act, section 512, emerged out of a larger effort to define the copyright rules of the road for the 'information superhighway' in the early- to mid-1990s. The Clinton Administration assembled a Task Force to provide what became a very contentious White Paper that would do so. The underlying theory of the White Paper was that the Internet was a dangerous environment for copyright owners because of the difficulties in identifying users and holding them responsible when they engaged in infringing activity. Its recommendations were justified on the basis of making the environment 'safe' for copyright owners to distribute their content. For this reason, among its recommendations was a rejection of any protection for Internet service providers from copyright infringement liability.[2] Coalitions of large corporate copyright owners pushed for legislative adoption of the White Paper's findings.[3] However, there was backlash from library groups, online service providers, Internet civil liberties groups, and others.[4] The Digital Future Coalition was formed by representatives from these groups, and it effectively stopped the hasty domestic adoption of the White Paper's recommendations.[5]

Policy attention shifted to the World Intellectual Property Organization (WIPO), through which two multilateral copyright-related treaties were negotiated shortly after the World Trade Organization's Agreement on Trade-Related Aspects of Intellectual Property Rights (TRIPS) had become effective.[6] Attempts by the United States delegation to incorporate many of the more-controversial proposals from the White Paper proved unsuccessful.[7] The compromises necessary to finalize the WIPO Copyright Treaty left considerable flexibility for national implementation.[8]

In the United States, treaty implementation became a platform to propose other revisions to the Copyright Act.[9] The legislative priority for large media companies was to add provisions making it

---

[2]   Jessica Litman, *Digital Copyright*, (Prometheus Books, 2001), p. 230.

[3]   Litman, n. 2 above, p. 123.

[4]   *Ibid.* p. 122.

[5]   P. Goldstein, *Copyright's Highway: From Gutenberg to the Celestial Jukebox* (rev. edn, Stanford, Stanford University Press, 2003), p. 172; Litman, n. 2 above, p. 128 ('Copyright owners remained unwilling to let service providers off the hook, and the providers and telephone companies were determined that the bill not move until their interests were addressed.').

[6]   See Litman, n. 2 above, p. 128 *et seq.*

[7]   *Ibid.* pp. 128–30.

[8]   See Goldstein, n. 5 above, p. 172 *et seq.* (detailing the negotiations and lack of agreement by the other member nations with all of the United States' agenda).

[9]   See Goldstein, n. 5 above, p. 172 *et seq.*

illegal to circumvent technological protection measures that controlled access to, or use of, copyrighted works and to traffic in technologies that enabled such circumvention. For service providers, the focus was on the background rules on direct and secondary liability that were under active development in the courts. Issues that were not fully resolved included whether a service provider or the user was directly responsible for infringing copies made by the service providers' machines in the course of an Internet transmission and what level of knowledge about, or control over, a user's infringing activities a service provider must have to be secondarily responsible for such conduct.

The sectoral approach to regulation taken in the United States meant that service provider responsibility would be established based on the source of law at issue. In 1996, service providers had persuaded Congress to immunize them from liability for defamation and related communicative harms caused by users of interactive computer services, such as chatrooms.[10] This statute, however, explicitly exempted harms caused by users' infringement of copyright and other forms of federal intellectual property from service providers' immunity,[11] leaving this issue to be resolved separately. Consequently, service providers found champions to introduce stand-alone copyright legislation that would provide immunity from infringement caused by users.[12]

In legislative hearings on this issue, witnesses from large media companies argued that Internet services were little different from services provided by other content intermediaries, and therefore no Internet-specific protection was required.[13] Moreover, these witnesses wanted to keep the status quo, including the specter of

---

[10]   Communications Decency Act of 1996, tit. 5, Pub. L No. 104–104, 110 Stat. 133 (1996) (codified as amended at 47 USC s. 230).

[11]   See 47 USC s. 230(e)(2) (2006).

[12]   See Goldstein, n. 5 above, pp. 171–73.

[13]   See House Judiciary Hearing, pp. 70, 79, 118, 130, 157, 168, 219 (statements of R. Hollyman, Business Software Alliance; J. Valenti, Motion Picture Association of America; K. Wasch, Software Publishers Association of America; L. Kenswill, Universal Music Group; A. Willis, Songwriter, Broadcast Music Inc.; J. Bettis, American Society of Composers; M. Kirk, American Intellectual Property Law Association); Senate Judiciary Hearing, pp. 10, 16, 20 (statements of F. Attaway, Motion Picture Association of America; C. Sherman, Recording Industry Association of America; D. Burton, Novell).

secondary liability, to give service providers an incentive to police their users' activities. Witnesses from the telephone companies, other ISPs and libraries argued that provision of Internet service was different in kind, and therefore required an Internet-specific solution. They argued that it would not be feasible – or even possible – to police their services to identify infringing material.[14] Service providers argued that the direct infringer should bear legal responsibility for her actions, not service providers.

As it became clear that some service provider measure would be necessary for the technological protection measures (TPM) provisions to also become law, the notice-and-takedown provisions were seen as a reasonable compromise. Copyright owners could obtain swift action from service providers through sending of notice alone, without adjudication or judicial supervision, but it would be the copyright owner's responsibility to monitor the provider's service for infringing content. Representatives from the Business Software Alliance (BSA) and the Recording Industry Association of America (RIAA) had shifted their position and testified in favor of safe harbors subject to the notice-and-takedown regime.[15] Although the general idea of safe harbor protection had been accepted, the

---

[14]   See House Judiciary Hearing, pp. 65 *et seq.*, 83, 114, 125, 151, 173, 250, 259 (statement of M.R.C. Greenwood, University of California, Santa Cruz; R. Neel, United States Telephone Association; T. Patel, US WEB; M. Jacobson, Prodigy Services; R. Oakley, Georgetown University Law Center; R. Dunn, Information Industry Association; C. Byrne, Silicon Graphics; E. Black, Computer and Communications Industry Association); Senate Judiciary Hearing, pp. 26, 29, 34 (statement of G. Vradenburg, ISP Copyright Coalition; R. Neel, United States Telephone Association; R. Oakley, American Association of Law Libraries).

[15]   WIPO Copyright Treaties Implementation Act: Hearing on H.R. 2281 Before the Subcomm. on Telecomm., Trade, and Consumer Protection of the H. Comm. on Commerce, 105th Cong., 1998 ('Business Software Alliance supports those provisions because they will promote cooperation and partnership between copyright owners and providers of online services, thus ensuring that the Internet does not become a haven for thieves') (statement of R.W. Holleyman, II, President, Business Software Alliance); *ibid.* p. 45 ('This section represents an historic achievement in establishing new rules of the Internet road, balancing the legitimate needs and concerns of copyright owners with those of Internet service providers') (statement of H. Rosen, President, RIAA).

legislative negotiations were not easy.[16] Eventually, however, the committee successfully produced a Bill that both houses enacted, and President Clinton signed the Digital Millennium Copyright Act (DMCA) into law on 28 October 1998.[17]

Born out of this hard-fought legislative compromise, the safe harbors for service providers in section 512 of the Copyright Act have proven stable even if they have required judicial interpretation to clarify the meaning of some of the language. The essential provisions are as follows. First, although service providers had sought to be held immune from *infringement liability*,[18] section 512 in its enacted form applies if liability has been established by limiting the *remedies* available to a copyright owner in cases in which the service provider qualifies for the safe harbor.[19] Specifically, section 512 provides that 'A service provider shall not be liable for monetary relief, or, except as provided in subsection (j), for injunctive or other equitable relief, for infringement of copyright by reason of' engaging in one of the four protected activities.[20] The 'monetary relief' that a qualifying service provider is spared is broad and is defined as 'damages, costs, attorneys' fees, and any other form of monetary payment'.[21] The conditions for injunctive relief in section 512(j) are also quite limited, making a service provider with a reasonable argument that it qualifies for safe harbor protection an unattractive target for litigation.

Congress identified four functions that service providers perform requiring safe harbor protection: Internet transmission (for example, basic Internet service);[22] system caching (for example, as done by

---

[16]   See J.M. Urban and L. Quilter, 'Efficient Process or "Chilling Effects"? Takedown Notices under Section 512 of the Digital Millennium Copyright Act' (2005) 22 *Santa Clara Computer and High Tech. LJ* 621, 633.

[17]   US Copyright Office, The Digital Millenium Copyright Act of 1998, Summary, December 1998.

[18]   See Online Copyright Liability Limitation Act of 1997, H.R. 2180, 105th Cong. s. 2 (1997); Digital Copyright Clarification and Technology Education Act, S. 1146, 105th Cong. s. 102.

[19]   See below.

[20]   See 17 USC s. 512(a)–(d) (2012) (beginning each subsection with the quoted text).

[21]   *Ibid.* s. 512(k)(2).

[22]   *Ibid.* s. 512(a).

search engines);[23] storing material at the direction of users (for example, web hosts or social media sites);[24] and linking to online locations (for example, search engines).[25] Focused on defining the protected activities of service providers, Congress left somewhat ambiguous in section 512 its implicit theory of liability for copyright infringement from which the service provider receives safe harbor protection. The Copyright Act grants to authors and their assigns six exclusive rights,[26] and the verbs used to define these rights do not align directly with the verbs used to describe a service provider's protected activities.[27] As a result, federal courts have had to explain, for example, which of the copyright owner's exclusive rights are subject to the safe harbor when a provider provides 'storage at the direction of a user' of infringing material.[28]

The basic structure of the legal analysis under section 512 is fairly straightforward. A defendant may successfully raise a section 512 defense to monetary relief if it shows that it: (1) is a 'service provider';[29] (2) has taken the necessary steps to be eligible for the safe harbor(s);[30] (3) has responded appropriately to qualifying communications from the copyright owner or to other relevant facts

---

[23] *Ibid.* s. 512(b).
[24] *Ibid.* s. 512(c).
[25] *Ibid.* s. 512(d).
[26] *Ibid.* s. 106.
[27] Compare 17 USC s. 106 (granting copyright owners exclusive rights to 'reproduce', 'distribute copies', 'perform … publicly', and 'display … publicly' the work of authorship or to 'prepare derivative works' from it) with 17 USC s. 512 (providing safe harbors for service providers that transmit, route, or provide connections to material; provide intermediate and temporary storage of material; store material at the direction of a user; and refer users to a location containing infringing material).
[28] See *UMG Recordings, Inc. v. Shelter Capital Partners LLC*, 718 F.3d 1006, 1015–20, 9th Cir. 2013 (devoting five reporter pages to the question and rejecting the argument that 'storage' is limited to a service provider's ingest of infringing material).
[29] See 17 USC s. 512(k)(1) (defining 'service provider').
[30] See *ibid.* s. 512(b)(2) (defining protected caching practice); (c)(2) (requiring designation of agent to receive notice of copyright infringement); (e)(1)(C) (requiring educational institution acting as service provider to provide to users information concerning compliance with copyright law); (i) (requiring of all service providers that they have a policy to terminate use of service by 'subscribers' and 'account holders' who are 'repeat infringers' and that they do not interfere with 'standard technical measures').

and circumstances that could affect the service provider's continuing eligibility for the safe harbor(s);[31] and (4) does not receive a direct financial benefit from infringing activity that the service provider has the right and ability to control in the case of hosting and linking service providers.[32]

Each of these elements has additional subsidiary inquiries designed to tailor the scope of safe harbor protection, while also attempting to deter potentially abusive conduct by copyright owners. For example, the initial inquiry of whether the defendant is a 'service provider' is actually more complex because the DMCA divides service providers into two classes and offers a different scope of protection to each.[33] Service providers of basic network transmission under section 512(a) receive broader protection than service providers protected under subsections (b)–(d) because knowledge of infringement does not disqualify a provider of network transmissions, whereas such knowledge would disqualify providers of other protected services.[34]

The second element of the legal inquiry is whether the service provider took the necessary preliminary steps to be eligible for safe harbor protection.[35] All service providers must have adopted and implemented a policy to terminate services for repeat infringers, and they must have set up their services not to interfere with standard technical measures.[36] Service providers who host content at the direction of their users must also have designated an agent to

---

[31]   See *ibid.*s. 512(b)(2)(B) (complies with website's reasonable caching policies); (b)(2)(E) (removes cached content upon receiving notice of infringement); (c)(1)(A) (removes infringing content expeditiously upon receipt of qualifying notice from copyright owner or when becoming aware of 'facts and circumstances from which infringing activity is apparent'); (d)(1), (3) (same as s. 512 (c)(1)(A)).

[32]   See *ibid.* s. 512(c)(1)(B); (d)(2).

[33]   See *ibid.* s. 512(a)–(d).

[34]   See *ibid.* s. 512(a)–(d).

[35]   *Ibid.*

[36]   See *ibid.*; see also *Ellison* v. *Robertson*, 357 F.3d 1072, 1080, 9th Cir. 2004 (holding that the District Court's grant of summary judgment for AOL, on the grounds it had reasonably implemented its s. 512(i) policy, was inappropriate because AOL had changed its email address for receiving infringement notifications without adequately providing a means to receive and respond to notifications sent to the old address).

receive email notifications[37] and must have registered the agent's information with the US Copyright Office, which keeps an online directory of such agents.[38] The DMCA does not expressly require caching and linking service providers to designate such an agent, but they are required to respond to a notice of infringement sent to such an agent.[39] Caching service providers must have aligned their practice to comply with reasonable caching policies of publisher sites,[40] and non-profit higher educational institutions acting as service providers must have provided to users information about legal compliance with copyright law.[41]

The third element is whether the service provider has responded appropriately to a qualifying notice from a copyright owner or to other relevant facts and circumstances.[42] This element has generated the most significant litigation to date because it effectively allocates the costs of enforcement between copyright owners and service providers. Litigants have contested how specific a notice of infringement must be to trigger a service provider's obligation to respond.[43] They similarly have sparred over when a service provider acquires actual knowledge of infringing activity, or so-called 'red flag' knowledge of facts and circumstances, from which

---

[37]   See 17 USC s. 512(c)(2).

[38]   See United States Copyright Office, 'Online Service Providers', available at www.copyright.gov/onlinesp/.

[39]   See s. 512(c)(3) (defining elements for a qualifying notice); see also s. 512(b)(2)(E) (incorporating (c)(3) notice requirements by reference for caching service providers); s. 512(d)(3) (same for linking service providers).

[40]   See *ibid.* s. 512(b)(2).

[41]   See *ibid.* s. 512(e)(1)(C).

[42]   See n. 36 above.

[43]   See *ALS Scan, Inc.* v. *RemarQ Communities, Inc.*, 239 F.3d 619, 625, 4th Cir. 2001 (finding adequate notice that the alleged two sites had been established to host infringing copies of plaintiff's photographs and therefore all of the content on each should be treated as infringing); *Wolk* v. *Kodak Imaging Network, Inc.*, 840 F.Supp.2d 724, 747 (SDNY 2012) ('Notices that do not identify the specific location of the alleged infringement are not sufficient to confer "actual knowledge" on the service provider'); *Hendrickson* v. *eBay, Inc.*, 165 F.Supp.2d 1082, 1089 (CD Cal. 2001) ('DMCA expressly provides that if the copyright holder's attempted notification fails to "comply substantially" with the elements of notification described in subsection (c)(3), that notification "shall not be considered" when evaluating whether the service provider had actual or constructive knowledge of the infringing activity').

infringing activity is apparent.[44] Two Courts of Appeals have rejected arguments that would impose on service providers an obligation to act when they have generalized knowledge that users are uploading popular titles, but without knowledge of specific allegedly infringing files.[45]

Last, hosting and linking service providers must not receive a direct financial benefit from infringing activity that they have the right and ability to control.[46] This terminology echoes the elements of the doctrine of vicarious liability as articulated by the lower courts.[47] A service provider otherwise liable for vicarious infringement has a 'right and ability to control infringing activity' for section 512 purposes – and thereby loses safe harbor protection – only when the service provider exerts 'substantial influence' over its users.[48]

---

[44]   See *UMG Recordings, Inc.* v. *Shelter Capital Partners LLC*, 718 F.3d 1006, 1025, 9th Cir. 2013 ('In other words, the actual knowledge provision turns on whether the provider actually or "subjectively" knew of specific infringement, while the red flag provision turns on whether the provider was subjectively aware of facts that would have made the specific infringement "objectively" obvious to a reasonable person'); see also *Viacom Int'l, Inc.* v. *YouTube, Inc.*, 676 F.3d 19, 31, 2d Cir. 2012 (fashioning an extra-textual standard for 'willful blindness' that could lead to finding of actual knowledge); *Viacom Int'l, Inc.* v. *YouTube, Inc.*, No. 07 Civ. 2103(LLS) 2013 WL 1689071, at *4–5, SDNY 18 April 2013 (applying willful blindness standard and holding that YouTube did not have actual knowledge of infringing activity). Further developments on this issue of law are forthcoming. See *Capitol Records, LLC* v. *Vimeo, LLC*, Nos. 09 Civ. 10101(RA), 09 Civ.10105(RA) 2013 WL 6869648 (31 December 2013) (certifying for interlocutory appeal the question '[w]hether, under Viacom Int'l, Inc. v. YouTube, Inc., a service provider's viewing of a user-generated video containing all or virtually all of a recognizable, copyrighted song may establish "facts or circumstances" giving rise to "red flag" knowledge of infringement').

[45]   See n. 43 above.

[46]   See s. 512(c)(1)(B).

[47]   See for example, *A&M Records, Inc.* v. *Napster, Inc.*, 239 F.3d 1004, 1023, 9th Cir. 2001 (defining elements of vicarious liability). The Supreme Court's articulation of vicarious liability, in passing, is more limited; see *MGM Studios, Inc.* v. *Grokster, Ltd*, 545 US 913, 930 (2005) ('[One] infringes vicariously by profiting from direct infringement while declining to exercise a right to stop or limit it.').

[48]   See *A&M Records, Inc.* v. *Napster*, n. 47 above, pp. 1026–31.

8.2.2 Europe

Within the European Union two related policy processes were running parallel to the policy conversation in the United States. One concerned the need for harmonization of copyright and related rights, framed by the European Commission's 1995 Green Paper on copyright reform, which also sought to chart a course for the digital future.[49] That initiative would eventually lead to the 2001 Copyright Directive. Separately, a broader initiative began in 1997 when the Commission adopted 'A European Initiative on Electronic Commerce'. Within this framework, the issue of service provider responsibility would be treated horizontally and would be dealt with for the full range of communicative harms that users of Internet services might cause. The initial proposal for the Directive in 1998 also called for legislation on this topic.[50] It declared that online service providers and intermediaries should be able to avoid liability in some way since they often do not have knowledge of infringing material.[51] The proposal noted that legislation would help clarify this branch of law, and dissuade forum-shopping if the law was allowed to develop solely at the national level within the EU.[52] When the E-Commerce Directive was finally released, articles 12–15 closely resemble the DMCA by exempting service providers from liability for certain functions they perform, subject to certain conditions.[53]

---

[49]   *Green Paper on Copyright and Related Rights in the Information Society*, COM(1995)382 final (19 July 1995), p. 6 *et seq.*

[50]   See M. Peguera, 'The DMCA Safe Harbors and their European Counterparts: A Comparative Analysis of Some Common Problems' (2009) 32 *Colum. JL and Arts* 481 ('The 1998 Proposal of Directive suggested safe harbors for the activities of "mere conduit", "caching" and "hosting", which were obviously inspired by those set forth in the DMCA. With only a few minor changes, those safe harbors made their way to the final text of the Directive.').

[51]   Proposal for a European Parliament and Council Directive on Certain Legal Aspects of Electronic Commerce in the Internal Market, COM(1998)586 final (18 November 1998), p. 12 *et seq.*

[52]   *Ibid.* p. 12.

[53]   Directive 2000/31/EC of the European Parliament and of the Council of 8 June 2000 on certain legal aspects of information society services, in particular electronic commerce, in the Internal Market ('E-Commerce Directive') [2000] OJ L178/14.

Articles 12–14 direct that 'Member States shall ensure that the service provider is not liable for' acting as a mere conduit for network transmissions (article 12), caching material to make such transmission service more efficient (article 13), or storing information provided by a recipient of the service (article 14). Each of these articles contains limiting conditions that mirror their counterparts in the DMCA, so, for example, service providers will not be liable for hosting material so long as it lacks actual or constructive knowledge of illegal activity and, upon obtaining such knowledge, it acts expeditiously to disable access to the hosted information.

Although these articles shield service providers from liability, they do not remove service providers entirely from enforcement proceedings. Under article 15, Member States may not impose a general obligation to monitor their users' communications in connection with providing transmission, caching or hosting services. Member States may require that service providers report information about illegal activities to competent authorities, and service providers may be required to furnish identifying information provided by recipients of their services.[54] In addition, articles 12–14 each provides that it 'shall not affect the possibility for a court or administrative authority, in accordance with Member States' legal systems, of requiring the service provider to terminate or prevent an infringement'. The horizontal nature of the Directive means that injunctive relief should be possible for infringement of any rights covered by it. However, with respect to copyright, Member States are further directed in article 8(3) of the EC Copyright Directive that they 'shall ensure that right holders are in a position to apply for an injunction against intermediaries whose services are used by a third party to infringe a copyright or related right'.[55]

These intersecting Directives, complemented by the Charter of Fundamental Rights of the European Union, and their national implementations have raised a number of issues for the Court of Justice of the European Union (CJEU). For example, the Court has preliminarily determined that a website that serves infringing

---

[54]   Case 275/06 *Promusicae v Telefónica de España SAU*, CJEU, Judgment of 29 January 2008. [2008] ECR I-271.

[55]   Directive 2001/29/EC of the European Parliament and of the Council of 22 May 2001 on the harmonization of certain aspects of copyright and related rights in the information society [2001] OJ L167/10.

audiovisual works is using the services of the viewer's or down-loader's service provider, and therefore such a service provider can be subject to an injunction to block access to the source website.[56] The most difficult issue for the Court has been to define a balance between a national court's power to issue injunctions against service providers to prevent prospective infringements of copyright, which would imply an obligation to have the ability to detect such infringements, against the protection in article 15 of the E-Commerce Directive, which prohibits national authorities from imposing a general obligation on service providers to monitor the communications of recipients of the service. This difficulty was noted in the European Commission's 2007 Study on the Liability of Internet Intermediaries, which said that '[i]njunctions – and closely related filtering and blocking – are one of the outstanding problems in the EU to be left untouched by the [Directive]'.[57]

Other sources of law require that a principle of proportionality govern the balancing of competing interests identified and protected in these Directives and the Charter, such as the rights of authors and the rights of service providers to conduct a business. Taking all of these legal mandates into account, the Court has determined that a national court that issues an injunction requiring a service provider to install a filtering system to detect infringing files has contravened EU law for more than one reason.[58]

8.2.3   Relationship Between the US and European Approaches

In light of the discussion of the US and European approaches to adapt the law to the digital environment with respect to copyright, a brief comparison of the similarities and differences between the two approaches follows. At a general level, the law in both territories identifies three Internet-based services that should be protected from overly expansive copyright liability that might otherwise

---

[56]   Case 314/12 *UPC Telekabel v Constantin Film* [2014] CJEU, Judgment of 27 March 2014.
[57]   European Commission, *Study on the Liability of Internet Intermediaries* (November 2007), p. 20.
[58]   Case 360/10 *SABAM v Netlog* [2012] CJEU, Judgment of 16 February 2012, 2 CMLR 18; Case 70/10 *Scarlet Extended SA v SABAM* [2011] ECR I-11959. C-70/10 *Scarlet v. Sabam*, CJEU, Judgment of 24 November 2011.

apply: providing basic network transmissions initiated and controlled by users, caching webpages, and storing information uploaded by users. Each shares essentially the same limits on the scope of service provider protection. Both approaches also make clear that service providers cannot be subjected to a general obligation to monitor or filter their users' communications. However, the service provider can be required to supply identifying information about users alleged to have engaged in infringing activities subject to certain privacy protections.

Noticeably absent from the E-Commerce Directive is any protection for search engines or providers of information location tools, in contrast to the protection offered by section 512(d) of the US Copyright Act. Article 21 of the Directive called for regular reports on the implementation of the Directive. The European Commission commissioned a report in 2007 about implementation of the intermediary liability provisions. That report noted that many Member States had implemented some protections for hyperlinking or providing search services, and the report recommended that protection should vary depending upon the level of control and knowledge that the linking party has about the content to be found at the destination site.[59]

With respect to the services covered by both the Directive and the DMCA, there are three significant differences between the approaches. First, is the basic difference between the United States as a single, federally governed state, and the European Union as a union of independently sovereign states. Legislation in the United States can be more specifically prescriptive because it is national law. In contrast, Directives need to allow space for some differences in national implementations. Second, there has been greater comfort in the United States than in the EU in regulating sectorally. For this reason, in the United States service provider liability varies depending upon the source of the rights asserted against the provider, whereas, the E-Commerce Directive applies horizontally to protected services.

Third, the two approaches differ in their conceptions of service provider responsibility for copyright infringement based on users'

---

[59] T. Verbiest *et al.*, *Study of the Liability of Internet Intermediaries*, Markt/2006/09/E Service Contract ETD/2006/IM/E2/69 (November 2007).

communications. In the EU, Member States are prohibited from holding service providers liable for infringement for providing the protected services if the provider meets the conditions of protection. In contrast, in the United States, provision of such services is assumed to be a legitimate basis for liability, and the protection is only from monetary remedies that would otherwise be available to the right-holder based upon the service provider's liability. However, in the EU, even if the service provider is not liable based upon users' communications, the service provider can still properly be subject to an injunction issued in response to users' infringing activities. As is discussed above, unlike in the US Copyright Act, the E-Commerce and Copyright Directives do not provide limitations on the scope of injunctive relief to which a service provider may be subject. It seems likely that the national courts and the CJEU will be called upon to continue to balance the rights of rights-holders and service providers when crafting injunctive relief in future cases.

8.3   INNOVATION ARGUMENT FOR PROTECTING SERVICE PROVIDERS

Experience with protecting service providers from the full consequences of liability for copyright infringement has shown that in addition to the original justification that focused primarily on keeping then-existing services economically viable, a second, compelling justification has emerged. These protections provide the space for new service providers to enter the market, to innovate, and to evolve in response to new developments in technology and to changing user tastes. Increases in bandwidth during the first decade of the millennium made possible the rapid growth in social media services, particularly video-sharing sites such as YouTube. As important, protection from copyright liability has made investing in these companies attractive. This investment capital has given these companies resource to develop new products and services that create significant economic value. After reviewing the original policy rationales for service provider protection, this section concludes with a brief case study of one beneficiary of this policy success, Pinterest, as an example of why this policy should be maintained even if other copyright reform initiatives move forward.

The preparatory materials and the original discourse around the rationale for protecting service providers' activities focused on users' needs to communicate through the services of providers and on providers' needs to be able to operate without the risk of liability for their users' conduct over which they lacked control or knowledge. For example, in its First Report on the implementation of the Directive, the European Commission explained that '[t]he limitations on the liability of intermediaries in the Directive were considered indispensable to ensuring both the provision of basic services which safeguard the continued free flow of information in the network and the provision of a framework which allows the Internet and e-commerce to develop'.[60]

This discourse recognized at a general level that limiting service provider liability would allow service providers to grow their businesses as new technologies were developed. But, law-makers on both sides of the Atlantic did not focus on, or perhaps fully understand, how existing services in the 1990s and early 2000s would likely develop as bandwidth and storage capacities increased. Social media was already part of the environment in the guise of companies such as GeoCities, which provided design templates and hosting services for user-generated websites. From these roots grew blogging services and subsequently YouTube and its competitors. Services that relied on user-generated content created and made available inside 'walled gardens', such as chatrooms hosted by America Online, gave rise to the model of limited Internet publication that fueled the growth of Facebook, Twitter and their competitors.

The growth of social media under the protection provided by the Directive and the DMCA illustrates a larger point about limitations and exceptions to copyright infringement. These are enabling provisions that fuel socially productive activities. In some cases, these activities are more connected to civil and political discourse, such as exceptions that recognize a right to make parodies of

---

[60] European Commission, *Report from the Commission to the European Parliament, the Council and the European Economic and Social Committee: First Report on the Application of Directive 2000/31/EC of the European Parliament and of the Council of 8 June 2000 on Certain Legal Aspects of Information Society Services, in Particular Electronic Commerce, in the Internal Market (Directive on Electronic Commerce)*, COM/2003/0702 final.

popular cultural works. But, in many cases, limitations and exceptions also provide a legal basis for investments and commercial risk-taking on innovative services that rely in part on the use of copyrighted works of authorship. As an illustrative case, consider the company Pinterest.

Pinterest is a company that has learned by doing – shifting its business strategy to respond to users' preferences and behavior. What was once a mobile shopping application is now a robust web-based platform, upon which a user population comprised mostly of women has built an extensive visual conversation using primarily photographs copied from the Web. Some uses of these photographs would qualify as fair use.[61] Uses of other photographs, such as those available under a Creative Commons license,[62] are licensed by the copyright owner.[63] However, some portion of these uses are likely infringing copyright, or are plausibly infringing to a sufficient degree to impose on Pinterest sizable potential litigation costs that would undermine its ability to raise investment capital to continue to innovate.[64]

Pinterest is more explicitly aimed at user copied content, but in the context of pictures and images that users have found in the vast array of content on the World Wide Web, and have 'pinned' to their electronic bulletin boards for future reference, and for sharing with others. The finding is often more work than the taking of the

---

[61]   See A. Mirsky, *Pinterest: Fair Use of Images*, Building Communities, Fan Pages, Copyright, Digital Media Law Project (22 October 2012), available at   www.dmlp.org/blog/2012/pinterest-fair-use-images-building-communities-fan-pages-copyright (discussing the applicability of copyright fair use in using Pinterest).

[62]   See generally about licenses and creative commons: http://creative commons.org/licenses/.

[63]   See T. Ratcliff, 'Why Photographers Should Stop Complaining about Copyright and Embrace Pinterest', *Stuck in Customs*, 13 February 2012, available at www.stuckincustoms.com/2012/02/13/why-photographers-should-stop-complaining-about-copyright-and-embrace-pinterest/.

[64]   See for example, *Rosen* v. *Hosting Servs, Inc.*, 771 F.Supp.2d 1219 (CD Cal. 2010) (photographer unsuccessfully suing service provider even in light of evident DMCA protection); see also *Corbis Corp.* v. *Amazon.com, Inc.*, 351 F.Supp.2d 1090, 1110 (WD Wash. 2004) (ruling on Amazon's s. 512 defense without deciding whether its hosting of celebrity photographs was infringing), overruled in part on other grounds, *Cosmetic Ideas, Inc.* v. *IAC/Interactive corp.*, 606 F.3d 612, 9th Cir. 2010.

photographs. This is not always true, particularly in the context of professional fashion and commercial photography. These photographers are the copyright owners most aggrieved by Pinterest's success. But, the overall economic and social value created by Pinterest derives primarily from creators other than the photographers, and from the conversational and inspirational nature of the communications enabled by Pinterest's platform.

As a start-up reliant on user growth, Pinterest's first few months showed only modest gains. However, some investors understood the site's potential and provided additional capital.[65] The site's popularity grew steadily throughout 2010, and by May 2011, it received a US$10 million investment at a US$40 million valuation.[66] Subsequent growth in 2011 was phenomenal. The number of Pinterest users grew by 4,377 percent, and the site quickly became one of the most popular social network sites on the Internet.[67] As speculation about a possible public offering increased in 2013, the company's value was estimated at US$2.5 billion.[68]

While dramatic in the speed of its growth, the evolving story of Pinterest's success demonstrates the importance of providing space for innovative new entrants in the digital economy to develop their business models and react to user preferences when offering new services. The balance encoded in both the Directive and the DMCA protects innovation in socially productive new services while discouraging models for services primarily dependent upon copyright infringement. Successful innovative services built upon the foundation of this balance strongly suggest that whatever imperfections there may be in this regime, it is worth maintaining for the foreseeable future to continue to enable this wave of innovation.

---

[65]   *Rosen v. Hosting Servs*, n. 64 above ('[Pinterest] got a very strong signal that their product was resonating. Unsolicited, former IAC M&A boss Shana Fisher called the company and said that she loved the product, and wanted to invest if they would let her.').

[66]   *Rosen v. Hosting Servs*, n. 64 above.

[67]   S. Rodriguez, 'Pinterest grew more than 4000% in one year, report says', *Los Angeles Times*, 15 June 2012, available at http://articles.latimes.com/2012/jun/15/business/la-fi-tn-pinterest-4000-percent-20120615.

[68]   J.J. Colao, 'Why is Pinterest a $2.5 billion company? An early investor explains …', *Forbes*, 8 May 2013, available at www.forbes.com/sites/jjcolao/2013/05/08/why-is-pinterest-a-2-5-billion-company-an-early-investor-explains/.

9. Exhaustion of rights: a concept for the digital world?

Ansgar Ohly

9.1 DEMATERIALIZATION OF MEDIA PRODUCTS AS A CHALLENGE FOR COPYRIGHT LAW

Digitization and the development of the Internet have given rise to a multitude of new business models, many of them involving the use of protected works. Since most national copyright laws were made in and for the analogue world, it is often not apparent from the statutory text if and to what extent these uses require the consent of the copyright owner. Judges then face the difficult task of deciding whether the old rules can be applied to new phenomena in accordance with established doctrinal principles, whether copyright policy allows an application of existing provisions by analogy, and whether the courts can take a pro-active role without overstepping the line between adjudication and legislation. The issue of exhaustion is an example in point.

The business of reselling media products is as old as printed matter itself. Used books have always been resold, as romantically evidenced by the stalls of the bouquinistes on the banks of the river Seine. The analogue model has been extended without major difficulty to carriers of digital data such as DVDs. But the business of reselling entirely digital products without transferring the corresponding data carriers is a new one. Two names have become associated with this new business model. UsedSoft, known from the leading Court of Justice of the European Union (CJEU) decision on digital exhaustion in the area of computer programs,[1] offers 'used

---

[1] C-128/11 *UsedSoft GmbH* v. *Oracle International Corp.* ECLI: EU:C:2012:407, [2013] RPC 6.

software', in other words, software licences which the former owner does not need any more, be it because he or she has given up business, be it because the licences are only available in larger packets which exceed the user's needs. ReDigi has launched a similar website for other types of 'used' digital media such as music and audio books. Users can upload their files to a 'digital locker' on ReDigi's servers. When a user wishes to sell a file, it is transferred from the seller's to the buyer's 'locker'.[2] Are these business models compatible with copyright law? Or, asking the question form the consumer's point of view: can I resell a digital book once I have read it, or an iTunes music file once I do not like the music anymore?

In the analogue context, the resale of books or records is governed by the principle of exhaustion.[3] Its basic idea is rather simple: when an embodiment of a work or of another intangible subject matter is first put on the market, there are two layers of legal regulation which need to be observed. Property law governs the entitlement to the tangible object, and the title can only be transferred by the owner or with the owner's consent. Intellectual property law constitutes the second layer. The first sale of a book, for instance, is also the distribution of a work, hence it requires the consent of the copyright owner. After first sale, the intellectual property level is stripped away with respect to the sold item. From then on the book is treated like a loaf of bread or like a watch, like any other good which can be freely resold. As Josef Kohler noted, the underlying concept is not the contractual notion of implied consent but a limitation in-built into the intellectual property right, a limitation *ex lege*.[4]

But copyright law is facing the challenge of dematerialization.[5] The sale of a DVD already represents the first step in this process:

---

[2]   The way ReDigi works is explained in *Capitol Rec.* v. *ReDigi*, 934 F.Supp.2d 640, 646 (SDNY 2013).

[3]   See for EU law Directive 2001/29/EC of the European Parliament and of the Council of 22 May 2001 on the harmonization of certain aspects of copyright and related rights in the information society ('Information Society Directive'), art. 4(2) [2001] OJ L167/10; for US law 17 USC s. 109(a).

[4]   J. Kohler, *Handbuch des deutschen Patentrechts in rechtsvergleichender Darstellung* (Mannheim, Bensheimer, 1900), pp. 452–9.

[5]   See H. Zech, *Information als Schutzgegenstand* (Tübingen, Mohr Siebeck, 2012), p. 167 *et seq.*

it is still a tangible object, but the digital content can be separated from the data carrier without any loss of quality. When a set of data is transferred, as done by ReDigi, no tangible object is given away, but it could at least be argued that the file changes possession. In the *UsedSoft* case, however, not even a particular set of data was transferred. The case was about client-server software which users could download directly from the producer's website. So the seller of 'used' software only passed on the access code to the buyer. In the brave new world of cloud computing, the buyer does not even receive a permanent copy of the work, but only the access to a website. Streaming, which is rapidly replacing filesharing, is an example in point. As Jeremy Rifkin famously put it, we are moving 'from ownership to access'.[6] It is the access which matters, not the tangible good.

Where on this road to dematerialization should copyright law draw the line with respect to exhaustion? The traditional view in Europe and the position endorsed by the US courts[7] is that exhaustion is only triggered by the sale of a tangible object. CDs and DVDs, albeit data-carriers, still constitute tangible objects and hence can be resold. The CJEU, however, has adopted a different and more revolutionary view, namely, that even the sale of software in intangible form can result in exhaustion.

Although this is still a rather new issue, articles and monographs on digital exhaustion abound.[8] This chapter cannot do justice to all

---

    [6]   J. Rifkin, *The Age of Access* (New York, J.P. Tarcher/Putnam, 2000), p. 5.
    [7]   For software see *Vernor* v. *Autodesk*, 621 F.3d 1102 (9th Cir. 2010), for digital music see *Capitol Rec.* v. *ReDigi*, n. 2 above.
    [8]   See the overview given by R. Hilty, K. Köklü and F. Hafenbrädl, 'Software Agreements: Stocktaking and Outlook – Lessons from the *UsedSoft* v. *Oracle* Case from a Comparative Law Perspective' (2013) *IIC* 263 and by L. Longdin and P.H. Lim, 'Inexhaustible Distribution Rights for Copyright Owners and the Foreclosure of Secondary Markets for Used Software' (2013) *IIC* 542. Perhaps not surprisingly, given that the *UsedSoft* case originated in Germany, much of the literature on EU law is in German; for an overview see M. Grützmacher, 'Endlich angekommen im digitalen Zeitalter!? Die Erschöpfungslehre im europäischen Urheberrecht: der gemeinsame Binnenmarkt und der Handel mit gebrauchter Software' 5 *ZGE/IPJ* 2013, 46; I. Hantschel, *Softwarekauf und –weiterverkauf* (Berlin, Duncker and Humblot, 2011), p. 207 *et seq.*; M. Leistner, 'Gebrauchtsoftware auf dem Weg nach Luxemburg', *CR* 2011, 209.

views expressed in scholarly publications. It can only highlight three dimensions of the problem: the doctrinal dimension, the economic dimension and the institutional dimension.

9.2 DOCTRINAL DIMENSION

On both sides of the Atlantic we agree that exhaustion has the following elements.[9] Exhaustion occurs when a copy of a work is first sold by the copyright owner or with his or her consent within a certain territory. Which territory is relevant is another very hotly debated issue. According to EU law it is the European Union, or to be more precise the European Economic area, where the sale will trigger exhaustion.[10] In the United States, the Supreme Court has recently endorsed the principle of international exhaustion in copyright law,[11] a very intriguing development which, however, cannot be analyzed in any detail here.

According to traditional doctrine, there are several reasons why exhaustion is restricted to the sale of tangible copies.[12] First of all, exhaustion is only triggered by a sale. Contracts concerning digital products, however, are regularly termed 'licences' by right owners. Indeed, these contracts differ from ordinary contracts of sale, which are discharged once both parties have fulfilled their obligations. Contracts concerning digital products quite often contain use restrictions. They may also be the source of ongoing obligations: software contracts, for example, often entitle the consumer to regular updates. So the contracts at issue here may not be 'contracts of sale'.[13] Secondly, only the distribution right is subject to

---

[9]   See n. 4 above.
[10] Information Society Directive, art. 4(2).
[11] *Kirtsaeng* v. *John Wiley & Sons*, 33 S Ct. 1351 (2013).
[12] See for example, T.J. Heydn, 'Anmerkung zu BGH, Beschluss vom 3.2.2011 – I ZR 129/08', *MMR* 2011, 309; U. Loewenheim in G. Schricker and U. Loewenheim (eds), *Urheberrecht* (4th edn, Munich, C.H. Beck, 2010), s. 69c para. 34; H. Schack, 'Rechtsprobleme der Online-Übermittlung', *GRUR* 2007, 643; G. Spindler, 'Der Handel mit Gebrauchsoftware – Erschöpfungs-grundsatz quo vadis?', *CuR* 2008, 70.
[13] See *Autodesk*, n. 7 above, p. 1108; see also Hilty, Köklü and Hafenbrädl, n. 8 above, p. 274 who also consider software agreements as licences, but who nevertheless argue in favor of digital exhaustion.

exhaustion, whereas the right owner retains the reproduction right. The offer of 'used software' is not a distribution in the classical sense. Rather, the seller invites the buyer to make a reproduction. Thirdly, the economic effects of digital exhaustion differ from those of exhaustion in the analogue world, as will be explained in more detail below.[14] Thus, a court which cautiously respects traditional doctrine will be likely to reject the concept of digital exhaustion. As the *Autodesk* Court put it: 'Congress is free of course to modify the first sale doctrine but under the existing doctrine, there is no exhaustion'.[15]

Under a more proactive perspective, which was adopted by the CJEU in *UsedSoft*, these three arguments are not conclusive. First, the CJEU held that whenever the buyer gets the right to permanently use the software or file the legal situation for a one-off payment the contract is for the sale of a product, however the parties choose to characterize the contract.[16] Secondly, the transfer of ownership changes an act of communication to the public, coupled with a reproduction, into an act of distribution.[17] Thirdly, the market does not make a difference between the online and the offline transfer of media products.[18] Quite often you can get both at the same price. So the law should not make a difference either. While the *UsedSoft* judgment, as the Court stresses, only concerns software, these arguments seem applicable to other types of work as well.[19]

Although the CJEU's reasoning is less than perfectly precise, all of these points are at least arguable. There are two issues, however,

---

[14] See *ReDigi*, n. 2 above, p. 656.

[15] See *Autodesk*, n. 7 above, p. 1115.

[16] *UsedSoft*, n. 1 above, pp. 42–9. Meanwhile the Federal Supreme Court has referred the case back to the Court of Appeal, because it still had to be clarified whether the software in the case had been transferred for permanent use: BGH *GRUR* 2014, 264.

[17] *UsedSoft*, n. 1 above, p. 51 *et seq.*

[18] *Ibid.* p. 61.

[19] Grützmacher, n. 8 above, p. 81; Hilty, Köklü and Hafenbrädl, n. 8 above, p. 284 *et seq.*; N. Malevanny, 'Die UsedSoft-Kontroverse: Auslegung und Auswirkungen des EuGH-Urteils', *CR* 2013, 426; the opposite view, however, is taken by OLG Hamm, *GRUR* 2014, 853; J. Marly, 'Der Handel mit so genannter "Gebrauchtsoftware"', *EuZW* 2012, 657; M. Stieper, 'Anmerkung zu EuGH, Urteil vom 3. Juli 2012 – C-128/11 – UsedSoft', *ZUM* 2012, 670.

which were only partly addressed in the judgment and which present grave doctrinal difficulties for any theory of online exhaustion.

First, the buyer of a 'used' digital product needs a right to use the copy. This is a fundamental difference between the analogue and the digital world. While you can use a book without interfering with the author's copyright, you need to download a copy and make more reproductions when using it afterwards. If the initial licence granted by the producer is non-transferrable, this right cannot be contractual, but only statutory. Under article 5(1) of the Computer Programs Directive,[20] which the CJEU considered applicable in this context, reproductions do not require the right owner's consent 'where they are necessary for the use of the computer program by the lawful acquirer in accordance with its intended purpose'. There is no similar provision for other types of works, but the exception for private copying, which exists in the copyright laws of most, but not all, EU Member States, may apply. The scope of what is allowed, however, does not coincide with the use restrictions stipulated in the contract between the producer and the first buyer. In the *UsedSoft* case, for instance, there was a restriction that the software could only be used at 25 terminals. Most commentators seem to assume that, in the case of exhaustion, the second buyer is also restricted to using the software at 25 terminals only. But this limitation cannot be accounted for under the doctrine of exhaustion. It stems from the first contract, but the first license is not passed on to the second buyer when it is non-transferrable.

This leads on to a related problem. In the *UsedSoft* judgment it remains unclear what the object is, the sale of which triggers exhaustion.[21] It could be one of three objects: the data carrier, the data or the licence to use the software. A data carrier was not sold in *UsedSoft*. Some passages in the judgment seem to indicate that the Court intended to treat the sale of a set of data like the sale of a data carrier. In particular, the Court insisted that exhaustion required the deletion of the data on the seller's computer. But the

---

[20] Directive 2009/24/EC of the European Parliament and of the Council of 23 April 2009 on the legal protection of computer programs [2009] OJ L111/16.

[21] H. Haberstumpf, 'Der Handel mit gebrauchter Software im harmonisierten Urheberrecht', *CR* 2012, 562.

data were not transferred either. As explained above, the buyers obtained the physical data from the software producer's website. So the only way of explaining the decision doctrinally is that it is the sale of the licence which results in exhaustion.[22] In *UsedSoft* as in many other cases, however, the licence was non-transferrable. At least under German law, which was the law applicable in this case, the transferability of rights can be excluded by the parties. The Civil Code only makes an exception for rights in land and in moveable, but tangible goods. Also German law provides that licences can only be transferred with the copyright owner's consent. In the absence of a full harmonization of copyright contract law, the CJEU had to respect the provisions of the applicable national law. Even apart from this technical point, allowing copyright licences to be freely transferred independent of the stipulations of the initial parties would be tantamount to making serious inroads into the freedom of contract.

It becomes clear that the doctrine of exhaustion is inextricably linked to the dichotomy of tangible copies and intellectual property. Intellectual property law adds a second layer to the sale of tangible goods. After first sale the copy becomes an ordinary commercial product: it can only be used by one person at a time (rivalry), the owner can exclude others from using it (natural exclusivity) and its value will diminish with use. Apart from the distribution right, which is exhausted, the buyer does not interfere with copyright when using the copy, and the copyright owner's interests are not unduly affected. In the digital world, this optimal balance of interests cannot be achieved, as data are non-rivalrous, non-exclusive and do not lose their value after use. If the second buyer can do with the acquired data as he or she pleases, there will be a massive interference with the copyright owner's interests. The only possible solution is to make copyright licences freely transferable, independent of agreements to the contrary between the right owner and the first buyer. Under this approach the second buyer would not acquire more rights than the first buyer had. At the same time the first buyer loses his or her licence so that the number of licenced users does not multiply. But doctrinally speaking this solution is

---

[22]   Hilty, Köklü and Hafenbrädl, n. 8 above, p. 281, who, however, underestimate the difficulties pointed out in the following text.

different from the principle of exhaustion. At the moment it cannot be reconciled with national provisions which allow right owners to grant non-transferrable licences. So this is not an option open to the courts. Parliament would need to change the law. Before it can be advised to do so, however, the economic aspects of the 'free movement of digital goods' should be taken into account.

9.3 ECONOMIC DIMENSION[23]

In the analogue world the principle of exhaustion strikes a fair balance. The owner has the possibility to calculate the price in order to make sure that he or she will receive full remuneration at first sale. After that, intellectual property law has served its purpose and the logic of markets for tangible goods is reinstalled. The result is that there can be competition between new and old products, between books fresh from the press and the used books sold by bouquinistes. Data, however, do not wear out. Buyers of 'used' digital products get exactly the same product as first-time buyers, only at a lower price. ReDigi's website shows this very clearly. If I want to download a song, I can either buy it in the iTunes store at €0.99 or from the ReDigi platform at, say, €0.50. Price discrimination between new and used products is undermined. As a result, the right owner's primary market will dry out. It is also almost impossible for the right owner to calculate the initial price in a way that will compensate him or her for all future uses. In the case of some digital products such as blockbuster movies the right owner may have an economically significant head start over competitors who sell 'used' copies, but this amortization period is short, and in other instances such as classical music even non-existent.

In addition, there are also the costs of verification: the right owner needs to make sure that the copy which is distributed is genuine. Verification may be possible but, of course, there are costs and these costs need to be taken into account in the economic

[23]   On the economics of digital exhaustion see A. Perzanowski and J. Schultz, 'Digital Exhaustion' (2011) 58 *UCLA L Rev.* 889; R.A. Reese, 'The First Sale Doctrine in the Era of Digital Networks' (2003) 44 *BCL Rev.* 577; T. Serra, 'Rebalancing at Resale: ReDigi, Royalties and the Digital Secondary Market' (2013) 93 *BUL Rev.* 1753.

analysis. There may be a difference between different kinds of work in this respect. If a computer game sells at €50, verification measures which cost €1 per copy may make sense. It is also easy to require registration or to tie the game to a user profile.[24] The digital version of a song, on the other hand, will sell at €0.99. There is not much room for expensive individual verification measures, and the market will not accept registration requirements.

It turns out that it would not make economic sense to treat digital media products exactly like books or records. This does not mean that the buyer's interest in reselling the media product and thereby partly refinancing the cost of acquisition can be completely discounted. But the economic analysis shows that a more nuanced approach may be preferable to the all-or-nothing approach adopted by the principle of exhaustion.

9.4 INSTITUTIONAL DIMENSION

Can the courts adapt the doctrine of exhaustion to the brave new digital world?

The CJEU has given an affirmative answer. Before criticizing the Court for having overstepped the line to legislation, one should take into account that the CJEU is not a specialist copyright court. First of all, the Court is always taking a proactive role when it comes to market integration. Thus, the *UsedSoft* decision is not so much motivated by copyright law considerations but rather by the EU fundamental freedoms.[25] Secondly, there seems to be a clash between the economic reality and what is increasingly perceived by outsiders as the self-referential nature of copyright law. Copyright lawyers are caught within that traditional doctrine, but the suspicion from outside is that they lose sight of the economic reality. The proper role of a Supreme Court may be to balance basic principles

---

[24] On the effects of exhaustion on the transfer of a user profile see *Half-Life 2*, BGH, GRUR 2010, 822.
[25] Grützmacher, n. 8 above, p. 59 *et seq.*; M. Senftleben, 'Die Fortschreibung des urheberrechtlichen Erschöpfungsgrundsatzes im digitalen Umfeld', *NJW* 2012, 2926.

and to tell the specialist court: 'We have determined the policy, now you deal with the dogmatic little details'.[26]

It has become clear, however, that the issue is more complex than the CJEU may have thought. Exhaustion in the doctrinal sense does not work in the digital environment. If the idea of restricting the exclusive right for the sake of the free movement of goods makes sense for the digital world, it will have to be recast into a 'doctrine of free transfer of licences'. The impact of such a doctrinal change on the freedom of contract and its economic implications require careful consideration. This is not a matter for judges but one of the most important tasks of copyright legislation in the digital age.

---

[26] See R.C. Dreyfuss, 'Percolation, Uniformity and Coherent Adjudication: The Federal Circuit Experience' (2013) 66 *SMU L Rev.* 526.

Index